UNIONS AT THE CROSSROADS

UNIONS AT THE CROSSROADS

Strategic Membership, Financial, and Political Perspectives

Marick F. Masters

QUORUM BOOKS
Westport, Connecticut • London

Library of Congress Cataloging-in-Publication Data

Masters, Marick Francis, 1954–
Unions at the crossroads : strategic membership, financial, and political perspectives / by Marick F. Masters.
p. cm.
Includes bibliographical references and index.
ISBN 1-56720-129-6 (alk. paper)
1. Trade-unions—United States. 2. Trade-unions—United States—Membership. 3. Trade-unions—United States—Finance. 4. Trade-unions—United States—Political activity. 5. Industrial relations—United States. 6. Labor policy—United States. 7. Labor laws and legislation—United States. I. Title.
HD6508.M353 1997
331.88'0973—dc21 96-40912

British Library Cataloguing in Publication Data is available.

Library of Congress Catalog Card Number: 96-40912
ISBN: 1-56720-129-6

First published in 1997

Quorum Books, 88 Post Road West, Westport, CT 06881
An imprint of Greenwood Publishing Group, Inc.

Printed in the United States of America

The paper used in this book complies with the Permanent Paper Standard issued by the National Information Standards Organization (Z39.48–1984).

10 9 8 7 6 5 4 3 2 1

This book is dedicated to my wonderful family—
Sally, Christopher, Jacquelyn,
Julie Ann, Catherine, and Jennifer

Contents

	Illustrations	ix
	Acknowledgments	xiii
	Abbreviations	xv
	Introduction	1
1	Strategic Perspectives on Union Resources: Human, Financial, and Political Capital	21
2	Union Density and Membership	43
3	Major Union Membership Trends	63
4	The Financial Capital of Unions	73
5	How Unions Raise and Spend Money	89
6	The Financial Performance of Unions	107
7	Union Political Capital and the Legal Enactment Strategy	117
8	Union Profiles	133
9	Baseline Union Budgets: Implications for Representational Services and Bargaining Clout	141
10	Strategic Union Resource Allocations	157
11	Union Growth Scenarios and Mergers	173
12	Strategies for Union Growth	185

13 The Future of U.S. Unions 203
Bibliography 209
Index 227

Illustrations

TABLES

I.1 Twenty-eight Major Unions' Membership 13
2.1 Aggregate Union Density Rates and Membership 44
2.2 Comparative Union Density Rates 47
2.3 Union Membership and Density by Major Industry Classifications 48
2.4 Union Membership and Density by Major Occupational Classifications 49
2.5 Union Membership and Density by Major Demographic Classifications 50
2.6 Percentage Change in Employment, Level of Employment, and Projected Change in Employment, by Occupation 52
2.7 NLRB Certification Election Results 55
2.8 Strike Activity in the United States 57
3.1 Aggregate Union Membership and Density 65
3.2 Twenty-Eight Unions' Membership Trends 68
4.1 Twenty-Eight Unions' Aggregate Real Assets and Wealth 74
4.2 Twenty-Eight Unions' Aggregate Asset Bases 76
4.3 Disaggregate Union Real Assets 78
4.4 Disaggregate Union Real Wealth 81
4.5 Average Concentration of Assets and Wealth 83

4.6	Disaggregate Union Liquid Asset Holdings	85
5.1	Twenty-Eight Unions' Aggregate Real Income and Operating Surpluses	91
5.2	Twenty-Eight Unions' Aggregate Real Member-Based Income and Selected Disbursements	94
5.3	Disaggregate Union Real Income and Operating Surpluses	96
5.4	Disaggregate Union Member-Based Income and Selected Expenditures as Percent of Operating Income and Disbursements	100
5.5	Real Per-Member Union Expenditures on Salaries and Administration	102
5.6	Union Dues Rates	104
6.1	Aggregate Union Financial Performance	109
6.2	Disaggregate Union Financial Performance	112
7.1	Trends in Aggregate Union and Corporate PAC Fundraising	122
7.2	Twenty-Eight Major Unions' Real PAC Receipts	124
7.3	Major Unions' Real PAC Receipts	125
7.4	Major Unions' Real Per-Member PAC Receipts	127
7.5	Major Unions' PAC Receipts as a Percentage of Member-Based Income	128
7.6	Private–Public Sector Union PAC Data	130
9.1	Aggregate Real Union Bargaining, Organizing, and Political Budget Estimates	145
9.2	Disaggregate Union Bargaining, Organizing, and Political Budget Estimates	147
9.3	Unions' Aggregate Real Strike Fund Capacity Estimates	151
9.4	Disaggregate Union Strike Fund Capacity Estimates	153
10.1	Unions' Aggregate Real Organizing Budget Increments	162
10.2	Union Organizing Budget Increments	164
10.3	Unions' Aggregate Organizing Squad Budget Estimates	165
10.4	Union Organizing Reserves	167
10.5	Unions' Aggregate Real PAC Receipt Increments	168
10.6	Disaggregate Union PAC Receipt Increments	170
11.1	Union Growth Scenarios	175
11.2	Membership Density Implications of Growth Scenarios	176
11.3	Estimated Costs of Union Growth	177

11.4 Capital Implications of Current Mergers and Superunions 181
12.1 Union Growth Target Opportunities 192

FIGURES

1.1 Strategic Framework of Analysis of Unions 23
1.2 The Role of Union Resources 32
8.1 Membership Dimension 134
8.2 Wealth Dimension 136
8.3 Income Dimension 137
8.4 Financial Performance Dimension 137
8.5 PAC Receipt Dimension 138
8.6 Composite Dimensions 139
12.1 Union Growth Strategies 187

Acknowledgments

A great deal of gratitude is owed to many who participated directly and indirectly in the development of this book, although all contents are the full responsibility of the author. In particular, I am indebted to the Joseph M. Katz Graduate School of Business at the University of Pittsburgh for providing the research support, release time, and environment for making this research project feasible. I also would like to recognize the intellectual insights of my colleagues Robert Atkin and James Craft for stimulating my thoughts in the development of this book.

In addition, I am grateful to the many persons in the union movement who have taken their valuable time to discuss with me various aspects of the operations of their organizations, both in preparation of this book and in other contexts, which have helped to give me broader insight into the condition and direction of organized labor.

I am also grateful to my graduate research assistant, David Eplion, for digging up some of the materials and doing painstaking tasks to help produce the final product.

Without doubt, this book could not have been written without the willingness of my secretary Pat Koroly to type its countless revisions. Her pleasant and supportive demeanor made this an enjoyable effort.

Last, I am thankful for my family, to whom this book is dedicated, for their continual support and understanding.

Abbreviations

ACTWU	Amalgamated Clothing and Textile Workers Union
AFGE	American Federation of Government Employees
AFL-CIO	American Federation of Labor-Congress of Industrial Organizations
AFSCME	American Federation of State, County, and Municipal Employees
AFT	American Federation of Teachers
ALPA	Airline Pilots Association
APWU	American Postal Workers Union
BRAC	Brotherhood of Railway and Airline Clerks
CJA	Carpenters and Joiners of America
COPE	Committee on Political Education, AFL-CIO
CWA	Communications Workers of America
FSLMRS	Federal Service Labor–Management Relations Statute
HERE	Hotel Employees and Restaurant Employees
IAFF	International Association of Fire Fighters
IAM	International Association of Machinists
IBEW	International Brotherhood of Electrical Workers
IBT	International Brotherhood of Teamsters
ILGWU	International Ladies Garment Workers Union
IUE	International Union of Electrical Workers

IUOE	International Union of Operating Engineers
LIU	Laborers International Union
LMRDA	Labor–Management Reporting and Disclosure Act
MEBA	Marine Engineers Beneficial Association
NALC	National Association of Letter Carriers
NEA	National Education Association
NFFE	National Federation of Federal Employees
NLRA	National Labor Relations Act
NLRB	National Labor Relations Board
NRLCA	National Rural Letter Carriers Association
NTEU	National Treasury Employees Union
OECD	Organization for Economic Co-operation and Development
PAC	Political Action Committee
PPI	Plumbing and Pipefitting Industry
PRA	Postal Reorganization Act
RLA	Railway Labor Act
RWDSU	Retail, Wholesale Department Store Union
SEIU	Service Employees International Union
UAW	United Auto Workers
UFCW	United Food and Commercial Workers Union
UMWA	Union Mine Workers of America
UNITE	Union of Needletrades, Industrial, and Textile Employees
UPIU	United Paper Workers International Union
URW	United Rubber Workers
USW	United Steelworkers of America
U.S. BLS	United States Bureau of Labor Statistics
U.S. DOL	United States Department of Labor
U.S. FEC	United States Federal Election Commission
U.S. OPM	United States Office of Personnel Management

Introduction

THE CONVENTIONAL VIEW

Labor unions in the United States have faced serious challenges in recent decades, as shown by a litany of downward trends. Union density (the percentage of the overall workforce belonging to unions) has fallen to its lowest level since the Great Depression era, and the actual number of union members fell in the 1980s, for the first time since the 1920s. To the alarm of union supporters, membership in the private sector has dropped to just above 10 percent. Formal elections to organize new members decreased, in part, because employers have used a variety of tactics, ranging from employee involvement and outsourcing to relocating plants and jobs to cheaper foreign labor markets, to resist and avoid unions (Kochan, Katz, and McKersie 1986; Voos 1994a). Major strikes have dwindled in number and economic consequence while emboldened employers have successfully replaced strikers (McCallion 1990; Goldfield 1987; U.S. DOL, BLS 1996b). Caterpillar's aggressive effort to maintain operations amid the United Auto Workers' (UAW) embarrassingly unsuccessful eighteen-month strike testifies to organized labor's diminished capacity to use the strike as a potent economic weapon (Kelly 1995; Kilborn 1995).[1] Similarly, the power of unions to gain "more" at the bargaining table has waned. Wage, benefit, and work-rule concessions have occurred in many industries.

Furthermore, Congress, even when controlled by Democrats, has enacted legislation hostile to unions. Witness the passage of the North American

Free Trade Agreement (NAFTA) and the General Agreement on Tariffs and Trade (GATT) in the Democratic 103rd Congress.[2] Deepening labor's political woes, the Republicans swept the 1994 congressional elections, gaining control of the U.S. House of Representatives for the first time since 1952. Under Republican control, Congress has vigorously assaulted many of organized labor's public-policy achievements and positions. It has challenged Fair Labor Standards Act limits on overtime work and pay, occupational safety and health regulations, and the Davis–Bacon Act of 1931, which requires construction contractors that receive federal money to pay "prevailing" area wage rates to employees. In addition, the Republican Congress passed the union-opposed Teamwork for Employees and Managers Act, which, had it not been vetoed by President Clinton, would have amended the National Labor Relations Act (NLRA) as follows: "That it shall not constitute or be evidence of an unfair labor practice . . . for an employer to establish, assist, maintain, or participate in any organization or entity of any kind, in which employees participate, to address matters of mutual interest, including, but not limited to, issues of quality, productivity, efficiency, and safety and health." Unions opposed this legislation because it would allow employers to establish employee involvement committees, which could arguably act as "company unions" and thwart independent union-organizing efforts.[3]

These developments have led to the popular view that unions are in serious, if not irreversible, decline, becoming ever more "irrelevant" to most workers (Swoboda and Hamilton 1996). Among labor scholars, "it is generally agreed that U.S. unions are in a crisis" (Strauss, Gallagher, and Fiorito 1991: v; see also Strauss 1995). Moreover, the crisis is at the point that "the issue of union growth had never been more critical than in the 1990s, since the extent of union decline, at least in the United States, has gathered a seemingly unstoppable momentum which threatens the very core of private sector collective bargaining" (Seeber 1991: 93). The bleak situation promotes cynical ridicule: "For too many years, the labor movement has been called a dinosaur. This is unfair and almost slanderous—not for labor, but for the poor maligned dinosaur" (Tasini 1995: C3).

Ironically, the decline in unions has concerned even erstwhile political foes. Conservative Republican Senator Orrin Hatch expressed the raison d'être of unionism: "There are always going to be people who take advantage of workers. Unions even that out, to their credit. We need them to level the field between labor and management. If you didn't have unions, it would be very difficult for even enlightened employers to not take advantage of workers on wages and working conditions, because of [competition from] rivals. I'm among the first to say I believe in unions" (Bernstein 1994: 70).

Indeed, as Senator Hatch and others (e.g., Freeman and Medoff 1984) have suggested, the decline in unionization has apparently contributed to some undesirable economic and social developments. Bernstein (1994: 70) cited "weakening unions as a key reason for the six-percentage-point slide in the 1980s in the share of employees with company pension plans, for the seven-point decline in those with employer health plans, and for a 125-fold explosion in unlawful discharge lawsuits now that fewer employees have a union to stick up for them."

This portrayal of dire union straits, however, must be put into a broader context (Goldfield 1987; Bennett 1991). It focuses almost exclusively on the condition and apparent result of declining union density and membership. But, as John Dunlop, former U.S. Secretary of Labor, comments, "The share of the nonagricultural workforce in labor organizations . . . is scarcely an all-purpose measure of union strength or influence—at the workplace, in a community, or in the larger society" (Goldfield 1987: 4). While the drop in union numbers is certainly of concern (to unions and their supporters), it does not necessarily mean that unions are weak institutions hopelessly beyond recovery. They still possess millions of current members and other possible sources of institutional sinew, including financial and political capital, which may increase notwithstanding or, ironically, because of otherwise difficult circumstances (Bennett 1991; Masters and Atkin 1996a; Willman, Morris, and Aston 1993). The availability of these other forms of capital has been linked to union successes in several important domains, including organizing new members and public-policy decision making (Voos 1983; 1987; Moore, Chachere, Curtis, and Gordon 1995). In addition, the ebb-and-flow in union membership in the United States can be fully comprehended only in historical and international perspective. Goldfield (1987: 8) correctly comments that "the nature of trade union decline . . . can only be ascertained in a many-decades-long historical context." Furthermore, the labor movement is by no means a monolithic community. Union conditions may vary widely, depending on the industry, leadership, and rank-and-file solidarity. Thus, the aggregate description of the labor condition may mask pockets of strength and dim insights as to where and how unions might strategically deploy their multifaceted resources for maximum gain.

To date, unfortunately, the analysis of the union "crisis," indeed of the union movement in general, mainly has focused on membership trends, bargaining impacts, and strikes, rather than on the broad condition of unions as institutions per se (see, e.g., Bennett and Delaney 1993; Kochan, Katz, and McKersie 1986). While this research has contributed significantly to our understanding of the role of unions in American society, it also has left major issues more or less ignored, especially with regard to the state of major national unions (the term national is used to refer to both national and international levels of union organization; for a discussion of this omission regarding national unions' organizing effectiveness, see Fiorito, Jarley, and Delaney 1995).[4] More generally, the topics of union finances and political resources (both of which fall under the broader rubric of union administration) have received relatively meager attention at a time in which they have arguably become much more important to the future of organized labor, as reflected in the revamping of the American Federation of Labor–Congress of Industrial Organizations (AFL–CIO) under the new leadership of John Sweeney, former president of the Service Employees International Union (SEIU):

> Although the administration of labor unions has long been of general interest, only fleeting attention has been devoted to the subject . . . In recent years, relatively little attention has been devoted to the structure and governance of unions, including the nature of union leadership, the management practices of unions, and *union finances* [emphasis added]. For several reasons, as scholars have recently suggested, this is potentially a major oversight . . . First, research by Bennett (1991) revealed that the real income of private sector unions increased by more than 25 percent over the years 1970–1987, a period during which membership declined by 5.3 million . . . Second, the decline in union membership has pressured unions to improve their efficiency. This has led to union mergers and smaller union staffs . . . Further, as many long-time union officials retire, changes may be easier to implement. Because the union movement in America may be permanently altered by some of these changes, it is an appropriate time for researchers to examine issues related to union management and administration. (Bennett and Delaney 1993: 99–100)

In particular, relevant questions for investigation include the following: To what extent have individual unions, as opposed to unions in the aggregate, gained or lost membership over the past several decades? To what extent have unions held on to the financial capital needed to conduct operations in relation to their membership trends? Has their capacity to raise political capital changed in the face of admittedly disappointing aggregate membership trends? In other words, to what extent have the various institutional resources (human, financial, and political capital) upon which national unions depend to operate changed or declined, not only in the aggregate but, more important, at the disaggregated union level? Further, what are the implications of strategic resource reallocations to achieve desired union objectives, particularly on the organizing front? Relatedly, how much might it cost for unions to pursue a massively expanded organizing program aimed at achieving a high growth rate? It may be argued that the future of organized labor will be determined more by variables beyond its control (e.g., global "competition propelling private unionism toward the twilight zone," Troy 1995: C3), but unions will nevertheless make a vigorous attempt to change the future for the better (from their perspective).

THE DECLINE IN MORE DETAIL

The consensus on the decline in U.S. unions revolves around several key indicators that may be conveniently grouped into three broad categories: organizing and membership; bargaining; and political. Developments in these areas, however, are not mutually exclusive. At the same time, these areas identify distinct but interrelated strategic approaches unions might take to influence a host of important outcomes (e.g., density, compensation, legislation).

Organizing and Membership

Union density has declined more or less continuously since the mid-1950s. From its pinnacle of approximately one-third of the workforce in the decade or so between the mid-1940s and mid-1950s, union membership had shrunk to 14.9 percent of the workforce in 1995. Today, in fact, only one of every ten private sector workers belongs to a union. Less than 18 percent of the manufacturing workforce, a traditional labor stronghold, is in the union ranks. Moreover, the actual number of union members has dropped by almost six million since the early 1980s. Several powerful unions, including the UAW, United Steelworkers (USW), and International Ladies Garment Workers Union (ILGWU), have had their memberships chopped in half during these troubling years.

The decline in general union membership and density in recent decades has both resulted from and contributed to a more specific drop in formal organizing efforts and successes. The certification of bargaining units under the National Labor Relations Board (NLRB), which is the principal mechanism unions use to gain members and represent employees in the private sector, has declined in several important areas: the number of certification elections held (which fell from 6,380 in 1960 to 3,079 in 1994); the number of employees voting in such elections (483,964 in 1960, compared to 188,899 in 1994); and the percentage of union victories (59 percent in 1960 versus 49 percent in 1994).[5] The decline in these absolute indicators, it is important to note, has occurred while the labor force has grown considerably. The sheer expansion in the labor force itself necessitates that union certification activity must increase simply in order to maintain an existing level of density, which is something unions obviously have been unable to do. At the disaggregate union level, in a study on the certification activity of eighteen U.S.-based unions (fifteen of which are studied here), Chaison and Dhavale (1990) found that each had conducted significantly fewer certification elections during 1983–1985 in comparison to 1973–1975. As an illustration, the number of (single-union certification) elections in which the USW sought bargaining recognition declined 55 percent, falling from 791 to 353 during these respective two-year periods. The UAW's and Machinists' (IAM) formal certification elections fell 47 and 74 percent, respectively. More generally, the number of union certification elections per 100 union members dropped from 3.6 to 2.0 between 1976 and 1985, and the number of employees which unions tried to certify as a percentage of union membership also declined from 2.1 percent in 1976 to 1.2 percent in 1985 (Rose and Chaison 1990).

On the surface, this evidence bolsters the longstanding criticism that unions have paid too little attention to organizing, though there is recent evidence of an expanded emphasis on this activity (Goldfield 1987; Block 1980).[6] Under aggressive new leadership, the AFL-CIO has established an Organizing Department led by Richard Bensinger, who stresses grassroots activism. In fairness, however, the drop off in organizing in recent decades may reflect greater employer resistance and reduced employee demand or employee willingness to express demand (Farber and Krueger 1993), thus putting unions into an unenviable vice: They became less active in organizing because their prospects of succeeding had diminished. Still, union neglect may have exacerbated the situation. Unions have paid insufficient attention to overcoming the numerous major obstacles they face in trying to protect and expand their base in the workforce (Goldfield 1987). Labor's timid commitment to this important function is testified to by an anonymously quoted AFL-CIO official who said: "Most of the labor movement is in total denial" (Swoboda and Hamilton 1996: H6). Further, some suggest that unions may have misspent even their limited organizing investments. Kochan and Katz (1988: 158) note that "while employment opportunities were shifting to the service sector, unions did not follow suit by reallocating their organizing resources to take advantage of that shift."

The upshot is that the decline in unionization is due at least partly to a reduced level of organizing in the private sector, which was occasioned by a weak union effort coupled with a higher level of effective employer resistance. In fact, as Dickens and Leonard (1985) reported in their study on the decline in union membership between 1950 and 1980, unions would have shrunk regardless of both structural economic changes and the slippage in certification success rates. The data indicate that "even if unions had continued to win representation rights for the same percentage of voters in certification elections as they did in 1950–54, their share of employment would still have fallen over this period [1950–1980] nearly as much as it actually did" (Dickens and Leonard 1985: 332) simply because of "the decline in organizing activity" (1985: 333). Thus, "those who explain the drop in percent organized since the mid-1950s by reference to the decline in the rates of organizing and election success derive more support from the results of this study than do those who suggest that there is something unusual about the economic position of the organized firms" (Dickens and Leonard 1985: 333).

Bargaining Clout

Union power at the bargaining table arguably also has deteriorated, particularly in the 1980s. The drop in union density and membership, almost by definition, entails a weakened position in bargaining with employers. An ample body of research, in fact, correlates union membership with economic power (Freeman and Medoff 1984; Kochan, Katz, and McKersie 1986; Voos 1983; 1987).

Two principal indicators are commonly cited to support this conventional opinion of organized labor's diminished negotiating clout. One is the decline in major work stoppages, coupled with several widely publicized examples of failed union strikes. While the number of stoppages involving bargaining units with 1,000 or more employees totaled 424 in 1950 and 381 in 1970, they have fallen to an average of less than 40 in the 1990s (1990–1995). Only thirty-one such work stoppages occurred in 1995. In the 1990s, strikes, on average, have involved only 273,000 workers per year, compared to 1.7 million in 1950 (U.S. DOL, BLS 1996b). The humiliating setbacks unions have experienced in the strikes involving Caterpillar, Eastern, Greyhound, Phelps-Dodge, and PATCO (the Professional Air Traffic Controllers Organization) serve to reinforce the view that these once economically shattering actions have lost their potency (Franklin 1995) or that unions, at least in several major instances, have woefully miscalculated employers' resolve and capacity to take a strike.

Likewise, numerously reported examples of concessionary bargaining—union "givebacks"—have firmly gripped public perceptions of waning bargaining muscle. According to Rose and Chaison (1996: 89), concessionary bargaining "became commonplace" among U.S. unions because of a combination of economic recession (in the early 1980s) and weakened union bargaining power, due to declining membership and density. In a similar vein, "reduced union bargaining power has encouraged a confrontational hard bargaining stance on the part of management in many companies continuing into the late 1980s and early 1990s" (Voos 1994a: 3). The mere fact that the UAW ordered its members back to work at Caterpillar in 1995 under a company-imposed contract that the rank and file refused to ratify exposes labor's bargaining weakness in key sectors. As a further illustration, General Motors recently has pursued an aggressive bargaining strategy to promote outsourcing (or the practice of subcontracting union work to nonunion firms) that precipitated a major UAW strike in March 1996. It has since been reported to be "preparing to attempt the most significant departure from industry-pattern labor-contract bargaining in about 17 years . . . to obtain new union concessions to make its manufacturing more cost-competitive" (Blumenstein, Christian, and Stern 1996: A2).

The wave of negotiated settlements involving flexible work rules, two-tier wage structures, reduced cost-of-living allowances, lower wage increases (especially those which are tied to base wages), and lengthier contracts led Goldfield (1987: 45) to conclude that these concessions have occurred in a scope unparalleled since the 1930s. Moreover, the same economic pressures that forced concessions at the bargaining table per se have led to even more fundamental changes in industrial relations. A transformation in American industrial relations has occurred, giving corporations more flexibility with regard to managing work and introducing change:

> The changes made to collective bargaining in the early 1980s entailed more than just adjustments in pay levels and work rules. As labor and management struggled to respond to environmental pressures, they made significant changes in the bargaining process as well . . . These process changes reversed many of the structures, patterns, and procedures that had taken years to build up within bargaining relationships . . . Important bargaining-process changes include a decentralization of bargaining structures; shifts in the role of internal industrial relations staffs and functions; new communication policies; an increased emphasis on contingent compensation criteria; and a changing pattern of strike activity (Kochan, Katz, and McKersie 1986: 128).

Political Influence and Public Opinion

Many observers and union leaders (and presumably rank and file as well) view the election of President Ronald Reagan in 1980 as ushering in a decidedly anti-union era. The Republicans took control of the Senate in that election year, which they retained until the 1986 elections, when the Democrats regained control for the subsequent eight years. With Reagan in the White House and Republicans in command of the Senate, labor's legislative support dropped. While labor won 63 percent of the key labor roll call votes (identified by the AFL-CIO's Committee on Political Education [COPE]) in the Senate in 1980 (the last year before the Republicans officially took control), backing dropped to 21 percent in 1981 (Masters, Atkin, and Delaney 1989–1990). In this climate, labor was forced into a defensive posture, relying on the Democratic-controlled House of Representatives to defeat numerous hostile legislative proposals. Unions "lobbied intensively against proposed reductions in social security benefits and other domestic spending programs, as well as proposals to weaken the Davis-Bacon Act" (Masters and Delaney 1987a: 15). While not battling these legislative initiatives, unions often had to combat equally threatening administrative efforts, including the appointment of conservatives to the NLRB and an attempt to prosecute the presidents of three major public sector unions (American Postal Workers Union [APWU], American Federation of Government Employees [AFGE], and National Association of Letter Carriers [NALC]) for violating the Hatch Act, which, until recently revised, prohibited federal employees from engaging in a myriad of partisan political activities (Masters and Bierman 1985).[7] Further, labor faced embarrassing defections in its own ranks. As Masters and Delaney (1987a: 2) note, "union members' loyalty to Democratic presidential candidates was much higher prior to the 1968 elections than it has been over the 1968–1980 period. In both 1980 and 1984, over 40 percent of union member voters cast their ballots for Ronald Reagan."[8]

Even when Democrats have controlled both houses of Congress and the presidency, labor has been unable to advance its agenda with much success, especially with respect to legislative proposals affecting union institutional rights per se. In the late 1970s, it failed to get labor law reform, which, among other things, would have eased the process of organizing new members. As noted earlier, labor was also unable to stop NAFTA and GATT in the 103rd Congress. In this vein, Masters and Atkin's (1992: 313) analysis of key labor votes in the Senate revealed that "labor's political support is limited even within a Democratic-controlled legislative body. On some issues, liberal Democrats may defect. This implies that labor needs to broaden its bases of appeal."

AN ALTERNATIVE VIEW?

Depending on one's point of view, the conventional thesis of union decline provokes deep pessimism (union admirers) or boundless optimism (union bashers). There are, however, detractors who believe that labor's best years are not in the past. Some cite labor's financial and political resources in making a case (e.g., Bennett 1991). More generally, the belief that unions may not be in irreversible decline is lent at least a ray of hope, however faint, by three recent developments.

First, reversing a more than decade-long trend, union membership per se increased in both 1993 and 1994, albeit insufficiently to keep pace with labor force growth. (Membership fell again, however, in 1995; see U.S. DOL, BLS 1996a). Second, a rebellious set of major unions ousted the unacceptably complacent former leader of the AFL-CIO, Lane Kirkland. After a spirited contest, the insurgent candidate, John Sweeney, defeated the old guard's pick, Thomas Donahue, then interim AFL-CIO president and former long-term secretary-treasurer of the federation, in October 1995. Mr. Sweeney won on a platform to pour considerably more union resources into organizing and political activities, and has demonstrated a willingness to use militant disruptive tactics to achieve labor's goals (Bernstein 1995a). Third, in a major surprise development, the UAW, USW, and the IAM announced their plans to merge into a 1.7-million-member mega-"Metals Union" in the year 2000. This merger was touted in part because the unions have a combined strike fund well in excess of one billion dollars, and their amalgamation will yield additional economies of scale in organizing workers and coordinating industry-related bargaining strategies (Griffith 1995; McKay 1995). A few more mergers have already taken place (Williamson 1995), and others are reportedly in the works, perhaps foretelling the formation of several superunions in the years to come, as has occurred in Britain and elsewhere (William and Cave 1994; Willman, Morris, and Aston 1993).[9]

AT THE CROSSROADS

Whether unions are in a state of unstoppable decline or demonstrating signs of renewal that will lead ultimately to membership growth and attendant muscle in the bargaining and political arenas, they clearly are *at the crossroads*. Indeed, the AFL-CIO argues that the stake as to whether unions grow or continue to wither on the vine is so great that it puts the "nation at a crossroad" (AFL-CIO 1994: 16). The strategic choices unions make, in order to turn the "right" way, will be affected by the availability of resources (Weil 1994). Even though the most effective and efficient use of these resources may not spawn a wave of union growth such as that which occurred in the 1930s, union strategies regarding how they deploy resources will nonetheless directly impact the thousands of employers and millions of employees with whom they currently deal and will come in contact with in what promise to be more confrontational years ahead. The labor movement may be a dinosaur, but it is not a passive institution. If it is destined to extinction, its passing will be littered with the sweat, blood, tears, and money of battles fought.

PURPOSE OF THIS BOOK

The basic purpose of this book is to provide a uniquely broad assessment of the institutional health of the twenty-eight major national unions in the United States. The first of this kind, it examines these unions' membership, finances, and political resources during the 1979–1993 period. It explores trends along these dimensions, mining data that are generally untapped in the literature on unions. In so doing, the book provides the most comprehensive assessment of the status of these unions to date, both on aggregate and disaggregate bases. Furthermore, it puts these resources into a strategic context, and provides information on the capacities of the unions to finance strikes, organize new members, and compete politically. The fundamental assumptions behind this book are (1) that unions' resources affect their capacities to undertake a variety of activities, including the pursuit of new strategies and tactics, and (2) unions have multidimensional sources of institutional strength, the status of which provides insight into how well they manage their organizations, adapt to change, and will be able to remain viable economic and political players in the future.

Chapter 1 presents the strategic framework for analyzing unions. Chapter 2 examines the ebb and flow of union membership during most of the twentieth century. It also puts U.S. developments into international context and explores some of the principal macro-level explanations of union decline. The plausible merits of these explanations shape the strategies unions might choose to gain new members.

Chapter 3 depicts the trends in these unions' membership levels since 1955 (to the extent consistent data are available). It also compares these roughly forty-year developments with more recent developments (1979–1993). These disaggregated data not only show the relative membership base of unions over time but also the extent to which trends among individual unions have compared favorably or otherwise to the macro-level trends reported in Chapter 2.

Chapter 4 focuses on the specific issue of how rich unions are. In particular, it examines the aggregate assets and wealth of the twenty-eight unions during the 1979–1993 period. It also disaggregates the data among the private and public sector unions. Chapter 5 explores how unions raise and spend their money. It examines union income and operating "surpluses," as well as union dependence on member-based income. In addition, it examines trends in union expenditures on officers' and employees' salaries and various other administrative items. Finally, Chapter 6 analyzes the financial performance of unions, measured according to several more or less standard accounting ratios. These measures tap the extent to which unions have avoided annual debt (solvency), maintained assets that are readily convertible to cash (liquidity), and accumulated financial reserves to fund union operations in case of a major emergency, such as a prolonged strike, that would disrupt the flow of regular income (reserve).

Chapter 7 presents data on the political capital of unions. It focuses on the trends in union political action committee (PAC) receipts and puts them into a broader interest-group context, comparing unions to corporate and other major economic interests represented in national politics. Chapter 8 presents composite measures of membership, financial, and political conditions to distinguish the general situations of the twenty-eight unions.

Chapter 9 examines the bargaining service and power implications by estimating the unions' baseline budgets and exploring their capacities to finance strikes. Chapter 10 examines the implications of reallocating union resources to increase organizing activities. Chapter 11 examines the possible outcomes of expanded resource investments in organizing. Specifically, the chapter provides estimates of current union membership trends to the year 2000 and the gains unions might expect to achieve from increases in their organizing budgets. It also assesses the resource implications of recently announced union mergers and other conceivable superunions. Chapter 12 suggests an array of strategies unions might pursue to achieve growth, and Chapter 13 explores the future condition of U.S. unions and recommends actions for renewal.

DATA, SAMPLE, AND MEASURES

Briefly, four principal sources of data are used. First, union membership data are obtained mainly from biennial reports compiled by the AFL-CIO as reported in Gifford (various years). Second, data on union finances are from annual LM-2 financial disclosure forms that unions must file under the 1959 Labor–Management Reporting and Disclosure Act (LMRDA).[10] Third, PAC receipts are from the two-year election cycle reports of the U.S. Federal Election Commission (FEC). Finally, several top union staff members were interviewed as to the status of unions, union finances, and organizing strategies for the future.[11]

Sample Table I.1 identifies the union sample, primary industries, and membership levels in 1993. Together, the unions' membership exceeded thirteen million, or almost four-fifths of the overall unionized U.S. workforce. They account for approximately 79 and 82 percent of private and public sector union memberships, respectively.[12]

Over the time period in which these unions are analyzed (i.e., principally 1979 to 1993), they each had autonomous status. Several mergers have since occurred or been announced for the near future: (1) The Retail, Wholesale and Department Store Union (RWDSU) will merge with the United Food and Commercial Workers (UFCW), effective 1997; (2) the Amalgamated Clothing and Textile Workers Union (ACTWU) merged with the ILGWU into the Union of Needletrades, Industrial, and Textile Employees, in 1995; and, as noted, (3) the IAM, UAW, USW will merge in the year 2000.[13] In addition, the United Rubber Workers (URW) merged with the USW in 1995. Discussions have also occurred between the National Education Association (NEA) and the American Federation of Teachers (AFT), which have an agreement not to raid their respective bargaining units, but have not yet reached successful closure. The twenty-eight unions are treated separately in the analyses below, in keeping with their independent status for the interval observed, though it is recognized that several of these unions have merged with or acquired smaller ones during the period under study (Chaison 1986; Williamson 1995). As will be discussed later, however, the data on these various unions' membership, financial health, and political capital trends point to some plausible incentives for merger activity.

At this point, a few words about the organizational unit of analysis are in order. The national union focus is chosen because it provides an organizationwide perspective. In the main, national unions are the only labor units with the capability of pooling resources and talents across locals and

Table I.1
Twenty-eight Major Unions' Membership (1993)

Union	Primary Industry Jurisdiction	Membership (1993)[1] (in thousands)
Private Sector		
Teamsters (IBT)	Transportation and Utilities	1,316
Food and Commercial Workers (UFCW)	Service	997
Auto Workers (UAW)	Manufacturing	771
Electrical Workers (IBEW)	Manufacturing	710
Machinists (IAM)	Manufacturing	474
Communication Workers (CWA)	Transportation and Utilities	472
Steelworkers (USW)	Manufacturing	421
Carpenters (CJA)	Construction	408
Laborers (LIU)	Construction	408
Operating Engineers (IUOE)	Construction	305
Hotel Employees (HERE)	Service	258
Plumbers (PPI)	Construction	220
Paper Workers (UPIU)	Manufacturing	188
Clothing Workers (ACTWU)	Manufacturing	143
Electronic Workers (IUE)	Manufacturing	143
Garment Workers (ILGWU)	Manufacturing	133
Retail, Wholesale Union (RWDSU)	Service	80
Total Membership		7,447
Percentage of Private Nonagricultural Employee Union Membership (1995)		.79
Public Sector		
National Education Association (NEA)	State and Local	2,100
State, County Employees (AFSCME)	State and Local	1,167
Service Employees International Union (SEIU)	State and Local	919
Teachers (AFT)	State and Local	574
Postal Workers (APWU)	Postal Service	249
Letter Carriers (NALC)	Postal Service	210
Fire Fighters (IAFF)	State and Local	151
Government Employees (AFGE)	Federal Service	149
Rural Letter Carriers (NRLCA)	Postal Service	81
Treasury Employees (NTEU)	Federal Service	74
Federal Employees (NFFE)	Federal Service	30
Total Membership		5,704
Percentage of Public Employee Union Membership (1995)		.82
28 Unions' Total Membership		13,151
Total U.S. Nonagricultural Union Membership (1995)		16,327
28 Unions' Membership as a Percentage of Total U.S. Union Membership (1995)		.80

Sources: AFL-CIO biennial reports for federation-affiliated unions as reported in Gifford (1994); self-reported union membership data for the NEA and NRLCA, as reported in Gifford (1994); and Masters and Atkin (1993), based on estimates calculated from dues rates and dues-based income, for NFFE and NTEU. These two unions' self-reported membership data in Gifford (1994) were known to be the unions' representation data in the federal sector, where high free-riding rates prevail. Industry classifications are from Masters and Delaney (1985).

Note: Individual union membership numbers in some instances are rounded to the nearest thousand. Percentage should be multiplied by 180 for conventional interpretation.

regionals for the purpose of developing and implementing broad-based strategies to revitalize labor (Fitzpatrick and Waldstein 1994). In addition, a substantial portion of union finances and political activities evidently occur at this higher level, recognizing the necessity of coordinating action on a national, or, in some cases, even international scale in order to achieve important union objectives (Troy 1975; Sheflin and Troy 1983; Masters and Atkin 1996c).

DATA SOURCES

Disaggregated union membership data, which are generally available for the 1955–1993 period, are principally from biennial AFL-CIO membership reports compiled by the federation and reported in Gifford (various years). Data on independent or unaffiliated unions' (e.g., the NEA) membership are from self-reported union surveys provided in Gifford (various years) and the U.S. DOL, BLS (1970; 1980). Unfortunately, for some public sector unions (i.e., NEA, NFFE, NRLCA, and NTEU) membership data are not readily available for the first two decades of this forty-year interval. It should be mentioned that the NEA was not officially classified as a union until the late 1960s, having been previously treated as a professional association.

Financial data are obtained from the LM-2 forms that the twenty-eight unions are required to file with the U.S. DOL under the LMRDA. Before regulatory changes that took effect at the start of 1995, unions with more than $100,000 in annual revenues were required to file LM-2 financial disclosure reports; unions with smaller amounts of total revenue had to file less detailed LM-3 forms (see Atkin and Masters 1995).[14] The changes in disclosure requirements that took effect in 1995 raised the revenue floor for LM-2 disclosure to $200,000.

For this study, the first two pages of the LM-2 forms filed by the national organization of each of the major unions were purchased for their fiscal years between 1979 and 1993. While the LMRDA requires unions to file their annual forms with the DOL within ninety days of the close of their respective fiscal years, it does not require that unions operate on the same fiscal year. Financial data were matched according to the calendar year in which a fiscal year ended. At the time this study was initiated (early 1994), 1993 was the latest year for which disclosure forms were available.

The first two pages of the LM-2 report include dues rates (which, parenthetically, are not consistently reported across unions), beginning- and end-of-year balance sheets (assets and liabilities); and income statements (revenues and disbursements). The balance sheet reveals the following sources of assets: (1) cash on hand; (2) cash in banks; (3) accounts receivable; (4) loans receivable; (5) U.S. treasury securities; (6) mortgage investments; (7) other investments; (8) fixed assets; and (9) other assets. A total assets figure is also reported, both for the beginning and end of the relevant fiscal year. Reported liabilities include (1) accounts payable; (2) loans payable; (3) mortgages payable; and (4) other liabilities. Specific definitions of these various categories are provided in documents and regulations promulgated by the U.S. DOL (Labor–Management Standards Enforcement, undated; and Office of Labor–Management Standards 1994). It should be mentioned, however, that unions may differ on how to classify and ascertain the value of particular assets and liabilities. Unfortunately, it is not possible to identify these accounting differences—and thus establish common reporting practices—without the availability of audits and accompanying detailed schedules.[15]

The income statement discloses cash receipts and cash disbursements in selected categories for each fiscal year. Sixteen specific revenue items are enumerated: dues; per capita tax; fees; fines; assessments; work permits; on behalf of affiliates for transmittal to them; sale of supplies; interest; dividends; rents; loans obtained; sale of investments and fixed assets; repayment of loans made; from members for disbursement on their behalf; and from other sources. A total receipts itemization is also reported. Cash disbursements fall into the following classifications: "Per capita taxes; fees, fines, assessments, etc.; to affiliates of funds collected on their behalf; for account of affiliates; to officers (gross)/(less deductions); to employees (gross)/(less deductions); office and administrative expense; educational and publicity expense; professional fees; benefits; loans made; contributions, gifts, and grants; supplies for resale; purchase of investments and fixed assets; direct taxes; withholding taxes; on behalf of individual members; repayment of loans obtained; for other purposes; total disbursements." Again, the DOL has regulations defining these items, but unions still may vary in terms of how they classify specific transactions.

Data on union PACs were obtained from reports (U.S. FEC 1982; 1983; 1985; 1988; 1989; 1991; 1993; 1995a) on PAC finances. As noted, the unit of analysis is the receipts of the principal PAC sponsored by each national union (thus excluding PACs sponsored by local and regional affiliates) for each of the two-year election cycles corresponding to the 1980, 1982, 1984, 1986, 1988, 1990, 1992, and 1994 elections for the U.S. Congress and presidency. Federal election laws permit unions to sponsor multiple PACs at various organizational levels: local, regional, and national. All of the PACs affiliated with a parent union, however, are bound by a $5,000-contribution ceiling to each congressional and presidential candidate per primary and general election (or a $10,000 maximum over both elections). Thus, altogether the PACs sponsored by a parent union may not exceed this contribution limit. Given that many unions sponsor multiple PACs (at local and regional levels) which may operate, within this constraint, more or less autonomously, the data reported here understate the unions' overall PAC fundraising. However, the focus on national unions' PACs is consistent with the unit of analysis regarding membership (i.e., total union rather than local union) and finances (national union). In addition, there has been a trend toward the consolidation and centralization of union PAC activity at the national level, as indicated by the drop in the number of union PACs making contributions to federal candidates from 293 to 255 between the 1982 and 1994 cycles.

Interviews also were held with six top-level union staff associated with four of the unions in this sample. The interviews focused on the relationship between union finances and organizing activities. They were conducted at the unions' headquarters in Washington, D.C., in late 1994 and the summer of 1995. Each interview, which was conducted with a semistructured questionnaire, lasted approximately one hour. Confidentiality and anonymity were assured. Together, the four unions have well over three million members located in the private and public sectors. The interviews provided important background information as to the emergence of organizing as a union priority and the strategies labor organizations are employing to boost their presence in the workplace.

DATA MEASURES

As noted, union *membership* data are primarily from biennial reports from the AFL-CIO (for affiliates of the federation) or biennial surveys conducted by Gifford (1982, 1984, 1986, 1988, 1990, 1992, 1994). AFL-CIO reports, which cover most of the unions in this sample, provide data on the unions' two-year membership averages ending in odd years (1979, 1981, 1983, and so on up to 1993). Union membership for even years (e.g., 1980) are interpolated, or calculated as the midpoint between the immediately preceding and following odd years. A similar procedure is used for the unaffiliated or independent unions (NEA, NFFE, NTEU, NRLCA, and IBT before 1987, when it reaffiliated with the AFL-CIO). Because the NFFE did not report its membership to Gifford for the 1992 and 1994 editions and the NTEU evidently reported its representation coverage rather than its membership (the former is twice as large as the latter), these unions' memberships were estimated based on their dues rates and dues income for the 1990s (see Masters and Atkin 1993c).[16]

Several measures of financial capital are reported. Unless otherwise noted, these measures are reported in real or inflation-adjusted dollars (Consumer Price Index=100; 1982–1984). More specifically, the issue of how rich unions are involves the unions' *total assets* and *wealth* (net assets, or total assets minus total liabilities reported at the end of each fiscal year). Total assets and wealth are also computed on a per-member basis (assets and wealth, respectively, divided by membership for the corresponding year). A subcategory of *liquid assets* (or cash and cash equivalents) is also examined. Liquid assets include cash (on hand and in banks), accounts receivable, and U.S. Treasury securities. *Working capital* is calculated as the sum of these assets minus the sum of accounts payable and the catch-all "other liabilities" (again, at the end of the fiscal year).

Union income is reported in three basic ways. The first is simply *total receipts* or revenues from all sources, in real-dollar terms, except as noted otherwise. To varying degrees, however, this measure may artificially inflate the actual income available to the national union for general-purpose use. Some unions collect revenue on behalf of affiliates for transmittal to them, thus serving simply as a financial conduit. Similarly, unions may collect money on behalf of members that is earmarked for specific purposes, such as donations to charities or contributions to welfare and benefit funds. In addition, unions often may sell large quantities of major investments (e.g., U.S. Treasury securities that have matured) or fixed assets (e.g., buildings) that generate impressive sums. However, these receipts are typically used to buy similar assets in the same fiscal year. Thus, the net revenue surplus or profit is minimal or nonexistent. For these reasons, a second revenue measure of *operating income* is reported as total income minus the sum of transmittals to affiliates, transmittals on behalf of members, and the sale of investments and fixed assets, each of which, as noted earlier, is separately itemized on the LM-2 form.

Total and operating surpluses or profits are the net revenue or income the unions have at the end of a fiscal year. Total surplus is total revenue minus total disbursements, and operating surplus is operating income minus *operating disbursements* (i.e., total disbursements minus transmittals to affiliates, transmittals on behalf of members, and purchases of major investments and fixed assets). In many instances, these income measures are also reported on a per-member basis. The third major income measure is *member-based income*, which consists of dues, per capita taxes, assessments, fees, fines, and work permits.

Three accounting measures of financial performance also are explored. *Solvency* is the ratio between operating income and operating disbursements, as previously defined. *Liquidity* is the ratio between current or liquid assets (the sum of cash, accounts receivable, and U.S. Treasury securities) and current liabilities (accounts payable plus "other liabilities"). Liquidity is a measure of the total liquid reserves or working capital that a union has (e.g., it is sometimes viewed as the equivalent of the strike reserve of a union). *Reserve* is the ratio between working capital and operating disbursements.

Three PAC receipt measures are reported. One is real *total PAC receipts* (adjusted by a two-year inflation factor corresponding to the election cycle). A second is real *PAC receipts per member* (with union membership averaged over the corresponding two years).[17] Third, *PAC receipts as a percentage of member-based income*, averaged over the two-year cycle, is examined. This last measure shows the participation of union members in PAC fundraising relative to the various other activities for which dues are assessed.

Two basic strike fund capacity measures are computed. One is the ratio between union wealth and the estimated costs of a major strike (wealth-to-strike cost ratio). The second is the ratio between working capital and estimated strike costs (working-capital-to-strike-cost ratio). Strike costs are the sum of estimated strike benefits (assumed to equal $175 per week per striker) and estimated losses in member-based income, based on the number of strikers involved. As appropriate, these various data measures are discussed further in the text.

NOTES

1. Caterpillar's workers were ordered back to work by the UAW leadership, despite having overwhelmingly rejected the company's last offer. According to Kilborn (1995: A18), the leadership believed that "a worse alternative to returning [existed] . . . They point to cases of strikes, like the one in the 1980's at Eastern Airlines, that ended with the collapse of the company—and all its jobs."

2. NAFTA and GATT were both strongly supported by President Clinton. The AFL–CIO had opposed President Bush's support for NAFTA, arguing "the Bush Administration's claim—that NAFTA will create good U.S. jobs—is without foundation in fact, based solely on questionable economic theory" (AFL-CIO 1992: 1).

3. The AFL-CIO ("Talking Points on the Team Act," faxed transmission to author) and labor unions generally argue that passage of the Team Act "would be a mistake. What the Team Act would do is change current law to allow employers to select the employees who would speak to them on behalf of other employees. We fundamentally believe that only freely chosen employee representatives should speak for employees with respect to wages, hours, and conditions of work."

4. Many U.S.-based unions have members located outside the United States, particularly in Canada. The organizational unit of analysis in this study is the national or international level of union organization, exclusive of union locals and regional or intermediate units.

5. These numbers pertain to the federal fiscal years (FY), October 1 to September 30. As recently as 1980, more than 7,000 union certification elections were held, in which almost 479,000 employees were eligible voters, with unions winning 48 percent of the contests. The numbers dropped precipitously after FY 1981. Illustratively, the number of elections and eligible employees dropped from 6,656 and 403,837 to 4,247 and 258,626 between FY 1981 and FY 1982.

6. Voos (1984a; 1984b; 1987) disputes this argument based on a study of manufacturing unions' organizing expenditures between 1953 and 1974. She (1984a: 44) argues that "insofar as the union commitment to growth can be defined as the aggregate amount of real resources allocated to organizing, it is obvious that a decrease in commitment was not responsible for the decline in the percent organized over this period."

7. Specifically, the Special Counsel of the Merit Systems Protection Board in February 1985 "initiated dismissal actions against three federal union presidents because they campaigned for Walter Mondale [the Democratic presidential nominee] in 1984" (Masters and Bierman 1985: 518).

8. However, it is important to bear in mind that while a sizable minority of union members voted for this Republican president in 1980 and 1984, a majority of U.S. voters did so as well. Thus, a union–nonunion voting gap remained, as union members, as a whole, bucked the national trend.

9. According to Willman and Cave (1994: 395), one of the most significant changes to have occurred in the U.K. trade union movement "has been the progressive and continued concentration of union membership within the largest unions, particularly since 1987, with the formation of 'super-unions,' including MSF [Manufacturing, Science, Finance] (1989), GMPU [Graphical, Paper and Media Union] (1991), AEEU [Amalgamated Engineering and Electrical Union] (1992), and Unison [an amalgam of health service, local government, and other public employee unions] (1993)."

10. Specifically, the first two pages of the unions' financial disclosure forms were purchased. These two pages report breakdowns of assets, liabilities, revenues, and disbursements. At the time this study was launched (early 1994), 1993 disclosures were the last available for study. Labor unions with more than $100,000 in annual receipts had to file LM-2s before 1995, when the floor was raised to $200,000. Smaller organizations (those with less revenue) have filed LM-3s, which are abbreviated forms of the LM-2.

11. Six semistructured interviews were conducted between winter 1994 and summer 1995. Each lasted about one hour and was conducted in the union's Washington, D.C., headquarters. The interviews covered the role of union financial and political capital in promoting a union growth strategy and the various efforts unions were undertaking to expand their membership.

12. It is realized that some of the unions in both sectors are "mixed," consisting of private and public sector employees. Nonetheless, the unions are nominally the largest in terms of membership in the private sector, the state and local sector of government, the postal service, and the nonpostal federal service.

13. During this time period, a significant number of union mergers occurred, in which the major unions acquired smaller ones (as opposed to merging among themselves). Williamson (1995) documents these mergers over the 1985–1994 period. For instance, (1) the USW acquired the Upholsters (1985); (2) the SEIU acquired the Georgia State Employees (1985), Connecticut Employees Union (1985), the Licensed Practical Nurses Association (1985), the Iowa State Police Officers Association (1986), Maine State Employees Association (1988), the National Union of Hospital and Health Care Employees (1989), Wyoming Public Employees Association (1993), and the International Brotherhood of Firemen and Police (1994); and the CWA acquired the United Telegraph Union (1986), International Typographical Union (1987), National Association of Broadcast Employees and Technicians (1992), and the Union of Professional and Technical Employees (1993). While these mergers have contributed, to varying degrees, to the expansion of the twenty-eight unions' human, financial, and political capital, no attempt is made here to disentangle the effects of the mergers/acquisitions.

14. Under current regulations, labor organizations with between $15,000 and $200,000 annual revenues file an LM-3; unions with less than $15,000 file LM-4s.

15. The LM-2 form requires fifteen detailed schedules on assets, liabilities, sales, loans, and selected disbursements, such as purchases of investments and fixed assets and salaries and expenses allocated to officers and employees of the reporting labor organization.

16. The NTEU reports its membership as 150,000, which is comparable to the 148,882 federal employees it represented in fifty-five bargaining units in 1992 (U.S. Office of Personnel Management 1992: part 1, page 4). In actuality, the NTEU's membership is about half this representation figure.

17. For the 1993–1994 election cycle, membership is not a two-year average as in prior cycles but rather the number reported for 1993.

Chapter One

Strategic Perspectives on Union Resources: Human, Financial, and Political Capital

As member-based organizations, unions derive their essential strength from the rank and file, measured in terms of total membership and density in the labor force. Yet, their institutional condition and power may be affected by resources that are somewhat independent of sheer numbers. Even as nonprofit organizations, unions need financial capital to pay officers and staff and otherwise to serve their members' interests (Clark 1989; Clark and Gray 1991). While the availability of money will depend in significant part on the dues members pay, it also will be affected by dues rates, alternative revenue sources, and financial management practices, regardless of membership levels per se (Troy 1975; Willman, Morris, and Aston, 1993). Similarly, unions are compelled to raise political capital in order to compete effectively in pursuing a legal enactment strategy. Because of restrictive federal election campaign laws (Epstein 1976; 1980), they must raise political action committee money separately from regular income sources in order to make direct contributions to congressional and presidential campaigns—a longstanding labor practice (Bok and Dunlop 1970; Delaney and Masters 1991b; Masters and Delaney 1987b).[1] Although unions are essentially restricted to raising PAC money from members on a strictly voluntary basis, their fundraising yield is not necessarily a function of total membership. Instead, it depends on the degree of rank-and-file participation, which can be influenced by the effectiveness of union political education and the commitment and solidarity of the membership (Fields, Masters, and Thacker 1987; Clark and Masters 1996; Masters and Atkin 1996b).

To sum up, financial, political, and human capital directly affect the capacity of unions to represent their members and expand their organizational base. How unions mobilize and allocate these resources involves strategic and tactical decisions which may determine the extent to which this organizational capacity is effectively deployed.

This chapter puts these resource issues into a broader industrial-relations-systems strategic framework. The model illustrates the role that human, financial, and political capital play in affecting the basic strategies unions might use to affect decisions at various levels within the system. The chapter also discusses the role that strategic planning might play in informing unions about the important resource allocation questions they will have to address if a revitalization of the labor movement through a massive growth campaign is to become a top priority.

STRATEGIC LEVELS OF DECISION MAKING AND UNION RESOURCES

Figure 1.1 portrays a strategic framework for analyzing union resources within an industrial-relations system. Building upon the models developed by Dunlop (1958), Derber (1970), Kochan, Katz, and McKersie (1986), Fiorito, Gramm, and Hendricks (1991), Lawler (1990), and Weil (1994), the framework identifies three types of strategies unions may use to influence decision making at distinguishable levels. An underlying assumption is that unions, like other organizations, make certain "strategic choices" which will influence their overall condition. One set of choices concerns how they allocate various resources. Lawler (1990: 2) put the argument well, observing that a central aspect "of the strategic choice paradigm is that key organizational decision makers have significant discretion in selecting organizational actions and what they choose to do matters." Further, he (1990: 41) hypothesizes that "*Labor unions are effective to the extent that exchanges are structured with the environment to ensure a predictable and steady flow of resources critical to the union's survival.* Critical resources include a wide range of tangible and intangible factors, including the recruitment of new and retention of existing members, employer cooperation, financial support, governmental support, and legitimacy in the broader community." The viability and effectiveness of any mix of strategies and related tactics are directly affected by the availability of capital and the environmental conditions unions face. These strategies may be evaluated in terms of their impact on selected key outcomes, which affect and reflect the institutional power of unions and the well-being of the employees who they directly or indirectly represent.

Figure 1.1
Strategic Framework of Analysis of Unions

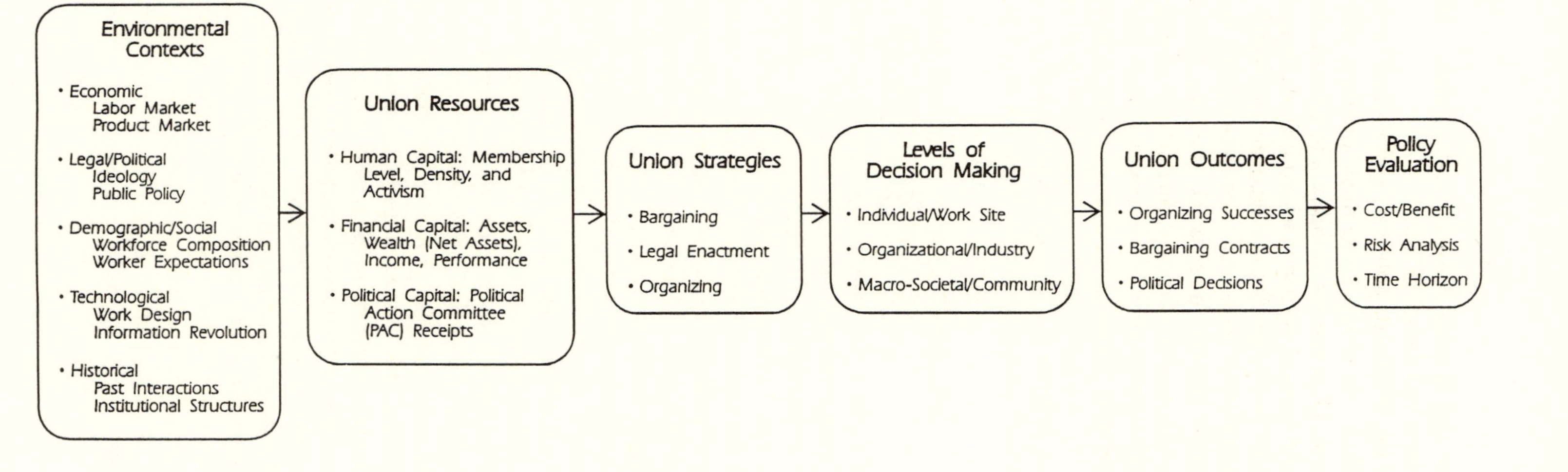

Levels of Strategic Decision Making

Unions represent and seek to influence employees (both members and nonmembers) through three basic levels of decision making which affect work-related conditions in one way or another (Kochan, Katz, and McKersie 1986). Specifically, they may focus on influencing decisions at the work-establishment or work-site level, where they interact with individual workers and local management on such matters as organizing new bargaining units, negotiating agreements, and handling grievances on the alleged improper administration of contracts or mistreatment of employees. Traditionally, unions have concentrated their organizing efforts, which have been largely ad hoc in nature, at this fundamentally work-site or shop-floor decision-making station (Barbash 1956; Craft and Extejt 1983). In this regard, efforts historically have not been characterized by broad-based, grassroots community mobilization in support of organizing. Instead, unions often have organized by "parachuting international representatives in for hot shot campaigns" rather than using a more proactive, *endemic* approach (Rogers 1995: 376).

The second level of decision making is the organizational point where basic terms and conditions of employment are often set. These terms and conditions of employment are established through unilateral, bilateral, or multilateral decision-making processes, depending in part on the extent to which an employer or employers coordinate employment-related decisions (e.g., allied into an association in which multiple employers negotiate with unions) and the degree to which employees are involved in decision making, perhaps through direct union representation. Decision making may occur at the level of a plant, a corporate division, the corporatewide level, or among an alliance of corporations within an industry formed for employment-related purposes.

Third, unions seek to influence community-level decision makers who affect the relative powers and prerogatives of employees (including unions) and employers in making decisions at all levels. Relevant parties include elected lawmakers, administrators, regulators, and judges, each of whom, to varying degrees, is subject to pressures from a variety of different interest groups. Further, to an increasing extent in recent decades, decision makers may be pushed to mandate basic terms and conditions of employment, as shown by organized labor's extensive lobbying for an increase in the minimum wage and to provide for more comprehensive health coverage. Broad-based community activism is one approach unions might use to influence these types of decision makers, particularly those who periodically stand before the electorate.

Union Strategies

To influence these decision-making processes, unions may use at least three basic types of strategies, each of which may apply to any decision level (Fiorito, Gramm, and Hendricks 1991; Hendricks, Gramm, and Fiorito 1993; Webb and Webb 1897). Collective bargaining "is typically the primary strategy used by unions in the U.S." (Fiorito, Gramm, and Hendricks 1991: 109). It focuses principally on the attainment of workplace goals through the negotiation and administration of contracts at the work site or organization/industry level, depending on the structure of bargaining (i.e., the range of employees and employers participating directly or indirectly in the negotiations). A bargaining strategy, however, also may be used to influence lawmakers or other community decision makers. For example, the 1981 strike by PATCO was intended in part to pressure members of Congress to pass legislation to raise pay and provide additional benefits to controllers employed by the Federal Aviation Administration (FAA). Specifically, PATCO struck over a bargaining impasse on economic matters over which, under the Federal Service Labor–Management Relations Statute (FSLMRS, or Title VII of the 1978 Civil Service Reform Act), Congress had primary jurisdiction (see Masters 1983; 1985).[2]

In addition, unions may negotiate contracts with provisions that facilitate ongoing or subsequent organizing efforts. A variant of this approach occurred in a "lease agreement between the City of Minneapolis and the Hilton's [the hotel chain] developer [which] guaranteed labor organizations rights of access to employees at work, voluntary card-check recognition, a pre-defined bargaining unit, and a neutral employer during any organizing drives" (Budd and Heinz 1996: 4). The Hotel and Restaurant Employees (HERE) union won the certification election thirty-two days after the hotel opened. While this lease agreement with the city has elements of a legal enactment strategy, it may be copied in collective bargaining contracts to promote the recognition of unions in new facilities opened by employees who are party to the initial contract. Obviously, the negotiation of such provisions presume a level of union bargaining power or employer cooperation which may not always be present.

Legal or legislative enactment often becomes the preferred or viable strategic alternative, because economic realities weaken union bargaining power or collective bargaining is limited in its coverage of employees. Legal enactment, for example, may promote basic workplace terms and conditions across union *and* nonunion employers, thus reducing the nonunion cost advantage. As a case in point, the minimum wage, which applies to union and nonunion employers, may raise the latter's average wage levels, thus reducing its labor cost advantage (Fiorito, Gramm, and Hendricks 1991; Kau and Rubin 1981). Thus, organized labor's support for the recently enacted increase in the minimum wage from $4.25 per hour to $5.15 (AFL-CIO 1995) is arguably in its institutional self-interest. (Congress passed a bill to raise the minimum wage from $4.25 per hour to $5.15 by September 1, 1997. The bill was enacted and signed into law by President Clinton in August 1996.) Similarly, unions may push for a comprehensive national health care program in order to reduce the extent to which unionized employers subsidize the provision of health care to nonunion employees who lack employer-provided health insurance.

At a fundamental level, legal enactment is the principal mechanism by which employees (through unions) and employers (through various other interest groups) establish their basic powers and rights vis-à-vis one another (Salisbury 1969). By granting employees the rights to form unions, bargain over major economic terms of employment, and strike, the NLRA has established a clear legal foundation for unions and collective bargaining. With the expansion of certain protections, unions might achieve greater recognition and power (Rose and Chaison 1995).

Organizing is a third basic strategy unions may use to advance their institutional position. It is aimed at increasing the membership level and density of unions. Although traditionally it has been operationalized in a relatively "ad hoc," "expedient," and "improvisational" manner (Craft and Extejt 1983; Barbash 1956), its strategic relevance lies in the objectives it seeks to attain. In other words, union organizing activity is pursued in part with the purpose of mind of enhancing the power of unions in negotiations with employers or on other fronts. Union density is associated with increased bargaining power (Freeman and Medoff 1984). As Voos (1987: 19) observes, "Those who have examined the costs and benefits that unions derive from organizing agree that a major economic incentive is the protection of union wage scales from the competition of low-wage nonunion firms." Thus, organizing is a strategy that unions may pursue in order to expand their economic power. With additional members, also, they may enhance their political power (Delaney and Schwochau 1993).

Operationally, the organizing strategy may focus on the work-site, organizationwide, and community levels. In fact, unions have increasingly experimented with departures from the traditional work-site focus, embarking on "corporate campaigns" and community-based organizing initiatives, and evidently intensifying their overall commitment to organizing vis-à-vis other union functions, such as collective bargaining and contract administration in the strictest sense of the terms (Craft and Extejt 1983; Jarley and Maranto 1990; AFL-CIO 1985; 1994a; CWA undated brochure; Grabelsky and Hurd 1994; Hurd 1989; Bennett and Delaney 1993).[3] Corporate campaigns, for example, exert financial leverage at the corporate level of organizational decision making. Developed in response to increasing difficulties in organizing on the shop floor, they may encompass an array of pressure tactics to move "toward the firm's strategic decision-making level in the hope of producing a long-term shift in firm practices that affect union objectives" (Jarley and Maranto 1990: 507).[4] The ACTWU pioneered this approach in its organizing campaign against a vociferously recalcitrant J. P. Stevens. In its campaign, the ACTWU challenged "the board of directors elections for New York Life

Insurance Company and Metropolitan Life Insurance Company—each of which had J. P. Stevens directors on its board and apparently had financial dealings with the company [i.e., J. P. Stevens]. The threat of adverse publicity and the cost of conducting the elections led these firms to oust the Stevens board members and exert pressures on Stevens to deal with the union" (Craft and Extejt 1983: 22).

More recently, the UFCW has been engaged in a massive campaign against nonunion Food Lion (a major retail grocer), which has filed a lawsuit charging UFCW with violating the Racketeer Influenced and Corrupt Organization Act (RICO), the Sherman Act, and the Clayton Act (for a provocative discussion of the UFCW's campaign, see DiLorenzo 1996).[5] Relatedly, unions may attempt to use general pension funds to promote membership. The AFL-CIO operates a program that invests pension funds in building projects to stimulate economic growth and union jobs. On a broader scale, unions have encouraged the "economically targeted investments" (ETIs) of pension funds into depressed areas on projects that would promote employment (and presumably union job growth). Further, they have attempted to change corporate behavior by mobilizing pension fund shareholders. A recent article in the *Wall Street Journal* (Lublin 1996: B1–2) highlights the role of Mr. William Patterson, corporate affairs director of the IBT, which has pension funds near $50 billion in total, in sparking shareholder activism. "Shareholder activism is wearing a union label . . . . The Teamsters may be leading the charge, but 11 other major unions, including the Service Employees and the Carpenters, are using shareholder activism as a bully pulpit—and scoring a growing number of victories . . . . With union pension funds now holding $250 billion of assets, 'governance structures affect the retirement income of the employees we represent.'"

Finally, unions have launched selective organizing campaigns to mobilize community coalitions to promote geographically broad-based initiatives (Hurd 1989; Jarley and Maranto 1990). The SEIU's "Justice for Janitors" campaign exemplifies this fundamentally grassroots approach. In this campaign, SEIU formed political alliances with various activist social groups, including immigrants' rights advocates, and mobilized marches and protests to encourage the bargaining representation of janitors across employers throughout the Los Angeles metropolitan region (Banks 1991–1992). The union succeeded in recruiting more than 35,000 new members.

Union Resources

The mix of strategies that unions may choose at any given point in time is constrained or facilitated by a set of organizational and environmental contexts. Apart from any internal political dynamics or ideological beliefs which may influence their strategic choices, unions are empowered or limited in the extent to which they may pursue any particular strategy by the resources that they have available. As noted, three sets of resources are relevant to defining their organizational capacity. First is human capital, which includes the number of members unions have at any given time, the density of representation within an industry or community in which they bargain with employers, and the relative activism of the rank and file. Obviously, more members, higher density, and greater activism will enhance union efforts to use any one of the principal strategies and to do so effectively.

Second, financial capital consists, among other things, of the assets, wealth (assets minus liabilities, or net assets), and income unions have at their disposal. Also relevant is their financial performance, such as the amount of liquid net assets (with liquidity referring to cash and more or less cash equivalents) relative to operating expenses. The performance of organized labor's assets "also provides information about the effectiveness of unions as managerial organizations" (Sheflin and Troy 1983: 149). Third, the availability of PAC money may affect the viability of a legal-enactment strategy (Steagall and Jennings 1996).

Environmental Contexts

Clearly, unions do not operate in a vacuum. Their resources, strategic choices, and ultimate influence will be affected substantially by a myriad of environmental factors, which will also influence the other parties which participate in key decision-making processes. The salient contexts of the environment deserve at least brief mention here.

The economic context is patently vital. Labor market conditions in particular will influence incentives that employees have to support unions. For instance, relatively high unemployment might discourage union-organizing efforts because employees fear the lack of other employment opportunities should they lose their jobs because they want union representation (Chaison and Rose 1991).

Product markets are also quite influential. Highly concentrated industries, in which a few employers have gained sizable market share, have proven more favorable to unions (Kochan, Katz, and McKersie 1986; Freeman and Medoff 1984). The more competitive the product market, however, the greater resistance unions might encounter, not only with respect to bargaining demands in situations where they have already achieved formal recognition, but also in their efforts to organize new sites. Many employers simply cannot afford higher labor costs and remain competitive at the same time. Indeed, unions vehemently opposed NAFTA and the GATT because increased international economic competition might export U.S. jobs (AFL-CIO 1992).[6]

The political–legal environment is important to organized labor's power as an institution in general and the strategies it might pursue to organize new members in particular (Barbash 1965; 1984; Aaron 1984). Many observers argue that the legal framework regulating labor relations in the U.S. contributes to the difficulties that unions face in organizing (Freeman and Medoff 1984; Weiler 1990; 1993). According to this perspective, the hurdles—and implied costs—of organizing are unduly high, especially in comparison to those conditions found in many other advanced industrial societies (e.g., Canada). Further, the sanctions against employers who violate employees' rights in this regard are considered too limited to deter illegal or unethical conduct (Freeman and Rogers 1993).

The political environment per se is important because it directly or indirectly molds the legal and regulatory conditions under which unions must operate on a daily basis. As noted, the Republican sweep of the Congress in the 1994 elections has sparked vigorous attacks on numerous landmark labor laws, including Davis-Bacon (AFL-CIO 1995c), the Fair Labor Standards Act (AFL-CIO 1995b), and occupational safety and health protections (AFL-CIO 1995e).[7] A possible or feared effect of these proposed legislative changes is to reduce the labor costs of nonunion employers (relative to unionized employers) and thus increase the incentives to secure union-free working environments. Unionized competitors would also face stiffer pressures to reduce labor costs.

Demographic changes and their implications regarding worker expectations also affect unions. The U.S. workforce has undergone profound demographic changes in recent decades and will continue to do so into the foreseeable future (U.S. Commission on the Future of Worker–Management Relations 1994a; 1994b). The workforce is increasingly female, minority, immigrant, and older. To appeal to this changing workforce, unions must broaden their message. They must also open their governing structures to groups that have been underrepresented if not largely excluded in the past (Needleman and Tanner 1987). In short, demographic shifts imply changing social and economic expectations that unions must address directly and promptly if their appeal among these groups is to keep pace with expected population growth. The heated contest between Thomas Donahue and John Sweeney for the presidency of the AFL-CIO was at least partly over the appeal (or lack thereof) that unions have had among these increasingly large groups of new entrants to the workplace (Bernstein 1995a).

Technology is also a powerful force. The mass production processes associated with the industrial revolution induced the wave of industrial unionism exemplified by the UAW and USW. As new technologies shift work away from mass production manufacturing, unions will inevitably have to change their emphasis or become less relevant. As the U.S. Commission on the Future of Worker–Management Relations (1994a: 7) noted,

"The new industrial composition of employment demands workers with different skills and with different responsibilities at the job than in the past and has contributed to the relative decline in the number of high paying jobs for manual workers." In this vein, technology will lead to job growth in many areas where unions are relatively unrepresented.

Historical relations among labor, employers, and government constitute another important set of external factors. For example, certain unions and employers may have had great antipathy for each other based on previous events (e.g., the UAW's bitter strike against Caterpillar) which may make it difficult to establish genuinely cooperative relationships. Thus, there is the danger that the parties' relationships will become self-fulfilling prophecies. Similarly, unions that have acquired reputations for illegal conduct, financial mismanagement, or insensitivity to minorities and women may experience greater difficulty in expanding their base of support, especially given today's workforce demographics, than unions that are not similarly tarnished.

Outcomes

The decisions of various parties at multiple levels will affect numerous outcomes of the system which are relevant to labor unions as institutions, their members and the employees they represent, and the realm of nonunion workers they seek to attract. Of particular relevance are organizing successes, favorableness of bargaining contracts, and desired political decisions that might, for instance, preserve union jobs (at least in the short term) and expand the rights of organized labor.

Evaluation

The last basic element of this strategic framework is the evaluation process. Often neglected, evaluation is essential if unions are to be able to determine which strategic choices to make and which have yielded dividends. Evaluating any organizational activity, however, is easier said than done, largely because many relevant factors may be unknown or unquantifiable at any given point in time. Also, especially in the organizing process, a long-term perspective (ten to twenty or more years) may be necessary.

Essentially, the evaluation process involves assessing the relative costs and benefits of the strategy or tactic pursued. Costs and benefits are either tangible or intangible. Tangible items may include monetary rewards (e.g., higher wages) or expenditures or the loss or gain of other assets to which it is possible to attach economic value. Another important tangible item is simply the time invested in pursuing certain activities. In this regard, organizing may involve many direct expenditures (e.g., organizers' salaries, travel, accommodations, media communications) plus the time of other union members and officers who are not directly compensated for performing this specific function. Intangible costs and benefits may include the public feelings of good or ill will unions create in organizing as well as the esprit de corps they can generate among rank and file. Another intangible is the net benefit that unions might have derived from the allocation of resources to pursuits other than chosen strategies. For example, if unions had selected another organizing tactic or invested their resources in serving current members rather than attracting new ones, how might they have benefited (or suffered) in relative terms? The answers to such questions are typically quite difficult.

Two other dimensions of the evaluation process complicate the assessment of costs and benefits. One is the assessment of the expected yield. In choosing strategies, unions make calculations as to the potential benefits, a determination which involves the relative risk or probability of success. Greater risks or chances of failure may involve higher yields if success is achieved. Conversely, low-risk strategies may yield fewer relative gains. The second dimension is the time horizon over which costs and benefits are evaluated. In some cases, unions may expect meager returns in the short run but comparatively large gains over the long haul. Thus, they may make a steep initial investment with little to show for it in the short term but with high yields expected in the more distant future.[8]

THE ROLE OF UNION RESOURCES

Model

Unions' human, financial, and political capital literally provide the inputs to permit and sustain their principal strategies, which in turn may impact organizing achievements, bargaining outcomes, and political decisions. Figure 1.2 illustrates some of the ways in which these forms of capital support union strategy (the litany of items is by no means intended to be exhaustive, but merely indicative of how such resources might tie into strategy development and implementation). With regard to human capital, union members constitute an important cadre of recruits to support not only bargaining activities (through their commitment to union objectives and participation in setting bargaining goals) but also political action and organizing. In this regard, many labor organizations, including the AFL-CIO, have intensified their efforts to increase union members' activism in all three strategies. The 1985 AFL-CIO report on *The Changing Situation of Workers and Their Unions* (AFL-CIO 1985) specifically recommended increasing rank-and-file participation in organizing,

Figure 1.2
The Role of Union Resources

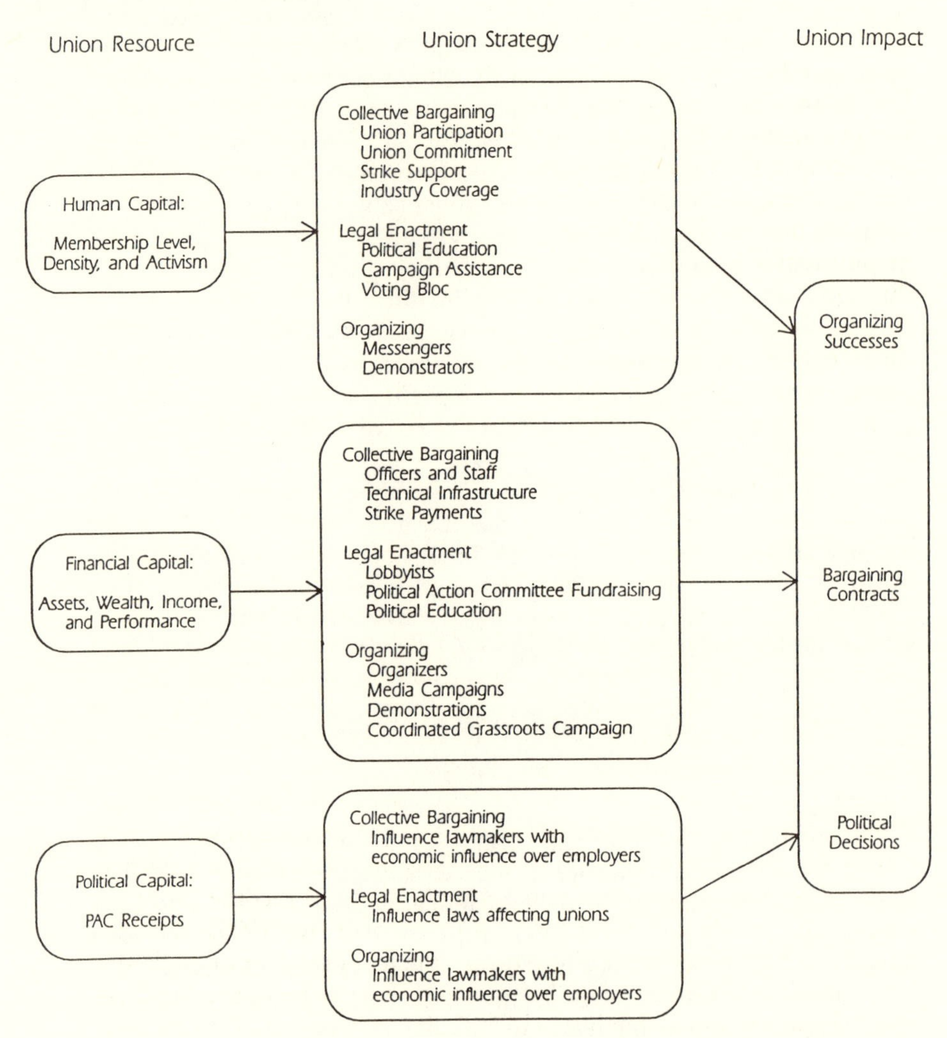

and Jarley, Delaney, and Fiorito (1992: 510) have reported that national unions have generally supported the "recommendations concerning member participation in union activities (particularly organizing and politics)." In fact, John Sweeney campaigned for the AFL-CIO presidency on a platform to create "a political training center to train [political] campaign organizers and campaign managers" and otherwise politicize union members (Nomani and Rose 1995: C13). He also pledged to deploy 1,000 new organizers over the next two years, concentrating on recruiting women and minorities.

As noted, human capital is important in two basic respects. First, the more members there are to begin with, generally speaking, the larger the base from which unions may recruit volunteers to support union activities in numerous ways, such as communicating their political message, providing assistance to political campaigns (e.g., staffing telephone banks), voting on election day, donating money to the labor PAC, and organizing new workers. Similarly, the more densely an industry or geographic region is unionized, the greater is the economic impact of a union through bargaining or a strike (Voos 1987; Freeman and Medoff 1984). Second, the relative activism of union members is also an essential part of the equation. In this regard, union members' participation in regular union activities and their "commitment" attitudes may strengthen bargaining effectiveness and solidarity in case of a strike (Fullagar and Barling 1987). It also has been shown to increase their willingness to support the union politically and to donate money to the labor PAC (Fields, Masters, and Thacker 1987; Masters, Atkin, and Schoenfeld 1990; Masters and Atkin 1996b; Clark and Masters 1996). Activism, as noted above, may also produce organizing benefits. As will be discussed in Chapter 3, the SEIU has defied the pattern of general union membership decline and grown considerably in the 1980s. Part of this gain is due to absorption of other unions, but Mr. Sweeney also attributes it in substantial part to SEIU's having "'resurrected 1930s-style campaigns that rely heavily on rank-and-file and turn membership drives into community issues involving church and nonprofit groups'" (Bernstein 1995: 87).

Financial capital is obviously critical to sustaining these strategies. While unions are not motivated, for political and legal reasons, to amass profits for their own sake, they nonetheless may accumulate wealth in order to provide a cushion against interruptions in income (due to a strike) and provide selected membership benefits (Troy 1975).[9] Put differently, as Barbash quotes Philip Murray, the first president of the USW: "'The modern labor union . . . has in many respects become a big business.' [However, it is a] 'big business' by union standards and not by business standards" (1956: 77).

Unions have traditionally managed their finances in such a way as to maintain a substantial portion of their assets and wealth in cash or investments readily convertible to cash (e.g., U.S. Treasury securities). As Barbash observed, "unions pursue extremely conservative policies in the investment of union funds. The union's assets are largely put in cash or government bonds" (1956: 80). The rationale for this investment policy—emphasizing liquidity or cash equivalency—rests, according to Troy on two grounds: "first, that 'profit-making' is of secondary consideration to them [i.e., unions] because they are nonprofit institutions; and second, that they require large cash resources to make the strike a credible weapon in industrial warfare" (1975: 38). Thus, there are internal political motivations, as well as financial or economic ones. Both union members and the general public will watch union finances to ensure that these nonprofit organizations do not pursue risky investments that jeopardize fiscal stability or viability. Also, as a matter of fiscal prudence, union investments should be relatively liquid to offer protection in case of adversity, like a strike or massive layoff, both of which disrupt the flow of normal income.

Although unions may divert some funds, apart from health and welfare benefits, for investments in order to generate additional money, they generally can be expected to spend the bulk of their regular income on behalf of their members. As Peterson notes, "the bulk of the unions' funds is used to advance the general economic interests of the millions of workers who support the unions, and to promote legislation and other measures which will improve the well-being of workers, nonunion as well as union" (1963: 92). Obviously, the more income a union generates, particularly in relation to the scope and diversity (occupational, geographic, or industrial) of its membership, the greater its financial capacity to provide these services.

In this spirit, unions take concerted measures to secure a dependable flow of revenue so as to support their array of representational functions and responsibilities. They commonly negotiate various forms of union-security arrangements (e.g., union and agency shops), except where prohibited from doing so by law (i.e., state right-to-work laws).[10] These arrangements require that employees (be they union members or not) belonging to duly certified bargaining units pay union dues or some equivalent, the justification being that since these employees enjoy the benefits of exclusive representation (regardless of membership status) they should also assume a fair share of the financial burden incurred in securing such benefits.

Turning more precisely to the use of financial capital, unions expend their regular income to pay officers, lobbyists, organizers, and clerical staff (Clark and Gray 1991; Clark 1989). In addition, they must supply administrative and technical infrastructure and other support. Furthermore, unions must often contract outside legal, financial analysis, political, and media consultants in order to provide expertise that might not be readily on hand. These external professional services may grow more significant as the economic, financial, legal, political, and public relations areas become more global, complicated, and sophisticated (Clark and Gray 1991; Clark 1992).

Programmatically, union expenditures serve to provide the staff and information necessary to planning and executing bargaining strategy, developing and lobbying legislative proposals, raising PAC money, and orchestrating various organizing campaigns. The plausible relevancy of financial resources to success on these matters is partly attested to by the CIO's aggressive organizing campaigns in the 1930s. According to Galenson (1960: 601), the industrial unions' organizing successes in the latter part of that tumultuous decade were due in no small measure to the relatively large sums of money the CIO poured into the effort: "There was no royal road to expansion. Cash was an essential ingredient, and if to John L. Lewis goes the credit for the first million-dollar organizing drive (steel), it must be said that the AFL leaders responded by loosening their normally tight purse strings when faced with the challenge of the CIO." In other words, the CIO's financial commitment to organizing reverberated throughout the labor movement, including the CIO's then rival, the AFL. "For all years between 1938 and 1941, organizing expenses constituted more than half of total AFL expenditures" (Galenson 1960: 595).

More contemporaneously, numerous unions have either substantially increased their financial commitment to organizing or pledged to do so in short order (Zachary 1995). While such commitments do not necessarily guarantee success, they are, according to William Gould, IV, current chairman of the NLRB, an "'essential condition for any revival'" (Zachary 1995: A1). Indeed, one of the principal reasons why John Sweeney won the AFL-CIO presidency may have been his union's well-known financial commitment to organizing. Bernstein (1995a: 87) reports that Sweeney's SEIU "sinks a third of . . . [its] $53 million annual budget into membership drives, vs. 2% to 4% at most unions." Parenthetically, the intensive focus on organizing displayed by UFCW, plus its willingness to confront a major nonunion employer, Food Lion, has led the target (i.e., Food Lion) of this allegedly illegal corporate campaign to challenge the use of union monies for such purposes. The objective of the litigation, in part, would appear to be to stymie the financing of certain types of anti-employer activities waged as part of an aggressive corporate-type organizing campaign.

Finally, political capital, as measured in part by PAC receipts, is used to influence lawmakers. While it may focus mainly on affecting the legal enactment strategy, it also may serve collective bargaining and organizing strategies in direct and indirect ways. For example, the IAM, which until recently was embroiled in a strike against the Boeing corporation, lobbied President Clinton's administration to prevent the aircraft manufacturing corporation from transferring technology and skilled jobs to China (Bernstein 1995b). Thus, the IAM attempted to exploit its political currency to bolster its collective bargaining (i.e., strike) strategy against Boeing. Unions also may lobby lawmakers, many of whom have received union money and in-kind donations, to pass legislation which would directly or indirectly preserve union jobs and otherwise promote union membership. Illustratively, Greenhouse (1995: A17) reports that "top union officials of the Northeast are urging their states to join forces to punish corporations that move operations to low-wage states and countries. The AFL-CIO presidents of New York, New Jersey, Connecticut and eight other Northeastern states are pushing for laws that would forbid states to sign contracts with such companies and prohibit public employee pension funds from investing in them." To the extent that such a policy arrests the exodus of union jobs, it would ease the task of organizing.

In conclusion, the human, financial, and political capital of unions influence the "strategic choices" (Weil 1994: 154) available at any given point in time, as vividly reflected in the AFL-CIO's thirty-five-million-dollar campaign (financed from affiliated unions' treasuries) to affect the 1996 congressional and presidential elections. Unions with greater resources usually have a broader panoply of options and potential to influence important outcomes. The status of these essential resource inputs also inform the membership as to how well the union is being led (Weil 1994). Unions with declining memberships, troublesome finances, and little political capital may want to reevaluate their organizational priorities. Those in particularly dire straits may seriously consider if they might benefit from a merger. Further, the status of unions regarding these dimensions serves to instruct management and the broader community about an institution whose future has important implications (positive or negative, depending in part on one's point of view) for the economic and political condition of the nation (Weil 1994).

Previous Research

Research on the human, financial, and political capital of unions is sketchy and sporadic, particularly as it relates to the interrelationship between these three dimensions. While a copious amount of research analyzes the determinants of individual and aggregate unionization (e.g., Chaison and Rose 1991; Wheeler and McClendon 1991; Farber and Krueger 1993; Fiorito, Stepina, and Bozeman 1996) and the impacts of aggregate union membership and density on economic and political outcomes (Freeman and Medoff 1984; Kochan, Katz, and McKersie 1986; Kau and Rubin 1981), less research systematically examines changes in union membership at the level of the national union (e.g., Fiorito, Jarley, and Delaney 1995; see Masters and Atkin 1989; 1990; 1996b; and 1996c for an examination of such data among selected public sector unions). With regard to union finances, only a handful of studies provide reasonably current treatments of the subject among U.S. unions (e.g., Troy 1975) and they tend to aggregate data across unions. Finally, few studies explore union PAC receipts, although a growing body of literature examines the impact of union PAC contributions on legislators (e.g., Moore et al. 1995). The purpose of this section is to provide a brief review of the literature, especially as it relates to the relationships between union membership, union finances, and political money.

At first blush, it appears intuitively convincing that union membership should be positively correlated with the other two dimensions of organizational wherewithal. In the main, as membership-based, nonprofit organizations, unions may be expected to derive the bulk of their income, and, by implication, their assets and wealth, from dues and other member revenue sources. The limited research on union finances attests to this relative dependency, at least at the aggregate level, with a few exceptions (Troy 1975; Sheflin and Troy 1983; for an exception pertaining to the UAW, see Perusek 1989). Thus, a decline in union membership would almost automatically imply a diminished base of revenue, unless offset with increases in dues rates and other member assessments. Such hikes, however, require direct or indirect membership approval under the LMRDA, and thus are often politically problematic for union leaders (Bok and Dunlop 1970).

Similarly, unions depend on the rank and file for PAC receipts. As a matter of fact, the dependency is well-nigh exclusive. The Federal Election Campaign Act of 1971, as amended, allows only very limited forays into broader employee ranks (U.S. FEC 1992). In reality, unions have drawn the overwhelming bulk of PAC receipts from member-based solicitations (Sabato 1985). Thus, other things being equal, it would seem that a decline in union membership would erode the capacity of unions to raise PAC money, unless the rate and degree of union members' PAC donation participation were to grow by an offsetting amount.

Interestingly, the research on union finances and PAC fundraising suggests some counterintuitive possibilities. In a study on aggregate private and public sector unions' finances (at the national, regional, and local levels combined), Sheflin and Troy (1983: 152) found that union income from various sources rose during the 1970s, despite a sizable drop in aggregate union density: "Consolidated union income rose by . . . 4 percent in real [i.e., inflation-adjusted] terms and .5 percent on a per member basis." However, it should be noted that this represented a significant drop from gains registered in the 1960s. Also, total union assets and wealth declined in the 1970s. "Real net assets per [union] member . . . declined . . . by almost 8 percent" (Sheflin and Troy 1983: 150).

In an analysis of member-based income (from dues, fees, fines, assessments, per capita taxes, and work permits), Bennett (1991) found that unions, at least in the private sector, gained in the 1970s despite membership losses. Real receipts from these sources climbed from $3.1 billion in 1960 to $5.7 billion in 1976 (although they had dropped from $5.9 billion in

1970). On a per-member basis, union member-based income rose (in real dollar terms) from $213 in 1960 to $350 in 1970 to $355 in 1976 to $444 in 1987 (Bennett 1991: 4). This led Bennett (1991: 9) to make the following emphatic statement about the state of private sector unions in the United States:

> Although private sector unions had experienced severe declines in union density and membership, particularly during the 1980s, these labor organizations are financially prosperous. By raising per capita income from members, private sector unions in the aggregate have been able to offset declines in revenues from reduced membership . . . . The conventional wisdom that unions are in a state of economic and political decline may be dismissed in the same way that Samuel Langhorn Clemens (Mark Twain) responded to premature reports of his death, that is, as 'greatly exaggerated'!

Willman, Morris, and Aston (1993) at least partially corroborate these findings in their comprehensive analysis of union finances among trade unions in the United Kingdom in the post–World War II era. Indeed, they (1993: 17) found a seemingly contradictory relationship between the state of union finances, on the one hand, and union membership, on the other hand:

> One of the more interesting contrasts to draw is that between the poor financial performance during [membership] expansion and the improved performance during rapid contraction in the 1980s. The increase in union real income and worth between 1980 and 1988 has not been matched before in the post-war period, nor has the rate of membership loss; the membership and real worth curves for the post-war period are almost mirror images. This contrast thus serves to emphasize that financial improvements do not depend solely on membership performance.

However, this observation must be tempered by Willman and Morris's (1995) update of British union finances into the 1990s. They found that union financial performance, measured in terms of real net worth and real income, deteriorated in the early 1990s, after peaking in 1987. This led them to conclude that there had been a long-term secular decline in union financial conditions since World War II which might have been partially alleviated in the 1980s but not fundamentally altered: "The key financial problems faced by British unions in the post-war years have not been solved . . . . Despite changes to financial management in the 1980s, the structural problems persist" (Willman and Morris 1995: 291).

With regard to political income, empirical research shows a positive but nonlinear relationship between union membership and PAC contributions (which are a subset of PAC receipts) to congressional and presidential candidates combined (Masters and Delaney 1984; 1985; Delaney, Fiorito, and Masters 1988).[11] In other words, while larger unions (in terms of total membership) tended to give larger amounts of PAC money in total to these candidates in selected election cycles, this relationship diminishes at some point. In fact, Masters and Delaney (1987a: 224) observed that "while large unions gave a substantial chunk of labor's total PAC contributions, they tended to give less on a per-member basis than smaller unions." Furthermore, Masters, Atkin, and Delaney (1990) found that total union PAC receipts jumped from approximately 86 cents per-member in the 1977–1978 federal election cycle to nearly $4.50 in 1987–1988 (unadjusted for inflation). Bennett (1991) confirms this growth in real dollar terms, finding that labor unions' real PAC receipts almost doubled between 1975–1976 and 1987–1988, despite sizable membership losses during this period.

These data suggest that it is at least plausible that unions may perform relatively well in raising financial and political capital at the same time their human capital base is shrinking. This possibility is important, particularly to the extent that these resources are somewhat independent sources of potential power and influence. As Willman, Morris, and Aston (1993: 19) comment: "A wealthier trade union movement might sustain a better membership performance than a poor one *ceteris paribus* through the devotion of more resources to membership retention and acquisition." Obviously, the unabated decline in union ranks would at some point exhaust any union's capacity to survive, either financially or politically. But, in the interim, financial and political resources might offset membership declines in stabilizing a drop in overall union capacity and at the same time offer currency unions can expend to seek outright advancement on the membership front. Thus, in a nutshell, it is salient to examine all three dimensions of union wherewithal. This examination is particularly crucial at the disaggregate as well as aggregate union levels, because the labor movement, as mentioned earlier, is by no means monolithic. Interunion differences may suggest strategies and tactics to promote union growth and viability well into the future.

STRATEGIC RESOURCE ALLOCATION PLANNING

At the crossroads, many unions are paying much more attention to strategic planning as they seek to transform or "reengineer" their organizations (Stratton and Brown 1989; Fitzpatrick and Waldstein 1994; Schurman and Stack 1994; Stratton-Devine 1992). According to a survey of 114 major national unions, approximately 35 percent engaged in some type of formal planning (Stratton and Brown 1989), and other research reports highly sophisticated strategic planning occurring among some of the unions (Fitzpatrick and Waldstein 1994). Interestingly, there is limited empirical evidence to support the proposition that such planning is associated with union membership growth (Stratton and Brown 1989), although what is cause or effect is not necessarily distinguishable from the data. In any event, the national union can serve the essential function of promoting planning. It has, as previously noted, the organizationwide perspective to push the institution forward. According to Fitzpatrick and Waldstein (1994: 76), it best serves strategic planning if it "coordinates the development of strategy by leading consensus building around problems and necessary strategic directions. In so doing, the central body must ensure that disparate or conflicting interests are understood and resolved."

The availability and allocation of resources is central to this overall process. Ideally, strategic planning unfolds in three stages: (1) setting goals and determining which strategic (e.g., legal enactment or organizing) and tactical approaches are best suited to their achievement; (2) assessing the organization and planning how to organize internally and allocate resources to achieve strategic objectives; and (3) implementing the organizational plan—that is, actually restructuring and reallocating resources if such is required (Fitzpatrick and Waldstein 1994; Weil 1994; Schurman and Stack 1994). If, for example, organizing new members is set as a principal union goal, then the current allocation of resources devoted to this function must be assessed relative to what are reasonable estimates of what is needed to achieve that mission. As Grabelsky and Hurd (1994: 103) observe, the "reallocation of resources and a restructuring of the union accompany" major changes such as transforming a union from one which focuses primarily on servicing *current* members to one which focuses on organizing *new* ones. Not only may financial capital be reallocated by setting new budgetary priorities, but human capital may need to be shifted and mobilized—motivated—as well. A logical part, then, of strategic planning would be the strategic allocation of human resources, including volunteers, to support overall union objectives—that is, to develop a comprehensive strategic human resource use plan (Stratton-Devine 1992).

NOTES

1. The Federal Election Campaign Act of 1971, as amended, prohibits labor unions from funneling their regular treasury monies (from dues, etc.) into the coffers of presidential and congressional candidates. However, they may establish separate segregated funds, or PACs, that raise money from union rank and file through voluntary solicitations. These separately accounted PAC funds may be used as contributions to these federal campaigns, with a $5,000-per-candidate maximum per general and primary elections (or a $10,000 overall limit). Unions may use their treasury monies to raise PAC funds, lobby Congress and the White House, engage in "partisan" communications with their memberships, and engage in "nonpartisan" communications with the general public. Also, union PACs may make "independent" expenditures on behalf of congressional and presidential candidates which exceed the limits on direct campaign contributions. (See U.S. FEC 1992 for a detailed discussion of campaign restrictions and allowances).

2. The FSLMRS contains a much more restricted scope of bargaining than the National Labor Relations Act and many state-level public employee bargaining laws. It bans negotiations on wages, fringe benefits, and union-security agreements (e.g., union and agency shops). The FSLMRS also prohibits strikes and other job actions, such as work slowdowns. Federal employees who strike in defiance of the law may face immediate dismissal, and the unions sponsoring such actions risk decertification by the Federal Labor Relations Authority, which is, in fact, what occurred in the PATCO case.

3. In its summer 1996 issue, the *Journal of Labor Research* (27: 327–424) published a symposium on "Corporate Campaigns." The seven articles in the symposium were introduced by the journal's editor, James T. Bennett (1996: 327), who observes that "the strategies that comprise corporate campaigns are by no means new, but their use has greatly intensified and become much more sophisticated over time." He quotes from the newly installed AFL-CIO president's (John Sweeney) acceptance speech: "'We will use old-fashioned mass demonstrations as well as sophisticated corporate campaigns to make worker [sic] rights the civil rights issue of the 1990s.'" The articles in the symposium discuss the use of regulatory agencies to further union objectives (Northrup 1996), the evolution of corporate campaigns (Perry 1996), the UFCW's corporate campaign against Food Lion (DiLorenzo 1996), the campaign waged by the UAW against Caterpillar (Gangemi and Torres 1996), the *Daily News* war of 1990–1991 (Vigilante 1996), a Capitol Hill perspective (Hoekstra 1996), and legal and regulatory responses to corporate campaigns (McGuiness 1996).

4. McGuiness (1996: 419) identifies "two prominent" elements of many corporate campaigns: "having the target company perceived as the villain by the company's investors, customers, employees and the public at large, and initiating enforcement and oversight actions by federal, state and local governmental agencies as a form of harassment."

5. On July 25, 1995, Food Lion filed suit against the UFCW in U.S. District Court (North Carolina, Statesville Division). The suit, as stated in the complaint prepared for Food Lion by the law firm of Akin, Gump, Strauss, Hauer, and Feld (1333 New Hampshire Avenue, N.W., Washington, DC 20036), "arises out of an ongoing pattern of extortionate, fraudulent, anticompetitive, and tortious activity of Defendants [the UFCW and various of its officers] designed to cause massive injury to Food Lion's business and reputation, and ultimately to drive Food Lion out of business."

6. In opposing NAFTA, the AFL-CIO argued that the free trade agreement would cost the United States thousands of high-pay jobs, citing an Economic Policy Institute study which projected "a job loss of 550,000 U.S. high wage jobs in the next ten years" (AFL-CIO 1992: 1).

7. Specifically the AFL-CIO and unions generally have opposed legislation (Senate bill #141 and House bill #500, introduced in 1995) to repeal the Davis-Bacon Act; opposed Senate bill #1129, which would weaken overtime pay provisions of the Fair Labor Standards Act; and opposed House bill #1834 to weaken the Occupational Safety and Health Act of 1970.

8. This perspective was stressed in the course of the interviews conducted. One union staff person said that his organization is willing to wait a generation or two for certain organizing campaigns to bear fruit.

9. The LMRDA, popularly known as the Landrum-Griffin Act, was enacted on the heels of revelations of union corruption and undemocratic practice. It "represented a comprehensive effort to deal with the abuses in internal union administration that . . . [congressional] investigations had shown to exist in important segments of the labor movement" (Seidman 1964: 24). The act regulates the election of union officers, establishes union members' rights within the union (to participate in setting dues rates, etc.), and requires annual financial disclosure statements. For an excellent discussion of the legislation and its historical context, see Estey, Taft, and Wagner (1964).

10. Section 14(b) of the Taft Hartley Act of 1947 allows states to enact right-to-work laws (RTWs), which forbid union-security arrangements. Twenty-one states, mainly in the southern region, have enacted such laws. An effect of these laws is free-riding (i.e., employees who are represented by unions need not pay dues). Thus, while 18.3 million employees are represented by unions in the United States, only 16.4 million are members, which is an 11 percent gap. The FSLMRS also disallows union-security agreements, as does the Postal Reorganization Act of 1970. The federal government is the nation's largest "open shop" employer. There is clear evidence of a massive free-riding problem in the federal service (i.e., the civilian wage-grade and general schedule employees; see Masters and Atkin 1989; 1990; 1993b; 1995).

11. In the 1994–1995 federal election cycle, labor unions, as a whole, raised $90,392,122 in PAC money, and spent $88,531,659 of that amount. Congressional and presidential candidates received only $41,867,393, or 46 percent, of the total receipts.

Chapter 2

Union Density and Membership

Unions have existed throughout the history of the United States (Perlman 1928). Originating primarily among skilled artisans, they have served a variety of economic and political purposes. In the process, union fortunes have also varied dramatically. The mystical Knights of Labor grew exponentially in the mid-1880s, but departed almost as quickly from the national stage.[1] In current form, unions stem mainly from the craft-type organizations that founded the AFL late in the 19th century and the industrial-based affiliates of the CIO, borne in the economic strife of the 1930s.[2] While contemporary unionism may have exhibited more stability than the Knights of Labor, it has nonetheless undergone several periods of rapid change in this century.

This chapter reviews aggregate trends in union density and membership. Specifically, it puts these trends into historical context and contrasts them with developments in other advanced industrial democracies. It also explores unionization trends across major industrial, occupational, and demographic classifications to show more current and precise sources of decline and growth. Finally, the chapter discusses the macrodeterminants of union decline with an eye toward suggesting where labor needs to concentrate its organizing efforts in order to grow.

AGGREGATE DENSITY AND MEMBERSHIP TRENDS

Density

Table 2.1 provides union membership and density data for selected years between 1920 and 1995. It also reports the percentage change in

Table 2.1
Aggregate Union Density Rates and Membership (Selected Years 1920–1995)

Year	Union Membership	Percentage Change in Decade	Total Union Density	Nonagricultural Union Density	Percentage Change in Decade[1]
1920	4,823		11.7%	17.6%	
1930	3,401	-29.5%	6.8	11.6	-34.1%
1936	3,989		7.4	13.7	
1940	8,717	156.3	15.5	26.9	131.9
1946	14,395		23.6	34.5	
1950	14,267	63.7	22.3	31.5	17.1
1956	17,490		25.2	33.4	
1960	17,049	19.5	23.6	31.4	-.0
1966	17,940		22.7	28.1	
1970	19,381	13.7	22.6	27.3	-13.0
1976	19,634		20.3	24.7	
1980	22,366	15.4	20.9	24.7	-9.5
1986	16,975		17.5	17.8	
1990	16,740	-25.1	16.1	16.3	-34.0
1991	16,568		16.1	16.4	
1992	16,390		15.8	16.0	
1993	16,598		15.8	16.0	
1994	16,748		15.5	15.7	
1995	16,360	-2.3	14.9	15.0	-8.0

Sources: 1920: Troy and Sheflin (1985); 1930–1980: Goldfield (1987); 1986–1995: U.S. DOL, BLS (1988; 1990; 1992; 1993a; 1994; 1996a).

1. Percentage change is based on nonagricultural density.

membership levels and density rates during the seven-and-one-half decades covered. The data reveal that union membership has fallen in only two full decades. In fact, the steepest relative drop occurred in the 1920s, when membership declined from 4.8 million to 3.4 million, or by almost 30 percent. While nearly four times as many members (5.6 million versus 1.4 million) were actually lost in the 1980s, the percentage decline (25 percent) was less than recorded sixty years earlier. Obviously, membership grew enormously in the 1930s and 1940s, and nontrivial increases also took place in the thirty years between 1950 and 1980. In addition, membership increased in 1993 and 1994, although it fell again in 1995, to a point where it is 2.3 percent less than it was in 1990.

In sharp contrast, union density (based on the nonagricultural workforce) fell during most of the seventy-five years, except for the 1930s and 1940s. The drops in density in the 1920s and 1980s are almost exactly comparable in scope, at 34 percent. Since the late 1940s and early-to-middle 1950s, union density has been more than halved, falling from 34.5 percent in 1946 to 15 percent in 1995. It is noteworthy, however, that the rate of decline has apparently leveled off in the 1990s, from the steep losses registered in the 1980s.

What these data unambiguously show is that unions have suffered severe losses in the past, even relatively greater than those recorded in the 1980s. Yet, the serious drop in union density in that decade followed two decades worth of significant retrenchment. Thus, the current membership problem cannot be fully ascribed to phenomena unique to the 1980s, such as the political climate under Ronald Reagan. Furthermore, the data also indicate that the key to labor's future, barring unforeseen events that might lead to the exponential upturn shown in the tumultuous New Deal–World War II era, is whether the increase in membership exhibited in 1993 and 1994 can be escalated to points above general labor force growth. To have maintained the same density rate in 1994 as they had the previous year, unions would have had to have added 315,000 more members to their ranks, or more than twice the 150,000 actual increment achieved in that year.[3] To have maintained the same 15.8 percent rate into 1995, an additional one million workers would have had to have been added to the union ranks above the 16.36 million. Thus, the difficulty in overcoming a decline in union density is one that is compounded severely over time.

INTERNATIONAL UNION DENSITY TRENDS

While there appears to be some divergence in density trends among advanced industrialized countries, the decline in the United States is not unique. Comparing density rates among Seventeen Organization for Economic Co-operation and Development (OECD) countries between 1970 and 1988, Freeman and Rogers (1993) found that the rates had declined in nine of the countries.[4] Troy (1990), in an analysis of density trends in selected European countries, the United States, and Canada, documented a fairly wide decline in unionization, particularly within the "market" segments of these economies.[5] Growth in public sector unionism had at least partially offset the aggregate drop in density, especially in Canada (for the reported period between 1975–1985).

More recently, Strauss (1995) reports that union density fell at a more rapid rate in France, Spain, and New Zealand than in the United States during the late 1980s and early 1990s. He further reported that union density had fallen significantly in Britain since 1979, and that the density rate in Australia had dropped from 48 percent in 1982 to 37.8 percent in 1993.[6] Also, Harbridge and Honeybone (1996) have reported that union density in New Zealand has plummeted from 43.5 percent in 1985 to 23.4 percent in 1994. In contrast, Canadian union membership (as a percentage of nonagricultural employment) rose from 32.4 percent in 1971 to 37.4 percent in 1992 (Bureau of Labour Information, Canada 1992–93), leading Rose and Chaison (1996: 78) to conclude that the U.S. and Canadian "labor movements, once so closely intertwined that comparative analysis almost seemed redundant, are moving in opposite directions."[7] Table 2.2 reports trends in union density among selected OECD countries, showing the global dimensions of the phenomenon.

The widespread decline in unionization has lent support to the relevance of structural explanatory factors, such as "the changing structure of employment, especially away from manufacturing and blue-collar work toward services and white-collar occupations" (Strauss 1995: 331). However, certain country-specific reasons, such as changes in labor laws, privatization, and deregulation, are also cited, as well as the underlying favorableness of public policy toward the organizing process (Strauss 1995; Chaison and Rose 1991; Rose and Chaison 1996). Whether union density results from or is the cause of such unfavorable developments, the international scope of union decline suggests the difficulty of the challenges facing unions in many countries. To the extent that the revitalization of U.S. unions depends on their capacity to exert international economic leverage, the drop in union densities in other major economies may have significant implications.[8]

UNIONIZATION BY INDUSTRY, OCCUPATION, AND DEMOGRAPHIC CLASSIFICATIONS

Although these aggregate union membership and density trends have raised legitimate voices of concern as to the future of labor unions in the United States, they may nevertheless mask considerable variation among particular economic segments. In this regard, private and public sector union density trends have reflected mirror images. While private sector density exceeded a third of the workforce in the 1950s, it has fallen to just above 10 percent in 1995. In contrast, public sector unionization has risen from less than 10 percent to nearly 40 percent during the same period. Because unions do not enlist new members per se at the macro or aggregate level but rather among individuals within particular industries, occupations, and demographic groups, it makes sense to decompose union density by major classifications along these lines. Focusing on the 1980–1995 period for industry and 1985–1995 for occupations and demographics, this decomposition permits a more precise determination of

Table 2.2
Comparative Union Density Rates

	Year		Percentage Change
Country	1970[1]	1990	1970-1990[2]
Australia	50	40	-.20
Austria	60	48	-.20
Belgium	46	51	+.11
Canada	31	36	+.16
Finland	51	72	+.41
France	22	10	-.54
Germany	33	32	-.03
Japan	35	25	-.28
Netherlands	37	25	-.32
New Zealand	46	45	-.02
Norway	51	56	+.10
Portugal	--	32	--
Spain	--	11	--
Sweden	68	83	+.22
Switzerland	31	27	-.13
United Kingdom	45	43[3]	-.04
United States	30	16	-.47

Sources: 1970: Freeman and Rogers (1993: 16); 1990: OECD (1994).

1. Freeman and Rogers (1993) numbers, which are based on OECD data, are kept for reasons of consistency, even though they may differ from other sources, such as the BLS data on U.S. union membership in 1970.
2. Percentage change numbers should be multiplied by 100 for conventional interpretation.
3. Data are from Andrews and Naylor (1994).

where unions have experienced the most difficulties and where renewal strategies will have to be targeted successfully if downward aggregate density trends are to be reversed.

Industry Data

Table 2.3 reports the union membership data by major industrial classifications. In this sixteen-year span, unions lost nearly half their private sector members, causing the density rate to be halved. This decline occurred

Table 2.3
Union Membership and Density by Major Industry Classifications (1980–1995)

Industrial Classification	Year 1980	1985	1990	1995	Membership Loss/ Gain	1980-1995 Percentage Change
Private Sector (nonagricultural)	18,232 (22.3%)	11,227 (14.6%)	10,227 (12.1%)	9,400 (10.4%)	-8,832	-48.4% -53.4
Mining	286 (32.1%)	153 (17.3%)	121 (18.0%)	84 (13.8%)	-202	-70.6 -57.0
Construction	1,574. (31.6%)	1,051 (22.3%)	1,073 (21.0%)	908 (17.7%)	-666	-42.3 -44.0
Manufacturing	6,771 (32.3%)	4,996 (24.8%)	4,197 (20.6%)	3,440 (17.6%)	-3331	-49.2 -45.5
Transportation	2,903 (48.0%)	2,118 (37.0%)	1,934 (31.6%)	1,792 (27.3%)	-1111	-38.3 -43.1
Trade	1,753 (10.1%)	1,400 (7.2%)	1,338 (6.3%)	1,401 (6.1%)	-352	-20.1 -39.6
Finance	190 (3.7%)	177 (2.9%)	173 (2.5%)	139 (2.1%)	-51	-26.8 -43.2
Service	4,743 (18.9%)	1,331 (6.6%)	1,391 (5.7%)	1,636 (5.7%)	-3107	-65.5 -69.8
Public Sector	5,695 (35.0%)	5,740 (35.8%)	6,484 (36.5%)	6,926 (37.8%)	1231	21.6 8.0

Sources: 1980: Gifford (1982); 1985–1995: U.S. DOL, BLS (1986; 1992; 1996a). Public sector membership data in 1980 are from Troy and Sheflin (1985).
Note: Membership in thousands; density in percentages.

throughout the seven private sector industrial classifications. In absolute terms, unions experienced the greatest membership losses in the manufacturing (3.3 million), service (3.1 million), and transportation (1.1 million) industries. On a percentage basis, they lost relatively more ground in the service and mining industries. These downward trends simply overwhelmed the public sector gains.

In short, U.S. unions have suffered severe reductions in each of the private sector industries where they had the largest numbers a decade and a half ago. In other industries (e.g., mining and finance), where total union membership has been relatively low, their presence also has faded. Today, less than 14 percent of the mining industry is unionized, compared with nearly a third in 1980. Across the major private sector industries, the data paint a bleak picture, offering little optimism for establishing a growth springboard within any particular segment, apart from the public sector.

Occupation Data

Union density and membership data in major occupations are reported in Table 2.4. The percentage of unionized employees fell in each of the classifications, most significantly (in percentage terms) in the production and operator classes, where unions had the most members in 1985. Further, even membership gains in the managerial/professional, technical, and service occupations lagged behind employment growth. Yet, it is still noteworthy that unions gained members in these three occupational categories, each of which is expected to grow in number in the future. Thus, a critical issue is how labor might accelerate its growth in these areas. This issue, it is worth noting, may prove a real challenge to the extent managerial and administrative employees are exempted from labor law protections, the lines between protected employees and supervisory ranks become increasingly blurred as managerial responsibilities are diffused, and the contingent workforce grows, much of which is also exempted from labor law protection (U.S. Commission on the Future of Worker–Management Relations 1994b).[9]

Demographic Data

Table 2.5 reports significant variation in union density rates and membership trends among selected demographic groups. Density rates declined among both men and women, but substantially more rapidly among the

Table 2.4
Union Membership and Density by Major Occupational Classifications (1985–1995)

Occupational Classification	Year 1985	1990	1995	Membership Loss/ Gain	1985-1995 Percentage Change
Managerial and Professional	3,307 (15.2%)	3,674 (14.3%)	4,116 (13.8%)	809	24.5% -9.2
Technical and Administrative	3,243 (10.8%)	3,462 (10.4%)	3,364 (9.9%)	121	3.7 -8.3
Service	1,922 (14.4%)	1,989 (13.8%)	2,112 (13.5%)	190	9.9 -6.2
Production	3,272 (28.5%)	3,011 (25.9%)	2,692 (23.3%)	-580	-17.7 -18.2
Operators and Laborers	5,157 (31.8%)	4,514 (26.4%)	3,983 (23.0%)	-1174	-22.8 -27.7

Sources: U.S. DOL, BLS (1986; 1992; 1996a).
Note: Membership in thousands; density in percentages.

Table 2.5
Union Membership and Density by Major Demographic Classifications (1985–1995)

Demographic Classification	1985	Year 1990	1995	1985-1995 Percentage Change
Gender				
Men	11,264 (22.1%)	10,564 (19.3%)	9,929 (17.2%)	-11.9% -22.2
Women	5,732 (13.2%)	6,175 (12.6%)	6,430 (12.3%)	12.2 -6.8
Race				
White	14,124 (17.3%)	13,798 (15.5%)	13,149 (14.2%)	-6.9 -17.9
African-American	2,445 (24.3%)	2,410 (21.1%)	2,519 (19.9%)	3.0 -18.1
Hispanic[1]	1,174 (18.9%)	1,209 (14.8%)	1,357 (13.0%)	15.6 -31.2
Employment Status				
Full-Time	15,717 (20.4%)	15,422 (18.1%)	14,790 (16.6%)	-5.9 -18.6
Part-Time	1,280 (7.3%)	1,318 (7.0%)	1,537 (7.5%)	20.1 2.7

Sources: U.S. DOL, BLS (1986; 1992; 1996)
1. Hispanics may be classified in any racial category; thus multiple counting exists.

former. Among men, absolute union membership also dropped by more than 1.3 million as density decreased to 17 percent. The number of women union members actually rose 12 percent, to narrow substantially the gender-based density gap. Still, the growth in union membership among women was insufficient to keep up with population growth in the labor force, meaning that density declined by almost 7 percent.

While actual union membership increased among African-Americans and Hispanics (who may be classified among all races) between 1985 and 1995, density rates declined in each of these racial categories at a more significant level than among whites. Among whites, membership fell by nearly one million, leading to a density rate under 15 percent.

Clear differences also exist in unionization rates based on employment status. Only 8 percent of the part-time workplace is unionized, despite a 20-percent hike in the total number of part-time union members between

1985 and 1995. Both membership and density fell among full-time employees. The projected expansion in part-time and other "contingent" workers in the United States portends further problems for union efforts to stimulate growth.[10]

To encapsulate, since 1980, union membership and density have declined significantly across all major industries in the private sector, and public sector growth moved too slowly to offset these trends. Union density also has fallen among the principal occupational classifications, but actual membership gains have been experienced among managerial/professional, technical, and service occupations since 1985. Unions also have recorded membership gains among women and minority groups in the past ten years, but by insufficient margins to keep up with employment growth. Interestingly, however, the occupational and demographic groups among which actual membership growth has occurred are also areas which are forecasted to become a larger share of the workforce.

MACRODETERMINANTS OF UNION DECLINE

What has caused the aggregate decline in unionization, particularly union density? Research in industrial relations and related disciplines has classified explanatory factors into individual, or microlevel, and macrodeterminants (for reviews of the literature, see Fiorito and Greer 1982; Heneman and Sandver 1983; Chaison and Rose 1991; Wheeler and McClendon 1991; Farber and Krueger 1993). In this regard, several macrodeterminants have received considerable attention: structural economic shifts, employer opposition, public policy, union organizing, and political conservatism. A brief review of these theses is provided in order to shed light on the approaches unions might take to promote organizing efforts.[11]

Structural Economic Shifts

This thesis holds that the decline in unionization in the United States since the 1950s is due in substantial part to the changing distribution of employment and composition of the workforce. These changes are structural and long-term rather than cyclical or transitory in nature. Specifically, employment has shifted from relatively unionized industries, occupations, and geographic regions to less densely organized counterparts. Thus, the shift in employment from manufacturing to nonmanufacturing, blue-collar to white-collar, and North to South and West, plus the feminization of the workforce, has contributed to the drop in unionization rates (e.g., see Farber 1985; Kochan, Katz, and McKersie 1986; Chaison and Rose 1991; Farber and Krueger 1993). Indeed, projected employment growth industries and occupations are relatively nonunionized, indicating that these structural shifts and their associated impacts on organized labor are likely to continue into the foreseeable future, barring a major shift in organizing successes. As shown in Table 2.6, two occupational classifications (i.e., production and operators) in which union density and membership levels historically have been high are expected to grow the least in terms of employment between now and the year 2005. In contrast, employment is projected to climb rapidly among professional, technical, and service occupations. Unions have comparatively low density rates among employees in these occupations, notwithstanding their actual membership growth among professional and technical employees.

Table 2.6
Percentage Change in Employment, Level of Employment, and Projected Change in Employment, by Occupation (1979–2005)

Occupational Classification	Percentage Change, Actual 1979-1992	Employment Level in 1992 (in millions)	Projected Percentage Change, 1992-2005
All Occupations	19.0%	121.1	21.8%
Executive, Administrative, Managerial	50.4	12.1	25.9
Professional Specialty	43.0	16.6	37.4
Technicians and Related Support	57.6	4.3	32.2
Marketing and Sales	30.7	13.0	20.6
Service Occupations	24.6	19.4	33.4
Administrative Support, Clerical	15.0	22.3	13.7
Precision Production, Craft, Repair	4.3	13.6	13.3
Operators, Fabricators, Laborers	10.3	16.3	9.5
Agriculture, Forestry, Fishing	-5.2	3.5	3.4

Source: U.S. Commission on the Future of Worker-Management Relations (1994a: 7).

Similarly, unions will need to gain significantly more women and minority members. The workforce will be substantially more diverse in the decades ahead, and unions will have to make appropriate inroads if further losses in density are to be avoided. It is reported that nearly "two-thirds of entrants to the civilian labor force in 1992 to 2005 are projected to be women and racial minorities and only one-third are projected to be White males" (U.S. Commission on the Future of Worker–Management Relations 1994a: 12).

While these structural shifts undoubtedly have some explanatory power, they do not fully account for the decline in union density. Chaison and Rose (1991: 14) argue that these shifts "cannot explain why union membership and density declined in the United States in all private sector industry categories—those of traditional union strength...and those in the expanding and less-unionized service sector." More broadly, Farber and Krueger (1993: 115) conclude that structural shifts in the industrial, occupational, regional, and demographic composition of work and the workforce account for "about 25 percent of the . . . overall [unionization] decline between 1977 and 1991."

Employer Opposition

Union advocates and many outside observers place much of the blame for the decline in unionization squarely at the doorstep of vehement and sometimes illegal employer opposition. Historically, U.S. employers have ideologically opposed unionization and aggressively resisted organizing efforts. This opposition arguably intensified in the 1970s and 1980s as employers faced mounting global competition to pare labor costs and increase productivity (Freeman and Medoff 1984; Kochan, Katz, and McKersie 1986; U.S. Commission on the Future of Worker–Management Relations 1994a; 1994b).

Employer opposition to unions may take many forms. According to a study on employment practices among several major nonunion firms, Foulkes (1979) found that a common resistance strategy was to substitute the supposed advantages of union representation. That is, employers adopted various positive employee relations policies and practices, including competitive pay scales and benefits, employee feedback and communications venues, and informal or formal grievance procedures (for a more detailed discussion of the latter as a union avoidance strategy, see Ewing 1989). Such a "union substitution" approach is clearly one way to reduce employee demands for union representation.

At the same time, however, employers also have pursued more aggressive and arguably less noble tactics to resist unions. They have allegedly relocated union facilities to nonunion U.S. sites, exported union jobs, and terminated employees for exercising their statutorily protected right to form unions (Freeman and Medoff 1984; Kochan, Katz, and McKersie 1986; Goldfield 1987; Voos 1994a; Chaison and Rose 1991; U.S. Commission on the Future of Worker–Management Relations 1994a). As Chaison and Rose (1991: 22) conclude, "There is growing recognition that employer opposition to unions is an increasingly important, if not dominant, determinant of changes in union density rates. Employer resistance can go beyond the legal opportunities to . . . oppose new organizing activity and can entail discriminatory discharges of union supporters." Labor leaders, as mentioned, have also attributed much of their organizing difficulties to the insidious nature of employer resistance: "The Commission [on the Future of Worker–Management Relations] received testimony from union leaders that the primary problem facing workers who want to organize is not the illegal actions of some employers (although those actions harm an organizing campaign). It is rather, in the words of AFL-CIO President Lane Kirkland, 'veiled threats and acts of discrimination which cannot be proven to be unlawfully motivated'" (U.S. Commission on the Future of Worker–Management Relations 1994a: 76–77).

In terms of trends in employers' alleged violations, Weiler (1993) has reported that the number of illegally terminated employees under the NLRA rose to 7,000 per year in the 1980s. Even more telling, the "ratio of workers offered reinstatement [for discriminatory discharge] to workers voting for unions" in certification elections held under the auspices of the NLRB rose from 1:689 in 1951–1955 to about 1:50 in 1986–1990 (U.S. Commission on the Future of Worker–Management Relations (1994a: 84). Further, a quarter to a third of the certification elections held in the 1980s produced reinstatement offers to employees who were found, by the NRLB, to have been discharged illegally.

Public Policy

U.S. public policies also may have contributed appreciably to the decline in union density in at least two fundamental ways. First, labor laws may have reduced the supply of union organizing services by aiding employer opposition. Under the NLRA, for example, the process of certifying union representation offers opportunities for employers to delay elections and increase the costs of organizing to unions and employees (e.g., see Hurd and McElwain 1988; Hurd 1989). To oppose the election of a union, employers may legitimately challenge the appropriateness of a proposed bargaining unit on several grounds. They also may wage aggressive anti-union media campaigns among employees, essentially holding employees captive in order to pursue their interests (Lawler 1990). Indeed, employers have become increasingly successful in winning union certification elections, as shown in Table 2.7. Also, the number of certification elections and eligible voters both have declined significantly. The total number of elections held in 1994 was much less than half the total held in 1970, with almost 400,000 fewer eligible voters involved.

This downward trend is further captured in data showing sharp decreases in several unions' formal certification activity between the mid-1970s and mid-1980s. Chaison and Dhavale (1990) document that fifteen unions in this sample were involved in anywhere from 25 to 76 percent fewer certification elections in 1983–1985 than a decade earlier.[12]

One commonly mentioned reason for the drop in certifications is the inadequate legal sanctions available to deter employer misconduct (Goldfield 1987). The law penalizes employers who illegally discharge employees

Table 2.7
NLRB Certification Election Results

	Total Elections Held	Elections Won by Unions	Percentage of Elections Won by Unions	Total Employees Eligible to Vote
FY 1940	1,192	921	77.3%	595,075
FY 1950	5,619	4,186	74.5	890,374
FY 1960	6,380	3,740	58.6	483,964
FY 1970	7,773	4,367	56.2	588,214
FY 1980	7,296	3,498	47.9	478,821
FY 1981	6,656	3,019	45.4	403,837
FY 1982	4,247	1,857	43.7	258,626
FY 1983	3,483	1,663	47.7	171,548
FY 1984	3,561	1,655	46.5	211,696
FY 1985	3,749	1,745	46.5	212,331
FY 1986	3,663	1,740	47.5	223,018
FY 1987	3,314	1,608	48.5	204,235
FY 1988	3,509	1,735	49.5	211,432
FY 1989	3,791	1,878	49.5	247,638
FY 1990	3,623	1,795	49.5	231,069
FY 1991	3,179	1,490	46.9	195,025
FY 1992	2,993	1,492	49.9	185,556
FY 1993	3,055	1,541	50.4	206,702
FY 1994	3,079	1,497	48.6	188,899
FY 1995[1]	2,911	1,468	50.4	192,934

Source: U.S. National Labor Relations Board (1996).
1. 1995 data are preliminary as of April 11, 1996.

essentially by providing for "make whole" remedies, such as reinstatement and back-pay. Even when victims win available remedies, they still may have suffered great pain. Months or years may have elapsed between their initial charges and subsequent relief as employers use administrative and judicial procedures to avoid penalties.

Unions also contend that employers skillfully exploit their right to replace strikers to erode labor's base further. In 1938, the U.S. Supreme Court ruled that employers have the right to continue their business operations by replacing, on a permanent basis, workers who have struck over a bargaining impasse (McCallion 1990). In several widely publicized situations, employers have exercised this right for the alleged purpose of subverting existing union representation. President Reagan's dismissal of the PATCO strikers in August 1981 arguably lent this strategy national approval, even though it occurred under a statute that strictly forbids strikes. More generally, strike activity has plummeted in recent decades, suggesting that unions have seen a once powerful weapon for protecting worker interests lose much of its practical utility (see Table 2.8).

In short, it is widely argued that existing labor law includes many provisions unfavorable if not blatantly hostile to unions, particularly as unions seek new members through the certification election process. Also, the U.S. government has allegedly been lax at times, such as during the Reagan administration, in enforcing available employee protections (Gould 1993; Greenhouse 1996). Goldfield (1987: 105) places much of the blame on the Taft-Hartley Act of 1947, which was mainly intended to curb union power. Parenthetically, the Taft-Hartley Act prohibited unions from using their treasury monies (e.g., dues) as sources of campaign contributions to federal office seekers (Cloke 1981).

A second public-policy contributor to union decline may be the proliferation of employee-protection legislation, quite apart from labor law per se. The legislation (EEO, OSHA, etc.) has arguably supplanted the potential need and, hence, demand for unions among many groups of employees. Current employment laws set minimum wages, mandate overtime pay, protect retirement plans, establish safety and health requirements, severely restrict the use of polygraph testing, and ban discrimination on the basis of race, gender, age, religion, and disability (Hunt and Strongin 1994). To the extent that unions have sought similar policies and practices through collective bargaining, their potential benefits have been at least partially usurped by legislation.

Union-Organizing

As previously mentioned, unions have been heavily criticized for their thrifty organizing pursuits (Rose and Chaison 1996). Instead of placing *new* membership high on the agenda, they generally have favored allocating

Table 2.8
Strike Activity in the United States (Selected Years, 1950–1995)

Period	Number of stoppages	Workers involved (thousands)
1950	424	1,698
1955	363	2,055
1960	222	896
1965	268	999
1970	381	2,468
1975	235	965
1979	235	1,021
1980	187	795
1981	145	729
1982	96	656
1983	81	909
1984	62	376
1985	54	324
1986	69	533
1987	46	174
1988	40	118
1989	51	452
1990	44	185
1991	40	392
1992	35	364
1993	35	182
1994	45	322
1995	31	192

Source: U.S. DOL, BLS (1996b).
Note: Data are collected from major bargaining units (i.e., units with 1,000 or more employees).

scarce resources to serve current rank and file (Block 1980). Intrinsically political institutions with democratically elected leaders, unions might understandably grant such preference to existing dues payers at the expense of attracting unorganized workers who do not have a current voice in internal union affairs. Block (1980: 101–102) stated: "One of the main reasons that union membership as a percentage of the private labor force and employment has declined in recent years is because unions in the 'traditional sectors' of manufacturing, mining, construction, and transportation . . . have not placed a high priority on organizing. If unions are basically democratic organizations, then it is logical to think that the reason that these unions have not placed an emphasis on organizing is because organizing new members may not be in the interests of the [current] membership of the union."

Most unions, in fact, have devoted somewhere between a paltry 2 to 4 percent of their annual budgets to attracting new members (Bernstein 1995a). In addition to "devoting too few resources to organizing," U.S. unions also have been attacked "for failing to coordinate their organizing campaigns and establishing clear long-term organizing goals and priorities" (Chaison and Rose 1991: 27). Goldfield (1987: 226) says that "unions themselves seem to have become less aggressive and, in general, less committed to new organizing campaigns in the private sector." Arguably, unions have paid a heavy price for neglecting this function. Indeed, the price may have become so steep that they no longer can afford to fail to devote more resources to organizing. Consequently, some in the labor movement are pushing unions to allocate roughly a third of their annual budgets to organizing.[13]

Political Conservatism/Public Opinion

It also is argued that the conservative bent of American politics has hurt organized labor (Goldfield 1987). The U.S. polity has never supported a sustainable independent labor party, nor have unions ever fully captured control of one of the major parties, at least at the national level (e.g., Greenstone 1977). According to Lipset (1995: 127), the "United States is the only industrialized country that has never had an electorally viable socialist party, and what little it once had has almost totally disappeared in the postwar years." Instead, unions have vied with various other groups to retain an influential position within the future of the Democratic party, which has of late shown remarkably little fealty to labor's agenda (witness President Clinton's vigorous backing of NAFTA and GATT). Freeman and Rogers (1993: 39) have perceptively stated:

> There is no labor nor labor-dominated party, and American politicians rarely articulate or explicitly direct issues to achieving the aims of workers qua workers.

> Since the New Deal, unions have been allied with the Democratic Party, occasionally dominating local party machines. But labor was a junior partner on the New Deal coalition and by the late 1970s had become an unfavored one . . . In the 1980s, it faced 'an indifference bordering on contempt' from party leaders. More broadly, unions have had a largely clientelistic relation to the Democrats, looking to the party for patronage, favors, and select program supports.

Labor's political agenda arguably has been further eroded as ideological conservatives have dominated national politics in recent decades. In the Reagan–Bush era, and now with the Republican sweep of the 104th Congress, market-based public policies have gained substantial favor over government regulation of approaches long pushed by labor unions and allied "liberal" groups (Garland and Regan 1996). The net result is a growing political constraint on government intrusion upon economic matters. Employers are thus encouraged to compete on the basis of wages and other labor costs, raising their incentive to remain nonunion or escape existing union relationships.

In sum, each of these macrolevel factors provides at least some plausible basis for explaining the decline in union density since the 1950s. None offers a universal explanation, but no one is mutually exclusive of the others. Research suggests that a combination of these (and various other) factors have caused unions to falter on the organizing front. To the extent that any one of these macrodeterminant factors holds merit, however, unions will need to gauge their growth strategies and tactics accordingly.

STRATEGIC IMPLICATIONS

The potential feasibility and effectiveness of union growth strategies will be substantially affected by impinging environmental contexts. To varying degrees, these contexts may prove amenable to change through union actions, although unions may be trapped in a vicious circle. The decline in density renders them less able to influence the contexts, which further erodes their base (Rose and Chaison 1996). As contextual factors unfold in ways largely beyond control or influence, unions must be facile in pursuing organizing strategies that both minimize anticipated losses and create new opportunities to exploit.

Fundamentally, the structural economic shifts have unalterable strategic implications. That is, profound changes have already occurred in the structure of work and the composition of the workforce, and they are likely to continue moving forward regardless of what unions may do. The only realistic issue, therefore, before unions is how to adapt strategically to these changes. In this vein, unions have no choice but to do better in organizing in industries and occupations where they have had relatively little presence or success in the past. Accordingly, their strategies must succeed in organizing professionals, technicians, and service employees and expanding gains among women and minorities, if only to keep pace with anticipated employment growth among these groups. Furthermore, unions need to maintain their gains in the public sector and stabilize if not reverse their hemorrhaging in the manufacturing and blue-collar sectors of the economy. As will be shown later, unions need to gain across the board if their current situation is to be markedly improved.

Similarly, these structural shifts, combined with intensified employer opposition that is bolstered by a market-based political ideology, will compel unions to devote more resources—including financial—to organizing. Bluntly, unions in the private sector can no longer afford a thrifty organizing program. There comes a point that membership or, more aptly, density falls to such a low level that it seriously weakens a union's capacity to service current members, let alone organize new ones. In this regard, it seems plausible that the mergers between ACTWU and ILGWU and the USW and URW, and the proposed one between the UAW, USW, and IAM, were consummated at least in part to offset the effects of or as a result of the hemorrhaging that has occurred in their respective manufacturing bases.[14] These mergers may enhance the capacities of these unions to pursue organizing on a greater scale.

Furthermore, the organizing strategies unions choose will have to be aimed at both circumventing employer opposition and facilitating union representation venues. The focus may need to move from formal bargaining recognition as the predominant objective to other forms of employee representation that entice membership but avoid costly head-on certification battles with employers, at least in the near term, when the odds of union success are relatively problematic. Unions may need to pursue representation policies that not only serve their exclusive bargaining rights but also the mutual interests of employees and employers in other representational forums.

NOTES

1. According to Foner (1947), the Knights of Labor had 9,287 members in 1878 and 51,914 in 1883. Between 1885 and 1886 it grew by 600,000. Controversial in many ways, which included organizing on a broad-based scale, the Knights collapsed rapidly under its own weight. The organization was challenged in 1886 by the formation of the AFL, which organized on a craft basis and favored a more moderate, work-related approach to solving workers' problems.

2. A group of industrial-based unions, led by John Lewis's United Mine Workers (UMWA), formed a Committee for Industrial Organization in 1936 within the AFL. Ordered to "disband or get out" (Holley and Jennings 1994: 54), the UMWA and six other unions formed a rival Congress of Industrial Organizations in 1938. The CIO unions continued their ambitious organizing thrusts in

steel, auto, rubber, and textile manufacturing. As will be noted, their organizing successes prompted accelerated organizing efforts by the AFL.

3. In 1994, approximately 17,062,262 employees would have had to have been unionized in order for the density rate to have been maintained at 15.8 percent.

4. These countries are Australia, Austria, France, Japan, the Netherlands, New Zealand, Switzerland, the United Kingdom, and the United States.

5. Troy (1990: 140) argues that "competitive markets 'repeal' the legal protection bestowed by governments on unions and collective bargaining. The process is slow and is typically unnoticed, but eventually the substitution of nonunion labor and products erodes the power of labor laws, union density, membership, and collective bargaining power." This argument, to the extent it holds, has obvious implications for labor's future as global competition intensifies and economies across the world privatize and deregulate industries.

6. Andrews and Naylor (1994) report that union density in the United Kingdom fell from 57.4 percent in 1979 to 43.5 percent in 1990, or by 25 percent. Actual union membership dropped from 13,289,000 to 9,947,000, or by 25 percent, which is quite comparable to the percentage decline in the United States between 1980 and 1990.

7. In this article, Rose and Chaison (1996: 100) make the important argument that the decline in density is both a function of and contribution to weakened performance on the strategic fronts of union activity, emphasizing "that declining density in the United States has lowered union performance in organizing, bargaining, and political activity and this brought about further declines in density." The question thus arises as to how unions in the United States extricate themselves from this vicious circle. One approach is to concentrate their energies and resources on organizing, which has evidently occurred in Canada: "Confronting expanded employment in lesser-unionized sectors, Canadian unions renewed their commitment to organizing, increased organizing resources, and attempted to develop new organizing strategies . . . . Although these efforts do not always achieve the desired results, Canadian unions did increase organizing expenditures by an average annual rate of 20 percent from 1984 to 1987" (Rose and Chaison 1996: 86–87).

8. It should be noted, however, that in several European countries there is a sizable gap between union density per se and bargaining coverage (i.e., the proportion of the workforce that is represented by unions). For instance, in Austria, the gap is 45 to 98 percent, respectively. In Belgium, it is 51 and 90 percent, and in Germany it is 32 and 90 percent. Also, in Australia, the gap is 40 and 80 percent. See OECD (1994).

9. The Commission (1994b: 35) found the following with regard to the use of "contingent workers" (broadly defined to include temporary, seasonal, leased, and part-time workers): "Unfortunately, current tax, labor and employment law gives employers and employees incentives to create contingent relationships not for the sake of flexibility or efficiency but in order to evade their legal obligations." Therefore, it (1994b: 36) recommended that "the definition of employee in labor, employment, and tax law should be modernized, simplified, and standardized . . . . [and] based on the economic realities underlying the relationship between the worker and the party benefiting from the worker's services."

10. For instance, the U.S. Commission on the Future of Worker-Management Relations (1994a: 21) reported that the "number of workers in temporary help services or help supply services industries more than tripled from 1979 to 1992." Thus, it noted (1994a: 22) that "the growing number of 'contingent' and other non-standard workers poses the problem of how to balance employers' needs for flexibility with workers' needs for adequate income protections, job security and the application of public laws that these arrangements often preclude, including labor protection and labor-relations statutes."

11. Again, the objective here is not a comprehensive review of the evidence but rather an attempt to highlight some of the principal reasons as to why unions in the United States have declined. To the extent any one of the theses holds, unions will have to adapt strategically and tactically.

12. Organizing activity in terms of formal single-union certifications declined by the following percentages among the fifteen unions: IBT (56.9%); UFCW (55.8%); IAM (73.8%); UAW (47%); IBEW (53.8%); USW (55.4%); SEIU (25.6%); HERE (44.7%); IUOE (53.8%); CJA (54.9%); RWDSU (51.9%); CWA (46.5%); LIU (60.9%); IUE (76.2%); and UPIU (53.9%) (Chaison on Dhavale 1990: 312).

13. This information was based in part on a telephone conversation the author had with a high-ranking union staff person in spring 1996.

14. It is important to observe that while membership decline and financial difficulty may create situations favorable to union mergers, they may not be the primary motivating factors, but rather symptoms thereof. For an excellent book on the phenomenon of union mergers, see Chaison (1986). It also must be recognized that unions face internal political incentives and barriers to merger. Regardless, mergers have significant membership, financial, and bargaining implications for those principally involved. As Chaison observes (1986: 156): "There is also a resurgence of interest in mergers as unions search for ways to adapt and survive in a challenging environment."

Chapter 3

Major Union Membership Trends

By definition, unions cannot exist or exert meaningful influence without members, or at least the genuine willingness of a sizable cadre of workers to support their cause in some tangible way. Admittedly, membership levels per se and union strength are not necessarily synonymous (certainly there are examples of relatively small unions, that have exercised considerable power at various points in time, such as the Airline Pilots Association (ALPA), Marine Engineers Beneficial Association (MEBA), and NALC.[1] Also, unions may increase financial and political capital even though membership is in decline by raising dues or increasing the voluntary "tax" of PAC donations.[2] Nonetheless, members provide the basic human capital from which unions draw the institutional fiber to exert economic and political influence. The rank and file are an integral source of intellectual and leadership talent, as well as the sheer brawn necessary to conduct battle against hostile employers. In addition, they are the principal base unions may tap for financial and political capital. The uninterrupted erosion of this base would eventually negate the possibility of raising these other resources. Obviously, the more efficient and effective unions are in using their members' talents and building coalitions of support among other active interests, the more extensive their influence will be in pursuing various bargaining, organizing, and political goals. Of relevance, it is important to reiterate, is not only the level of membership but also the industry penetration and solidarity that unions have been able to attain.

While the aggregate decline in union membership and density, particularly since the late 1970s, should give union backers cause for concern, it may nonetheless mask important interunion differences. As demonstrated in Chapter 2, clearly divergent membership trends have occurred between unions which operate primarily in the private sector versus those which are preponderately public sector. Still, sizable differences may exist not only between private and public sector unions but also among unions within each sector. Patterns of interunion variation may provide insight into where pockets of union membership strength exist and where they might be exploited in the future. Moreover, unions that have experienced a sharp decline and operate in employment or industry sectors unlikely to grow much in the future may need to consider bold strategies to cease the bleeding and position themselves for growth. Mergers, such as the prospective IAM, UAW, and USW mega-union, may emerge as an increasingly attractive option to achieve this objective (Carlisle 1996c).

This chapter explores the membership trends among the twenty-eight unions. First, it examines the twenty-eight unions' combined memberships (to the extent data are available) as a percentage of the total *unionized* workforce since 1955. These data reveal the extent to which union membership has become more concentrated, or lodged within these major unions, which is a trend that has been observed in the United Kingdom (Willman and Cave 1994). They also show the extent to which the major unions' trends have contributed to and comported with the aggregate trends. Second, the chapter disaggregates these data among individual unions in the private and public sectors. To the extent data are available, it compares trends between (1) 1955 and 1993 and between (2) 1979 and 1993. This latter comparison indicates how the 1980s in particular impacted these unions' membership.

A couple of observations about the membership data seem appropriate at this point. For most unions, data come directly from AFL-CIO reports covering 1955 to 1993. Between 1955 and 1979, four unions (ACTWU, APWU, UFCW, and UPIU) were formed by mergers.[3] Data on their membership levels during this earlier period include the combined ranks of the principal unions that formed the mergers. Otherwise, membership growth due to union merger is reflected only after the mergers have actually taken place.[4] In this regard, it is important to observe that mergers have contributed to some unions' growth over the past several decades. For instance, according to Williamson's (1995) report on union mergers, at least nine unions merged with the SEIU between 1985 and 1994. The LIU and SEIU adopted their current names in 1965 and 1968, respectively.[5]

Pre-1975 data on union membership are limited for four unions (NEA, NFFE, NRLCA, and NTEU). The NEA was considered a professional association per se rather than a union until 1968 (Stern 1979).[6] The NTEU (previously named the National Association of Internal Revenue Employees) had at that time a relatively restricted organizational jurisdiction, confined mainly to employees of the Internal Revenue Service. More recently, it has adopted more of a government-wide charter, though its bargaining representation is still predominantly concentrated among white-collar employees in the Treasury department (Masters 1983).[7] In any event, to the extent these data are unavailable (or even inapplicable in some years, as might be the case with regard to the NEA), the subsequently reported data on the degree to which union membership (across all labor unions) has been concentrated among these major unions understate the degree of actual concentration.

TWENTY-EIGHT MAJOR UNIONS' AGGREGATE MEMBERSHIP

Table 3.1 compares the twenty-eight unions' aggregate membership to the overall situation in the United States between 1955 and 1993. As reported earlier, union density in the U.S. nonagricultural workforce was more than halved during this period. Union membership was also lower in 1993 than 1955, as a result of the sharp loss in the 1980s.

Table 3.1
Aggregate Union Membership and Density (Selected Years)

Year	Total U.S. Union Membership (in thousands)	Nonagricultural Union Density	Twenty-eight Major Unions' Membership (in thousands)	Major Unions as Percentage of Total Union Membership
1955	17,246	34.0%	9,352	54.2%
1965	17,299	28.4	10,322	59.7
1975[1]	22,361	28.9	14,978	67.0
1979[1]	22,579	25.1	15,221	67.4
1985	16,996	18.2	14,005	82.4
1991	16,568	16.3	13,509	81.5
1993	16,598	16.0	13,151	79.2
Percentage Change				
1955 - 1993	-.04		.41	
1979 - 1993	-.26		-.14	

Sources: 1955: Goldfield (1987), interpolated between 1954 and 1956; 1965–1979: U.S. DOL, BLS (1970) and Goldfield (1987); 1985–1993: U.S. DOL, BLS (1986; 1992; 1994). Major unions' membership are from AFL-CIO reports in Gifford for affiliates of the federation and from other union reports to Gifford (1982; 1984; 1986; 1988; 1990; 1992; 1994), and U.S. DOL, BLS (1970; 1974; 1977; 1979; 1980).

1. Estimates from Goldfield (1987) include members of employee associations

As a group, the major unions' membership expanded considerably between 1955 and 1979, rising by six million in number to 15.2 million. Obviously, a non-trivial portion of this increase is due to adding the NEA, NRLCA, and NTEU to the totals in 1975 and these three unions plus NFFE in 1979. Also, some of the growth is because of amalgamation with or absorptions of smaller unions, but it is noteworthy that union merger activity was slower during the 1955–1975 period than in subsequent decades. Williamson (1995) reports forty-eight mergers between 1955 and 1975, compared with forty-five between 1976 and 1985 and forty between 1986 and 1994. Even if one were to eliminate the NEA, NFFE, NRLCA, and NTEU from the 1955–1979 growth calculations, the remaining unions still grew by 43 percent. Total union membership, in contrast, jumped by only 31 percent between 1955 and 1979.

However, the major unions also experienced significant membership reductions in the 1980s, but less steep than the losses among all unions generally, a differentiation which may be due in part to growth among public sector unions and heightened merger activity. Specifically, their ranks shrank by 14 percent between 1979 and 1993, or by a little more than two million in number, compared to 26 percent overall. Given that the major unions' membership (for whatever reason, including the official recognition of the NEA as a union) climbed by 41 percent over the entire four-decade period, during which total union membership fell by 4 percent, their representation in the aggregate unionized workforce grew considerably. The concentration of total union membership among these majors rose from 54 percent in 1955 to approximately 80 percent in the mid-1980s, and it has since held more or less steady. Increased concentration is certainly consistent with the just-mentioned acceleration in union mergers and would be even higher if the recently announced or planned mergers among the major twenty-eight were factored into the calculations. In other words, twenty-five rather than twenty-eight unions would account for 79 percent of total union membership.[8] Also, these major unions have included a high proportion of public sector union membership, which has been almost exclusively responsible for any union growth since the 1970s.

DISAGGREGATED MAJOR UNION MEMBERSHIP TRENDS

Table 3.2 reports the twenty-eight unions' disaggregated memberships for 1955, 1979, and 1993. The data show that while six private sector unions actually had more members in 1993 than they did nearly forty years before (UFCW, CWA, IBEW, LIU, IUOE, and PPI), each of the seventeen had fewer members in 1993 than they did in 1979. While caution must be exercised in making any specific year-to-year comparisons (because a given year might be aberrational), the data are nonetheless compelling in several respects. Also, they do show the difference in the membership status of the unions at the beginning and end points of two periods (1955–1993, 1979–1993) that have involved a continual decline in aggregate union density.

First, considerable variation exists in the rate of growth or decline among the unions in both sectors. While four unions (UFCW, CWA, IBEW, and IUOE) had memberships that were at least 50 percent greater in 1993 than in 1955, five lost nearly half or more (ACTWU, ILGWU, USW, IUE, and CJA). The ACTWU and ILGWU, in fact, had 65 percent fewer members in 1993 than they did in 1955. Focusing on the 1979–1993 period, four of the private sector unions (ILGWU, USW, ACTWU, and UAW) lost half or more of their members. Another five saw their ranks shrink by somewhere between almost one-third and one-half (IUE, CJA, RWDSU, IBT, and HERE). Only four unions in the private sector held their losses to less than 10 percent (IUOE, PPI, CWA, and UFCW). In total, the private sector unions had 14 percent fewer members in 1993 than they did in 1955, and 30 percent less in that year than in 1979. In fifteen years, they lost almost 3.3 million members. The UAW and USW alone had their memberships shaved by 1.3 million.

Second, the public sector union situation in the main stands in sharp contrast. Excluding the NEA, NFFE, NRLCA, and NTEU, the seven remaining unions' combined membership was nearly 400 percent greater in 1993 than in 1955. Unsurprisingly, not a single one of these seven public sector unions ended the four decades with fewer members than they had at the beginning. For some, in fact, growth was almost phenomenal. AFSCME and AFT, for example, added more than 1,000,000 and 500,000 members, respectively, to their ranks, expanding by more than 1000 percent. Indeed, the rapid growth of the AFT in the 1960s was one of the key factors that led the NEA to transform itself from a fundamentally professional association into a union that is now the largest in the United States (Stern 1979; 1988).

Growth has evidently slowed since the 1970s, but nine of the eleven unions in this sector nonetheless ended the 1979–1993 period with more members. Overall, they gained 27 percent (which is essentially the flipside of the private sector loss of 30 percent). Consequently, while the public sector unions accounted for just 7 percent of the major unions' total membership in 1955, they constituted 43 percent in 1993.

It is interesting to observe that the two public sector unions that actually lost members in the 1980s are located in the nonpostal federal service. The AFGE and NFFE, which had 37 percent and 40 percent fewer members, respectively, in 1993 than in 1979, operate in a public sector jurisdiction (i.e., Title VII of the Civil Service Reform Act, which covered

Table 3.2
Twenty-Eight Unions' Membership Trends (1955–1993)

Union	1955	1979	1993	Average Member 1979-1993	Percentage Change[1] 1979-1993	Percentage Change[1] 1955-1993
Private Sector						
IBT	1,330	1,924	1,316	1,665	-.32	-.01
UFCW[2]	522	1,076	997	1,009	-.07	.91
UAW	1,260	1,534	771	990	-.50	-.39
IBEW	460	825	710	778	-.14	.54
IAM	627	664	474	561	-.29	-.24
CWA	249	485	472	512	-.03	.89
USW	980	964	421	622	-.56	-.57
CJA	750	619	408	575	-.34	-.46
LIU	372	475	408	419	-.14	-.10
IUOE	200	313	305	330	-.02	.52
HERE	300	373	258	312	-.31	-.14
PPI	200	228	220	224	-.03	.10
UPIU[3]	254	262	188	227	-.28	-.26
ACTWU[4]	413	301	143	210	-.52	-.65
IUE	271	243	143	190	-.44	-.47
ILGWU	383	314	133	216	-.58	-.65
RWDSU	97	122	80	119	-.34	-.17
TOTAL	8,668	10,722	7,447	--	-.30	-.14

PATCO) that severely limits the scope of bargaining (excluding wages and other main economic items), bans strikes, and prohibits any form of union-security arrangement (see Masters and Atkin 1989; 1990; 1993c). These limitations, combined with the two unions' vast representational obligations (the AFGE and NFFE represent approximately 750,000 federal employees scattered across a large number of governmental agencies and locations), have contributed to a severe free-riding problem, in which federal employees support union representation per se but do not join the union or otherwise contribute financially to attaining the benefits, however limited, of such representation.[9] In this regard, it is noteworthy that the NTEU, which operates in the same sector, did not lose members and also

Table 3.2 *(continued)*

Union	1955	1979	1993	Average Member 1979-1993	Percentage Change[1] 1979-1993	Percentage Change[1] 1955-1993
Public Sector						
NEA	NA	1,696	2,100	1,816	.24	--
AFSCME	99	889	1,167	1,036	.31	10.79
SEIU	205	528	919	713	.74	3.48
AFT	40	423	574	500	.36	13.35
APWU[5]	121	245	249	235	.02	1.06
NALC	100	151	210	186	.39	1.10
IAFF	72	150	151	145	.01	1.10
AFGE	47	236	149	184	-.37	2.17
NRLCA	NA	60	81	66	.35	--
NTEU	NA	70	74	65	.06	--
NFFE	NA	51	30	42	-.40	--
TOTAL	684	4,499	5,704	--	.27	7.34 (3.99)[6]
GRAND TOTAL	9,352	15,221	13,151	--	-.14	.40 (.19)

Sources: Major unions' membership are from AFL-CIO reports in Gifford for affiliates of the federation and from other union reports to Gifford (1982; 1984; 1986; 1988; 1990; 1992; 1994) and U.S. DOL, BLS (1970; 1974; 1977; 1979; 1980).

1. Percentage should be multiplied by 100 for conventional interpretation.
2. The UFCW was formed in 1979 by a merger between the Meat Cutters and Retail Clerks International Union. Membership data for UFCW prior to the merger consists of the combined ranks of the two merging unions.
3. The UPIU was formed in 1972 by a merger between the Pulp Workers and the United Paperworkers and Papermakers, which was formed by an earlier merger between the Paper Makers and Paper Workers. Prior membership data for UPIU reflect these sets of amalgams.
4. The ACTWU was formed by a merger between the Amalgamated Clothing Workers and the Textile Workers of America in 1976. Earlier membership data reflect these two unions' combined ranks.
5. The APWU was formed in 1971 by a merger between the United Federation of Postal Clerks (formed by an earlier merger), Post Office Maintenance Employees, Post Office Motor Vehicle Employees, and the Special Delivery Messengers. Prior membership data reflect the combined ranks of these merging entities.
6. Percentages in parentheses exclude the NEA, NFFE, NTEU, and NRLCA from calculations.

has had a much less severe free-riding problem (Masters and Atkin 1989; 1990; 1993c; 1995). The NTEU's relative success in this regard may be attributed to its narrower structure of bargaining (83 percent of the roughly 149,000 members it represents are in the U.S. Department of Treasury) and its widely reported effectiveness in handling employee grievances and litigating disputes, thus providing potentially quite valuable individual as well collective benefits to represented employees (Masters 1983).

Nonetheless, the public sector unions that grew in the 1980s are in the state, local, and postal sectors of government. SEIU grew the most, by 74 percent, fueled in substantial measure by mergers, which still signal a growth strategy or emphasis. For instance, in mid-1983, SEIU absorbed the National Association of Government Employees (NAGE), which then reported 200,000 members (Gifford 1984), although its actual membership may have been considerably smaller (Stern 1988).[10] AFSCME and AFT grew by at least a third, as did NALC and the NRLCA. While the NEA's 24 percent hike may thus seem comparatively small, it still reflects a gain of more than 400,000 members, which exceeded the SEIU's 390,000 increase in its ranks.

CONCLUSIONS

The data yield several conclusions. First, the fate of the labor movement as a whole hinges much more on what happens to a relative handful of unions than was the case forty years ago. If anything, labor union membership will become even more concentrated as recently announced mergers are implemented and new ones are consummated.[11]

Second, enormous differences have emerged both within and between private and public sector unions in terms of membership trends. Unfortunately, while public-employee unions as a whole have experienced significant growth, most of them may offer little potential hope for the broader labor growth in the future, unless organizational jurisdictions are changed. The primary federal-employee unions (AFGE, NFFE, and NTEU) are relatively small and either flaccid or declining in terms of membership. Moreover, the highly circumscribed labor relations legal framework within which they operate seriously limits the incentives for membership expansion (Masters and Atkin 1989; 1990; 1993c; 1995).

Furthermore, with their jurisdictions confined to postal employment, the major postal-employee unions (APWU, NALC, and NRLCA) also face limited growth opportunities. Mounting efforts to privatize the Postal Service promise to make it increasingly difficult for these unions to expand their positions by substantially increasing employment. Similarly, the AFT and NEA have restricted growth opportunities in an occupation (teaching) where fiscal constraints also may limit employment expansion, unless organizing efforts in nonteaching education-related employment accelerate.[12] The net result is that, barring major jurisdictional changes, the burden of future public sector growth (arguably of increasing relevance to organized labor) would appear to rest heavily on the shoulders of AFSCME and SEIU. These two unions appear to have the occupational and governmental breadth from which to grow significantly. The others, as noted, would seem to be somewhat encumbered by a combination of occupational confinement (e.g., rural letter carriers), limited governmental jurisdiction (e.g., federal or postal service), and fiscal constraints that promise to limit employment growth and, hence, membership expansion via accretion.

Finally, the major private sector unions would seem to be well advised to consider whether their current jurisdictional alignments make sense for future organizing purposes. Unions need to strike a balance between conveying a public image that is open to expansion in growth areas of the economy while maintaining their traditional bases. In this regard, unions that are nominally identified with a specific manufacturing industry may have become somewhat mislabeled, at least to the extent that they have already diversified their membership and organizing efforts (Chaison and Dhavale 1990). A breakdown of USW membership (pre-merger with the URW) reveals that only 31 percent are in the primary metals manufacturing sector. Another 31 percent are in such industries as furniture and fixtures; electric services; store, glass, and clay; and health services and retail trade (DaParma 1994: H1). To broaden their appeal to more diverse employee audiences, these unions may need to shed the labels and images of a past era. Still, as noted in Chapter 2, most of the manufacturing sector is nonunion, leaving plenty of opportunity, at least in theory, to organize new members and reverse the decline in a traditional bastion of union strength.

NOTES

1. In 1993, these unions' membership totals were 31,000 (ALPA); 52,000 (MEBA); and 210,000 (NALC). Yet, these unions raised very large sums of PAC money in 1993–1994. ALPA raised $1,254,938, or $40 per member; MEBA raised $1,261,160, or $25 per member; and NALC raised $1,600,399, or $7.60 per member. In comparison, the IBT, which raised $9,190,610, raised less than $7 per member. Also, because of their somewhat strategic positions within their respective transportation and postal industries, ALPA, MEBA, and NALC may exert more economic influence than reflected by sheer membership numbers.

2. The point here is not that PAC donations are a tax per se but that unions may stress to their members the critical importance of political participation (hence donating to the PAC) in order to achieve successes on the organizing and bargaining fronts, toward which unions expend dues-related income which is compelled via union-security agreements.

3. These mergers resulted in the creation of these four unions. Over the past several decades, however, many of the other unions (e.g., SEIU, USW) have acquired or absorbed other unions but nonetheless retained their nominal titles. The mergers resulting in the formation of ACTWU, APWU, UFCW, and UPIU are described in Table 3.2.

4. For example, USW membership data incorporate mergers with the Mine, Mill, and Smelter Workers (1967), Stone and Allied Product Workers (1971), Allied and Technical Workers (1992), and the Upholsterers International Union (1985). See Chaison (1986) and Williamson (1995) for specific information on union mergers.

5. Before 1965, LIU was known as the International Hod Carriers, Building, and Common Laborers Union of America. SEIU was named the Building Service Employees International Union before 1968.

6. According to Stern (1979: 63), "The predecessor organization to the present-day NEA was founded in Philadelphia in 1875 by educational administrators and college professors. For most of its long existence, it has functioned as a professional organization promoting the cause of public education and the improvement of teaching. In the 15 years since 1962 when the NEA was defeated by the AFT in the battle to represent New York City school teachers, however, the organization has undergone a sharp metamorphosis."

7. The NTEU has fifty-five bargaining units representing 148,882 employees, 99 percent of whom are white-collar. In contrast, NFFE has 370 units with 146,767 employees, 81 percent of whom are white-collar (U.S. Office of Personnel Management 1992).

8. This calculation reflects the mergers (in place or to be completed) between the ACTWU and ILGWU; RWDSU and UFCW; and IAM, UAW, and USW.

9. Masters and Atkin (1995; 1996c) report that the AFGE and NFFE had free-riding rates equal to 76 and 79 percent, respectively, in their 1991 bargaining units. Thus, more than three-fourths of the federal service employees these unions represented did not actually belong to the two unions.

10. These NAGE membership data may be overstated. Stern (1988: 54) reports the union's having 23,000 public-employee members in 1983, and Chaison (1986: 44) reports its overall membership at 100,000 in 1982 (having fallen precipitously from 200,000 in 1978).

11. In the course of interviews with staff at four unions it was revealed that each of the unions was contemplating mergers with several other unions, in part because of the economic integration of the various industries in which they and other unions operate.

12. The AFT and NEA both organize education-support personnel, and both organize somewhat outside of educational institutions, particularly health care and state civil service (Stern 1988).

Chapter 4

The Financial Capital of Unions

This chapter examines the general question of how much financial capital the twenty-eight major U.S.-based national unions have had. More specifically, it examines the unions' aggregate assets and wealth during the 1979–1993 period. In addition, it dissects the unions' assets, showing the percentage held in various categories which are more or less distinguishable in terms of their liquidity (i.e., convertibility to cash). The chapter also compares assets and wealth held by individual unions to show the extent to which there is variation on these financial dimensions and to explore how unions have fared over time. Comparisons are made not only in terms of total assets and wealth but also on a per-member basis. Finally, the degree to which assets and wealth are concentrated among a few of the major unions is examined.

UNIONS' AGGREGATE ASSETS AND WEALTH

Table 4.1 reports the twenty-eight unions' aggregate total assets and wealth during the 1979–1993 period and their aggregate per-member assets and wealth. Their assets exhibited a somewhat bell-shaped curve during the fifteen years, rising, albeit unevenly, from $2.3 billion in 1979 to a peak of $2.6 billion in 1984 and then falling to slightly above $2.2 billion in 1993. Interestingly, the unions' assets grew most when their membership losses were heaviest. While the unions' ranks shrank by more than one million in number, or nearly 7 percent, between 1979 and 1984, their

Table 4.1
Twenty-Eight Unions' Aggregate Real Assets and Wealth (1979–1993)

Year[1]	Total Assets[2] (in millions)	Per-Member	Total Wealth[3] (in millions)	Total Liabilities (in millions)	Per-Member Wealth
1979	$2,302	$151.12	$1,778	$524	$116.73
1980	2,196	147.26	1,770	426	113.99
1981	2,275	155.92	1,804	471	123.65
1982	2,399	165.69	1,924	475	132.89
1983	2,524	175.63	2,020	504	140.58
1984	2,600	183.47	2,097	503	147.98
1985	2,251	160.73	2,092	159	149.35
1986	2,270	163.81	2,119	151	152.93
1987	2,259	167.19	2,105	154	155.78
1988	2,253	168.16	2,071	182	154.55
1989	2,196	165.10	2,015	181	151.45
1990	2,188	163.25	1,997	191	149.05
1991	2,222	164.50	1,995	227	147.71
1992	2,189	164.21	1,956	233	146.73
1993	2,230	169.58	1,880	350	142.97
Percentage Change 1979-1993	-.03	.12	.06	-.33	.22
Average	2,290	164.37	1,970	320	141.76

Source: Unions' LM-2 financial disclosure forms.
Note: Totals rounded to nearest million.

1. The unions operate on different fiscal years, as will be noted in Table 4.3. The years are matched according to the calendar year in which their fiscal years' end.
2. Assets are adjusted for inflation (consumer price index = 100; 1982–1984); total assets are reported for the end-of-year period, based on all asset sources. Per-member assets are total assets divided by the unions' aggregated membership for each year.
3. Wealth is total assets minus total liabilities, or net assets, reported at the end of the fiscal year. Again, wealth is adjusted for inflation, as noted above. Per-member wealth is computed in the same fashion as per-member assets.

assets rose by 13 percent during the same five-year interval. Still, despite the membership losses and the drop in assets since 1984, the unions' total assets averaged almost $2.3 billion during this period or only three percent lower in 1993 than in 1979.

Indeed, on a per-member basis, the unions ended the decade-and-a-half with 12 percent more assets than they had at the beginning. Specifically, their assets totaled nearly $170 per member in 1993, compared to

$151 in 1979. Again, however, the trend was more or less bell-shaped, with per-member assets peaking in 1984 at $183.

The unions' real aggregate wealth demonstrated a smoother bell-shaped pattern during the fifteen-year period. It rose 18 percent from almost $1.8 billion in 1979 to peak at $2.1 billion in 1986, but then proceeded to fall 10 percent to just above its 1979 level. In 1993, the unions held 6 percent more wealth than they recorded fifteen years earlier, but $100 million less than their average during this entire period. On a per-member basis, however, the unions ended the period with 22 percent more wealth than they had at the start, but with almost $13 less than their 1987 peak of $156. Yet, in 1993, they had slightly more wealth per member than their $142 average.

Interestingly, over the entire fifteen-year period, the unions' wealth averaged nearly 87 percent of their total assets. This in effect means that the unions' assets have been relatively large compared to their liabilities, which are also shown in Table 4.1. The data reveal that their liabilities were well above $400 million each year between 1979 and 1984, but dropped in 1985. Although the unions' liabilities have grown in the 1990s, relative to what they were in the last half of the 1980s, they nonetheless were 33 percent less in 1993 than at the start. Thus, the data would suggest that the unions have maintained their assets without adding to their liabilities, thereby permitting their wealth to grow, however slightly, over the period observed.

Aggregate Liquid Assets

How do unions invest their assets? To what extent are their assets held in relatively liquid investments? These issues are addressed in Table 4.2, which reports the percentage of the aggregate assets held by the unions in seven specific types of investments enumerated explicitly on the LM-2 financial disclosure forms. Specifically, a breakdown of assets held in the following categories is provided for each year between 1979 and 1993:

1. *Liquid* assets
   a. cash on hand and in banks
   b. accounts receivable
   c. U.S. Treasury securities
2. *Other* assets
   a. mortgages
   b. other investments
   c. fixed assets
   d. "other assets"[1]

The data illustrate an important trend, namely, the percentage of aggregate union assets held in U.S. Treasury securities has grown noticeably. While the unions held less than 25 percent of their total assets in this

Table 4.2
Twenty-Eight Unions' Aggregate Asset Bases (1979–1993)

	Percentage Asset Holdings[1]						
	Liquid Assets			Other Assets			
Year[2]	Cash	Accounts Receivable	U.S. Treasury Securities	Mortgages	Other Investments	Fixed Assets	Other Assets
1979	.11	.02	.24	.10	.38	.12	.01
1980	.11	.03	.22	.10	.39	.13	.02
1981	.12	.02	.24	.09	.38	.11	.02
1982	.13	.02	.26	.09	.36	.10	.02
1983	.11	.02	.27	.07	.39	.10	.02
1984	.10	.02	.27	.06	.42	.10	.02
1985	.17	.03	.33	.02	.30	.11	.02
1986	.16	.03	.33	.02	.31	.11	.03
1987	.14	.03	.34	.04	.29	.10	.03
1988	.12	.03	.35	.04	.28	.10	.03
1989	.11	.03	.40	.04	.25	.11	.04
1990	.09	.03	.41	.04	.24	.12	.04
1991	.10	.03	.41	.04	.23	.12	.04
1992	.08	.03	.43	.04	.23	.13	.04
1993	.07	.04	.44	.04	.22	.12	.04

Source: Unions' LM-2 financial disclosure forms.

1. The numbers refer to the percentage of total assets held in each category. Percentages should be multiplied by 100 for conventional interpretation. Cash includes cash on hand and cash in banks.
2. Year refers to the unions' fiscal years, which are matched as described in Table 4.1, as is the case in all subsequent tables, except where noted.

form in 1979, they held 45 percent in U.S. Treasury securities in 1993, representing an 87 percent increase. Given that their accounts receivable, as a percentage of total asset holdings, grew from 2 to 4 percent, and their cash remained close to 10 percent of the total, the unions' liquid assets climbed from approximately 37 percent of total assets in 1979 to more than 55 percent in 1993.

In contrast, the unions' mortgages and other investment holdings declined. Mortgages dropped from 10 percent of total assets in the late 1970s to less that five percent in the late 1980s and early 1990s. These investments actually fell to an even lower level in the mid-1980s. Other investments, decreased from roughly 40 percent of total assets in the late 1970s and early 1980s to 22 percent in 1992 and 1993. Other assets jumped 400 percent during this period, but still accounted for only 4 percent of total assets. Overall, as mentioned, the data reveal a shift in the distribution of union assets. The trend has been for these unions, as a whole, to increase their liquidity, particularly with respect to assets held in U.S. Treasury securities.

DISAGGREGATE UNION ASSETS AND WEALTH

These aggregate data, while providing insight into the overall financial condition of unions, may nonetheless mask considerable interunion variation. Unions differ not only in terms of their membership level, which has direct implications for their long-term financial security, but also in terms of the degree to which they centralize organizational activities at the national levels of operation (Troy 1975; Fiorito, Gramm, and Hendricks 1991; Fiorito, Jarley, and Delaney 1995). The centralization of decision-making authority at these higher levels, in turn, may directly affect the extent to which finances are centralized, or, in other words, the relative financial resource bases of the national office vis-à-vis local and regional offices. On the one hand, decentralized financial operations may simply reflect the variation in the unions' bargaining structures, which are substantially influenced by the product market structure of the industry (Katz and Kochan 1992). Thus, a union negotiating in an industry in which few employers dominate the product market (i.e., a relatively concentrated industry) may perforce have a commensurately centralized bargaining structure with financial operations thus gravitating to higher organizational levels (Hendricks and Kahn 1982; Hendricks, Gramm, and Fiorito 1993). Conversely, unions which negotiate with numerous employers in an unconcentrated and geographically dispersed industry may adopt, again of necessity, a decentralized bargaining structure in which local and regional affiliates are organizationally dominant. On the other hand, unions may also have made the internal political decision to operate in a relatively centralized or decentralized manner, somewhat irrespective of the nature of their bargaining structure (Bok and Dunlop 1970).[2] Thus, the extent to which financial operations are centralized may reflect both the economic and bargaining contexts within which unions operate, as well as various political considerations. In any event, these conditions may substantially affect the degree to which the nationals of unions are financed, at least on a relative basis (Troy 1975).

Table 4.3 reports the twenty-eight unions' assets, comparing 1993 to (1) 1979 and (2) average levels during the fifteen-year period. Clearly, substantial differences exist in the assets levels of unions both within and

Table 4.3
Disaggregate Union Real Assets (Totals in Millions, Except in Percentage Change Column)

			Assets[1]					
UNION[2]	1993		1979		1979-1993 Percentage Change[3]		1979-1993 Average	
Private Sector	Total	Per-Member	Total	Per-Member	Total	Per-Member	Total	Per-Member
IBT	$77	($58.52)	$187	($97.28)	-.59	(-.40)	$161	($98.01)
UFCW	83	(83.02)	32	(29.38)	1.62	(1.83)	65	(64.44)
UAW	764	(990.46)	555	(361.71)	.38	(1.74)	681	(716.20)
IBEW	138	(194.53)	467	(566.53)	-.70	(-.66)	246	(309.34)
IAM	106	(223.42)	134	(201.78)	-.21	(.11)	126	(224.17)
CWA	71	(151.08)	41	(85.15)	.73	(.77)	52	(102.85)
USW	146	(345.99)	223	(230.97)	-.35	(.50)	193	(323.02)
CJA	103	(252.33)	102	(165.10)	.01	(.53)	140	(243.61)
LIU	111	(271.80)	68	(142.76)	.63	(.90)	89	(215.29)
IUOE	66	(217.19)	50	(160.08)	.32	(.36)	45	(137.99)
HERE	12	(47.74)	20	(54.42)	-.39	(-.12)	16	(53.23)
PPI	53	(239.68)	65	(284.20)	-.19	(-.16)	68	(302.95)
UPIU	25	(132.39)	18	(67.24)	.41	(.97)	23	(102.21)
ACTWU	9	(65.72)	26	(88.22)	-.65	(-.25)	14	(67.62)
IUE	33	(229.69)	31	(122.59)	.05	(.87)	36	(197.88)
ILGWU	145	(1092.19)	166	(529.49)	-.13	(1.06)	142	(724.16)
RWDSU	19	(242.97)	10	(81.26)	.96	(1.99)	16	(137.25)

between private and public sectors. Among the major private-sector-based unions, assets totals ranged from a low of roughly $9 million (ACTWU) to more than $760 million (the UAW) in 1993. In the public sector, the range was much more restricted but still sizable, as the NFFE had total assets slightly above $1 million ($1.42 million) compared to the NEA's nearly $90 million. Between sectors, the unions also differ, as the private sector unions held an average of $115 million in total assets in 1993 in comparison to the public sector unions' $24-million average holdings.

To some extent, these differences may be due to interunion variation in membership. At first blush, for example, one might not expect the NFFE to harbor the assets level held by the 2.1 million NEA or the more than 770,000-strong UAW. However, the data demonstrate significant

Table 4.3 *(continued)*

	Assets[1]							
UNION[2]	1993		1979		1979-1993 Percentage Change[3]		1979-1993 Average	
Private Sector	Total	Per-Member	Total	Per-Member	Total	Per-Member	Total	Per-Member
NEA	88	(42.07)	36	(21.23)	1.45	(.98)	52	(28.01)
AFSCME	23	(20.11)	17	(19.17)	.38	(.05)	19	(18.11)
SEIU	32	(34.71)	22	(41.41)	.46	(.16)	24	(33.29)
AFT	39	(68.59)	7	(15.97)	4.83	(3.29)	17	(33.52)
APWU	18	(71.35)	4	(15.87)	3.57	(3.50)	14	(60.65)
NALC	34	(160.77)	6	(37.37)	4.98	(3.30)	20	(104.67)
IAFF	7	(45.80)	2	(11.05)	3.17	(3.14)	4	(24.14)
AFGE	16	(108.48)	8	(32.33)	1.12	(2.35)	15	(87.56)
NRLCA	6	(77.46)	1	(18.73)	4.55	(3.05)	4	(59.44)
NTEU	4	(51.19)	3	(41.87)	.30	(.22)	4	(58.66)
NFFE	1	(46.78)	2	(32.88)	-.15	(.42)	2	(44.33)

Source: Unions' LM-2 financial disclosure forms.
Notes: Totals are rounded to the nearest million.

1. Assets are adjusted for inflation, as described in Table 4.1; per-member assets are computed by dividing total real assets by the union's membership in 1979 and 1993, respectively.
2. Union fiscal years vary from (a) January 1 – December 31: IBT, SEIU, UAW IAM, ACTWU, CJA, LIU,IUOE, CWA (after 1982), USW, UPIU, IUE, ILGWU, RWDSU, AFGE, APWU (after 1983), AFSCME; (b) May – April 30: UFCW, HERE; (c) July 1 – June 30: IBEW, PPI (after 1986), AFT, NRLCA, NFFE; (d) October 1 – September 30: NTEU, IAFF (after 1981); (e) September 1 – August 31: NEA; and (f) April 1 – March 31: NALC. Union fiscal years were matched according to the calendar years in which their fiscal years ended.
3. Percentages should be multiplied by 100 for conventional interpretation.

interunion differences on a per-member basis. In the private sector, the range in per-member assets extended from less than $50 (HERE) to more than $1,000 (the ILGWU). In fact, on a similar basis, two unions (ILGWU and UAW) in that sector had roughly $1,000; eight more (IAM, USW, CJA, LIU, IUOE, PPI, IUE, and RWDSU) had greater than $200; and another three (IBEW, CWA, and UPIU) had over $100. It is noteworthy that the top three unions (ILGWU, UAW, and USW) in per-member assets have manufacturing as a primary industrial jurisdiction.

In contrast, only two of the public sector unions had assets totaling more than $100 per member (i.e., the NALC and AFGE). Although the differences among these unions on this dimension are substantial, they, again, are much more restricted than found among the private sector unions. Nonetheless, membership would still seem to be a rather limited predictor of assets. On a strictly per-member basis, the NFFE actually had more real assets than the NEA, and the NALC had nearly four times as much assets as the NEA, which has almost ten times as many members.

The unions also varied widely in terms of their asset holdings over the fifteen-year time period. Eight of the private sector unions (IBT, IBEW, IAM, USW, HERE, PPI, ACTWU, and ILGWU) ended the period with fewer real assets than they started with, but only five of them (IBT, IBEW, HERE, PPI, and ACTWU) actually lost assets on a per-member basis. The biggest losers in this regard would appear to be the IBEW, ACTWU, and IBT, each of which ended the period with substantially fewer than half of the total assets they had at the beginning.[3] As a further indication of these unions' standing over time, nine unions (IBT, IBEW, IAM, USW, CJA, HERE, PPI, ACTWU, and IUE) had fewer assets in 1993 than they averaged during the 1979–1993 period, but only six (IBT, IAM, IBEW, HERE, PPI, and ACTWU) had fewer than they averaged on a per-member basis.

Although they generally hold fewer assets, particularly on a per-member basis, the public sector unions tend to experience sizable asset gains during this period. All but one of the eleven ended the period with more total assets, and all, in fact, ended it with more assets per member than they had at the beginning. Further, all but the NTEU had more assets per member in 1993 than they averaged during the fifteen-year interval. In this regard, the postal service unions (APWU, NALC, and NRLCA) each grew considerably (relative to most other unions in either sector) on both total and per-member asset bases. Yet, as indicated above, the public sector unions lag behind their private sector counterparts in terms of how extensively they are financed, at least in terms of asset holdings. Overall, while the eleven public sector unions account for more than 40 percent of the twenty-eight unions' total membership, they held less than 12 percent of the total union assets in 1993. Because of their relative asset growth during this period, however, this percentage more than doubled from 4.7 percent in 1979.

Given that the unions' aggregate wealth has constituted the overwhelming majority of their total assets throughout this period, it is unsurprising that the disaggregate union patterns are somewhat comparable, with differences, across both financial dimensions (see Table 4.4).

First, in terms of general patterns, as was the case with regard to total assets, the unions' wealth varied widely within and between sectors. In particular, it ranged from –$26 million (UFCW) to $758 million (UAW) among private sector unions; the range extended from $400,000 to $28 million in the public sector. Across both sectors, only six unions (UAW,

Table 4.4
Disaggregate Union Real Wealth (Totals in Millions, Except for Percentage Change Column)

	Wealth[1]							
UNION	1993		1979		Percentage Change 1979-1993[2]		1979-1993 Average	
Private Sector	Total	Per-Member	Total	Per-Member	Total	Per-Member	Total	Per-Member
IBT	$44	($33.63)	$183	($94.90)	-.76	(-.64)	$153	($92.42)
UFCW	-26	(-26.21)	25	(23.69)	-2.02	(-2.11)	46	(45.89)
UAW	758	(983.58)	548	(357.03)	.38	(1.75)	689	(710.40)
IBEW	129	(182.02)	41	(49.36)	2.17	(2.69)	96	(118.09)
IAM	105	(221.78)	121	(182.52)	-.13	(.21)	115	(209.34)
CWA	59	(124.42)	28	(57.09)	1.12	(1.18)	34	(66.06)
USW	116	(276.55)	209	(216.94)	-.44	(.27)	179	(296.67)
CJA	90	(219.87)	101	(163.30)	-.11	(.35)	135	(233.65)
LIU	107	(262.09)	67	(141.97)	.58	(.85)	86	(209.15)
IUOE	65	(213.59)	49	(157.25)	.32	(.36)	44	(134.73)
HERE	11	(43.78)	19	(50.78)	-.40	(-.14)	15	(48.85)
PPI	51	(231.44)	63	(276.81)	-.19	(-.16)	66	(294.50)
UPIU	21	(112.73)	18	(67.09)	.20	(.68)	19	(78.38)
ACTWU	7	(50.94)	23	(75.54)	-.68	(-.32)	12	(56.93)
IUE	30	(212.08)	30	(118.91)	-.00	(.78)	35	(188.87)
ILGWU	144	(1083.76)	163	(520.74)	-.12	(1.08)	140	(714.73)
RWDSU	19	(242.49)	10	(80.86)	.97	(2.00)	16	(135.48)
Public Sector								
NEA	27	(12.90)	27	(16.20)	-.01	(-.20)	27	(15.16)
AFSCME	10	(8.77)	12	(13.31)	-.13	(-.34)	10	(10.22)
SEIU	28	(30.58)	22	(41.38)	.29	(-.26)	22	(32.00)
AFT	27	(46.47)	4	(10.18)	5.19	(3.56)	11	(21.61)
APWU	16	(64.89)	4	(15.55)	3.24	(3.17)	12	(51.24)
NALC	28	(135.61)	3	(17.88)	9.55	(6.58)	16	(82.80)
IAFF	5	(32.59)	1	(10.17)	2.22	(2.20)	2	(15.23)
AFGE	3	(18.93)	4	(16.43)	-.28	(.15)	1	(7.53)
NRLCA	2	(21.15)	.4	(6.90)	3.12	(2.07)	2	(27.81)
NTEU	2	(21.32)	2	(22.26)	.02	(-.04)	3	(39.90)
NFFE	.4	(14.87)	.4	(8.82)	.00	(.69)	.7	(17.81)

Source: Unions' LM-2 financial disclosure forms.
Note: Totals are rounded to nearest million.
1. Wealth is adjusted for inflation, as described in Table 4.1; per-member wealth is total real wealth divided by the union's membership in 1993 and 1979, respectively.
2. Percentages should be multiplied by 100 for conventional interpretation.

ILGWU, IBEW, USW, IAM, and LIU) had more than $100 million in net assets. The sizable gap in wealth between unions in the private and public sectors is revealed in the disparate averages these two sets of unions held in wealth between 1979 and 1993: $109 million among private sector unions vis-à-vis less than $10 million among the public sector organizations.

Second, vast interunion differences in per-member wealth are also observed. For instance, the NALC held more wealth in 1993 than either the NEA or AFT, both of which are substantially larger in terms of membership. More generally, the private sector unions' per-member wealth averaged $214 between 1979 and 1993 and was $263 in 1993, compared to $29 and $37, respectively, among the public sector unions.

Third, ten private sector unions ended the 1979–1993 period with less wealth (a larger number than was the case with regard to assets), but only five of them (IBT, UFCW, HERE, PPI, and ACTWU) ended the period less wealthy on a per-member basis. Relatedly, nine unions ended the period with less wealth than they averaged over the fifteen years, but, again, fewer (IBT, UFCW, USW, CJA, HERE, PPI, and ACTWU) lost on a per-member basis.

Fourth, somewhat similar to the situation among the private sector unions, more public-employee unions ended the period with less wealth than occurred regarding assets. Three such unions (NEA, AFSCME, and AFGE) in particular had less wealth, but the loss for the NEA was minimal. Four actually suffered on a per-member basis (i.e., NEA, AFSCME, SEIU, and NTEU), but only one union (NTEU) ended the period with less wealth than it averaged. As was the case with regard to assets, the public sector unions generally exhibited growth, and the postal unions (APWU, NALC, and NRLCA) in particular had uniformly impressive expansions.

Concentration

The disaggregated data on union assets and wealth point out the widely disparate levels of financial resources available to these national organizations. They also illustrate the relative concentration of money in the coffers of a few organizations. Table 4.5 reports the concentration ratios for assets and wealth, averaged over the 1979–1993 period. The ratios show the percentage of assets and wealth, respectively, held by the top three, five, and ten organizations (in terms of asset and wealth holdings) over the fifteen years.

The data show that three of the twenty-eight unions held roughly half of the total assets and wealth, averaged over the fifteen years. In particular, the UAW, IBEW, and USW held an average of 30, 11, and 8 percent of the total assets, respectively. The UAW, USW, and IBT held approximately

Table 4.5
Average Concentration of Assets and Wealth (1979–1993)

Union Set[1]	Percentage of Assets	Percentage of Wealth
Top 3	.49 (UAW, IBEW, USW)	.51 (UAW, USW, IBT)
Top 5	.62 (Plus IBT, ILGWU)	.65 (Plus ILGWU, CJA)
Top 10	.83 (Plus CJA, IAM, LIU, PPI, UFCW)	.86 (Plus IAM, IBEW, LIU, PPI, UFCW)

Source: Unions' LM-2 financial disclosure forms.

1. The percentages refer to the proportion of the twenty-eight unions' total real assets and wealth, respectively, held by the top three, five, and ten unions with the most assets and wealth, averaged over the 1979–1993 period. Percentages should be multiplied by 100 for conventional interpretation.

34, 9, and 8 percent of the total wealth. What emerges from these data is the towering financial resources of the UAW relative to the other unions.

Carrying the analysis a bit further, the top five unions in terms of assets and wealth held 62 and 65 percent of the unions' overall resources in these dimensions. The top 10 held over 80 percent of the assets and wealth. Interestingly, none of the union leaders in either category is in the public sector. Altogether, in fact, the public sector unions averaged only 7.8 and 5.4 percent of the total assets and wealth, respectively, held in 1979–1993.[4]

Disaggregate Liquid Asset Holdings

Just as unions vary in the overall amount of assets and wealth they hold, they also may differ in the composition of these financial bases. An important consideration in this regard is the relative liquidity of their assets. Liquidity arguably enhances the financial flexibility of an organization, as assets may be more or less readily converted into cash and hence deployed for any number of important organizational needs or purposes, assuming of course that the union's debt is not so seriously steep as to limit the availability of assets (a point addressed in Chapter 6, which discusses union financial performance).

Table 4.6 shows the percentage of union assets held in cash, accounts receivable, and U.S. Treasury securities in 1993 and averaged over the 1979–1993 period. It also reports the total percentage held in all three more-or-less liquid categories, again both in 1993 and averaged over the fifteen years. The data reveal vast interunion differences in the percentage of assets held within these various categories. In 1993, the range in relative cash holdings varied from a negligible amount to 52 percent of total assets among private sector unions. Only six unions (HERE, ACTWU, CWA, RWDSU, CJA, and IUE) held more than 10 percent of their combined assets in cash. Most of the public sector unions, however, held 10 percent or more of their assets in this form in 1993, but it is important to bear in mind that their overall holdings are comparatively small vis-à-vis their private sector counterparts. Three public sector unions (APWU, AFT, and IAFF) held well over half of their assets in cash in 1993, and the APWU and AFT did so over the 1979–1993 period, as did the NRLCA as well.

Averaged over the fifteen years, three private sector unions (UAW, CJA, and IUOE) held 50 percent or more of their assets in these three asset forms, and two of these (UAW and IUOE) held their assets principally in U.S. Treasury securities. Another six unions in this sector (CWA, CJA, USW, HERE, IUE, and RWDSU) held more than 40 percent of their assets in liquid form over the fifteen-year span, while another six held more than 20 percent (IBT, UFCW, IBEW, IAM, UPIU, and ACTWU). Thus, only three private sector unions held less than 20 percent of their assets in these liquid forms (ILGWU, PPI, and LIU).

Among unions in the public sector, only two (AFSCME and SEIU) held more than 10 percent of their assets in U.S. Treasury securities in 1993, and only three (the two aforementioned plus the NTEU) averaged 10 percent or more of such holdings. However, seven of these unions (NEA, AFSCME, AFT, APWU, IAFF, NRLCA, and NTEU) held more than 50 percent of their assets in one or more of these liquid forms over the fifteen years. Only the NALC and NFFE held less than 20 percent in such categories. On average, the public sector unions held 50 percent of their assets in either cash, accounts receivable, or U.S. Treasury securities, compared to 36 percent in the private sector.

CONCLUSIONS

Several conclusions follow from the data. First, the twenty-eight major unions maintained their financial capital base (assets and wealth) during a period of sizable membership losses. On a per-member basis, they actually had more assets and wealth at the end of the period than at the start. Obviously, they maintained their assets without incurring additional liabilities that would effectively trim their wealth. Relatedly, the unions increased

Table 4.6
Disaggregate Union Liquid Asset Holdings (Percentages in Categories)

Union	Cash		Accounts Receivable		U.S. Treasury Securities		Total Liquidity	
	1993	1979-1993 Average	1993	1979-1993 Average	1993	1979-1993 Average	1993	1979-1993 Average
Private Sector								
IBT	.08	.11	.06	.01	.13	.10	.28	.22
UFCW	.08	.06	.11	.16	.10	.13	.29	.35
UAW	.00	.02	.00	.00	.93	.81	.93	.83
IBEW	.03	.17	.01	.01	.19	.04	.22	.23
IAM	.08	.27	.00	.02	.08	.04	.16	.33
CWA	.18	.33	.02	.01	.36	.08	.56	.42
USW	.01	.01	.01	.00	.49	.42	.51	.44
CJA	.14	.30	.03	.04	.48	.16	.66	.50
LIU	.06	.07	.02	.02	.02	.02	.10	.10
IUOE	.03	.04	.04	.04	.80	.52	.87	.60
HERE	.52	.40	.00	.00	.03	.05	.55	.45
PPI	.01	.03	.00	.00	.00	.08	.01	.11
UPIU	.07	.22	.06	.07	.00	.00	.13	.29
ACTWU	.22	.15	.20	.13	.00	.03	.42	.31
IUE	.13	.41	.00	.00	.00	.03	.13	.45
ILGWU	.02	.06	.02	.01	.00	.02	.04	.10
RWDSU	.15	.26	.00	.00	.31	.20	.46	.47
Public Sector								
NEA	.12	.19	.24	.36	.00	.00	.36	.55
AFSCME	.14	.25	.20	.19	.40	.12	.74	.57
SEIU	.10	.18	.21	.05	.18	.17	.50	.40
AFT	.68	.59	.18	.23	.00	.00	.86	.82
APWU	.86	.77	.04	.03	.00	.00	.90	.81
NALC	.03	.05	.09	.11	.02	.03	.14	.18
IAFF	.63	.44	.10	.11	.00	.01	.73	.56
AFGE	.04	.04	.12	.14	.00	.08	.17	.26
NRLCA	.22	.52	.05	.08	.00	.00	.27	.60
NTEU	.30	.26	.09	.12	.09	.27	.49	.65
NFFE	.08	.03	.12	.08	.00	.00	.21	.11

Source: Unions' LM-2 financial disclosure forms.
Note: Percentages are rounded up and may not add exactly across categories. They should be multiplied by 100 for conventional interpretation.

the liquidity of their financial reserves. In 1993, they held 56 percent, or more than $1.2 billion, of their more than $2.2 billion in total assets in liquid form, principally U.S. Treasury securities. This compares to 37 percent, or $852 million, in similar holdings in 1979. Thus, these findings are consistent with Willman, Morris, and Aston's (1993) and Bennett's (1991) observations that unions may improve their financial position, at least in certain respects, while still losing members. Further, to the extent liquidity gives unions some additional financial sinew, their combined capacity to withstand difficult circumstances, such as a major strike, has arguably been enhanced over this time period, which is a point explored in more detail in Chapter 9.

Second, a vast gap exists between the evident financial wherewithal of private and public sector unions, at least at the national level. Bluntly put, the private sector unions—in absolute and relative or per-member terms—swamp their public sector counterparts on both dimensions of financial capacity (i.e., wealth and assets). Because of the highly decentralized nature of government especially at the state and local level, and the attendant balkanization of the structure of unions and collective bargaining in these areas, this comparison may not be strictly fair. Local and regional affiliates of unions in this sector may play a far more significant role in the financial and other affairs than is the case with regard to unions that are more centralized organizationally or in their structure of bargaining. As Stern observes, "In education, as in other parts of local government, the national union usually is not involved in the collective bargaining process. The key decision-makers are either local union officers or officials of district councils, UniServe districts [which are the local units of service for bargaining in the NEA]..., or state councils. For this reason, national office-holders and national policy are less important in these organizations than in industrial unions in the private sector" (1979: 63). Nonetheless, the private–public sector union financial gap is consistent with Sheflin and Troy's (1983) empirical observation that public sector unions' finances lagged behind those found in the private sector in the 1960s and 1970s.

Third, although sector, as well as membership size, may explain some of the considerable interunion variation in assets and wealth, there are clearly significant intrasector differences. Also, these differences within sector cannot be explained by membership alone. In this regard, both assets and wealth have been relatively concentrated in a handful of unions, exclusively in the private sector. Clearly, then, other factors must be looked at as possible predictors. According to Troy (1975), one major explanatory factor is bargaining centralization, or the extent to which a union's structure of bargaining centralizes decision-making power at the national or international level.

Finally, the data permit distinguishing between unions that suffered financially in the 1980s, versus those that gained. In particular, three unions

(IBT, IBEW, and ACTWU) lost at least 25 percent of both their assets and wealth, measured in either absolute or per-member terms, between 1979 and 1993. In contrast, ten unions (the UAW, CWA, LIU, IUOE, RWDSU, AFT, APWU, NALC, IAFF, and NRLCA) ended the 1979–1993 period with 25 percent more assets and wealth—both in absolute and per-member amounts—than they had at the beginning. Unsurprisingly, five of these unions are in the public sector, including all three of the major postal-employee unions. For example, the postal unions' combined wealth was 520 percent higher in 1993 than 1979.

NOTES

1. "Other assets" is a catchall category that includes all assets apart from cash, accounts receivable, loans receivable, U.S. Treasury securities, mortgage investments, other investments, and fixed assets.

2. It is arguable that a decentralized system of governance in a union may enhance union democracy, as the point of decision making lies closer to the rank and file, given that local leaders represent smaller constituencies and, hence, are more likely to be in regular contact with the membership. Although there may be drawbacks in decentralization, they may be the "price that must be paid to achieve a democratic union" (Bok and Dunlop 1970: 152).

3. Between 1979 and the mid-1980s, the IBEW held vast amounts of assets in the mortgage investments and other investments categories. For instance, it held nearly $150 million (unadjusted for inflation) in mortgage investments and $124 million in other investments in 1979; the IBEW listed a "Special Reserve" liability of more than $308 million in that same year. By 1986, these respective assets had shrunk to $8 million and $64 million, and no special reserve liability was listed. Thus, the IBEW's assets had fallen from $339 million in 1979 to $112 million in 1986, but its liabilities shrunk from $309 million to slightly less than $1 million during the same period. Consequently, its net asset situation improved.

4. As suggested earlier and will be discussed in more detail, this situation may be substantially attributable to the relative decentralization of some public sector unions.

Chapter 5

How Unions Raise and Spend Money

Understandably, unions should not be expected to measure their success as organizations in terms of the accumulation of sizable annual surpluses or "profits." Such revenue generation would certainly raise serious reservations about whether the union was operating in the members' real interests, especially if the bulk of income came from member-based sources. At the same time, however, the scope and stability of a union's annual revenue stream is an important determinant of its capacity to undertake various organizational activities. In addition, unions, like any other type of organization (perhaps apart from the federal government), cannot continually incur budget deficits (expenses in excess of revenues) without jeopardizing their institutional security and ultimate viability.[1]

Accordingly, it is important to examine how unions raise and spend their money. In particular, it is instructive to examine the scope or size of their annual revenue stream and their dependence on member-based income. Obviously, the extent to which unions are so dependent has direct implications for understanding the financial consequences of membership losses. Eventually, income lost due to membership reductions will translate into a diminished capacity to offer various union goods and services to the rank and file, at least on an absolute, if not a per-member, basis. Also, it is important to examine the operating surpluses that unions have been able to sustain, particularly during periods when their membership has declined. In other words, to what extent have unions been able to avoid annual financial deficits by generating sufficient revenues, paring expenditures, or some combination of the two?

In addition, it is relevant to examine union expenditures on such key items as salaries and administration. In this regard, Clark (1989: 585) found that several major unions (such as the IBT, USW, AFSCME, SEIU, and AFT) "acquired larger and larger numbers of full-time, paid employees" between 1961 and 1985. While he observed a positive relationship between membership and union staff growth, noting "that as the membership of many American unions increased through the 1950s, 1960s, and 1970s, so did the number of professional staff" (Clark 1989: 594), he has also commented that "the challenges unions face and the services they provide have become increasingly complex" (Clark and Gray 1991: 183). Thus, it may not be intuitively obvious that a decrease in membership implies fewer union staff and related administrative costs particularly relative to overall union operating costs. In fact, the decline may cause unions to experience strong opposite pressures. They face growing demands to expand organizing and political efforts, thus necessitating more organizers, lobbyists, and PAC fundraising (Masters and Delaney 1985; Delaney and Masters 1991a; 1991b). Also, to maintain an effective bargaining presence in the face of economic globalization and a wave of complex corporate mergers and acquisitions, they have a need for greater expertise in business finances. As mentioned, the USW recently hired a full-time investment banker who has an MBA from Harvard, and significant experience in employee buyouts of companies (Norton 1996b). Directly to the point, the newly appointed special assistant to the president of the USW says that "unions were being backed into corners by companies and couldn't understand on a sophisticated level the company's arguments. . . . Labor needed to be armed with the equivalent skills" (Norton 1996b: B1).

AGGREGATE UNION INCOME AND OPERATING SURPLUSES

Table 5.1 reports the unions' aggregate income and operating surpluses. As previously described, total income consists of revenues from all reported sources, including transmittals and sales of fixed assets. Total surplus is simply total income minus total disbursements. Operating income omits transmittal revenues and the sales of investments and fixed assets from total income, and operating surplus is operating revenues minus operating disbursements (total disbursements minus transmittal expenditures and purchases of investments and fixed assets). Operating measures provide a more stable and realistic indication of the general-purpose money these national organizations have to spend on their own activities.

The data show that total union income, like total assets and wealth, exhibited a bell-shaped trend during the 1979–1993 period. Total income rose more than $1.6 billion between 1979 and 1987, reflecting a 56-percent in-

Table 5.1
Twenty-Eight Unions' Aggregate Real Income and Operating Surpluses (1979–1993)

Year	Total Income (in millions)	Total Surpluses (in millions)	Operating Income (in millions)	Operating Surpluses (in millions)	Surplus as Percentage of Operating Income	Per-Member Operating Income	Per-Member Operating Surpluses
1979	$2,907	$17	$1,623	$224	(.14)	$106.52	$14.72
1980	2,878	32	1,536	119	(.08)	103.01	8.01
1981	2,777	55	1,555	279	(.18)	106.60	19.14
1982	3,051	55	1,567	270	(.17)	108.20	18.67
1983	3,092	-32	1,485	175	(.12)	103.31	12.20
1984	3,284	-6	1,517	205	(.13)	107.02	14.44
1985	3,286	68	1,488	188	(.13)	106.25	13.41
1986	3,967	-12	1,540	28	(.02)	111.15	1.99
1987	4,536	-41	1,541	38	(.03)	107.36	2.81
1988	4,412	-25	1,406	85	(.06)	104.96	6.34
1989	4,431	-15	1,488	47	(.03)	111.89	3.55
1990	3,114	-27	1,411	96	(.07)	105.28	7.19
1991	2,977	19	1,364	130	(.10)	100.94	9.65
1992	3,145	-25	1,384	63	(.04)	103.78	4.71
1993	2,905	-28	1,253	99	(.08)	95.24	7.52
Percentage of Change 1979-1993	-.001	-2.65	-.23	-.56	(-.43)	-.11	-.49
Average 1979-1993	3,384	2.4	1,471	136	(.09)	105.49	9.62

Source: Unions' LM-2 financial disclosure forms.
Note: Numbers in columns are rounded to nearest million; percentages should be multiplied by 100 for conventional interpretation.

crease. It fell rapidly thereafter to just slightly below the 1979 level. On a per-member basis, however, total income was $221 in 1993, compared to $191 in 1979, or 16 percent higher (per-member total income data are not reported in Table 5.1). Total income per-member also reflected a bell-shaped trend, peaking at $336 in 1987. Thus, once again, despite heavy membership losses, these twenty-eight unions maintained their aggregate income level and actually improved their per-member revenues by a substantial amount.

As expected, the unions typically spent most of, if not slightly more than, what they took in as income. Their total surpluses (or lack thereof) ranged from a $41 million deficit to $68 million, the latter of which still amounted to less than three percent of total revenues ($3.28 billion) in 1985. Although nominally minor, the unions incurred deficits in seven of the eight years since 1986. Over the fifteen years, however, the unions enjoyed a net surplus of $35 million.

The operating income data are noteworthy. The national unions have a much smaller revenue base to fund regular operations than their total receipts would suggest. On average, the twenty-eight national unions derived 57 percent of their total receipts from transmittals or sales of investments and fixed assets. These transactions contributed to the bulge in total receipts in the mid- to late 1980s. In 1987, for instance, the year in which total income peaked, operating income comprised less than 34 percent of all receipts. In 1993, despite the $1.6 billion drop in total income from 1987, operating revenues accounted for only 43 percent of total receipts. Thus, while total receipts may accurately reflect the magnitude of union financial transactions, they may vastly overstate the steady income national unions have had at their command for discretionary use.

Second, operating income declined significantly in the 1980s. The unions ended the period with nearly a quarter less in such revenue. This decrease outpaced the drop in union membership. Per-member operating income dropped 11 percent. For all practical purposes, the unions had less money to spend on behalf of members. To avoid a diminution in services, unions would have had to engage in deficit spending, tap their wealth or assets (which they evidently did not deplete in the 1980s), or gotten more "bang out of the buck" reordering organizational priorities and improving operations.

Third, the unions, in the aggregate at least, clearly did not deficit finance their operating budgets. Quite to the contrary, they maintained operating surpluses in each year between 1979 and 1993. On average, the surpluses amounted to almost 10 percent of operating income, and were as high as 18 percent in 1981. While the surpluses have been relatively small since the late 1980s, they still account for a nontrivial portion of income. Thus, the unions evidently chose to curb their operating disbursements. In reality, they spent 18 percent less in 1993 than in 1979, or $1.1 billion compared to almost $1.4 billion (in real operating disbursements). On a per-member basis, operating disbursements dropped from $92 to $87 between 1979 and 1993. The upshot of these data is that unions chose to reduce their spending in order to maintain a "balanced" budget. On average, they held $10 per member in surpluses. Given that their total receipts over the entire fifteen years exceeded total disbursements, and that operating income exceeded operating expenditures, the unions would seem to have maintained fiscal integrity.

Income Sources and Selected Expenditures

Table 5.2 reports on aggregate unions' income derived from member-based sources (i.e., dues, per-capita taxes, assessments, fees, fines, and work permits) and on aggregate union expenditures dedicated to salaries (both officers and employees) and administrative-related expenses, which include the LM-2 line items on office and administration expenses, educational and publicity expenses, professional fees, and direct taxes paid by the union as an organization.[2] These data indicate that approximately two-thirds to three-quarters of the unions' operating income has come from member-based sources, with the average being 72 percent between 1979 and 1993. Unsurprisingly, then, member-based income drifted downward, as did operating income. In fact, both fell by the same percentage, comparing 1993 to 1979. The loss in union membership would thus seem to have hit the unions hard in this regard. On this matter, the decline in member-based income would likely have been much steeper had not several of the unions substantially increased their dues during this time period, a topic to be discussed in detail later.

In a relevant vein, the data also speak to the relatively minor amount of total income that unions derive from member-based sources. On average between 1979 and 1993, the twenty-eight unions' raised less than a third of their total revenues from member-based dues, excluding transmittals, at the national level. However, transmittal income includes dues, fees, fines, assessments, and work permits collected on behalf of affiliates for transmittal to them. During the 1979–1993 period, transmittal income averaged $262 million, or approximately a quarter of the member-based income that is not directly reallocated to affiliates or members. Still, member-based income plus transmittal revenues averaged only $1.33 billion dollars, or slightly less than 40 percent of total union income.

The data regarding the disbursements on salaries and administration also point to some distinctive aggregate trends. The unions have spent a relatively constant amount of their budget, in percentage terms, on officers' and employees' salaries (combined). The percentage has ranged from 26 to 32 percent, with the average being 29 percent. In absolute terms, however, the amount spent actually decreased, falling by 15 percent between 1979 and 1993.

Expenditures on administrative-related items, however, actually increased significantly, particularly in the mid- to late-1980s. Comparing 1993 to 1979, the unions spent $78 million more (again in real dollar amounts) on administration, which represents a 35-percent hike. As a percentage of operating disbursements, administrative-related spending rose from 16 to 26 percent. Within this spending group, office and administration expenditures rose by 34 percent between 1979 and 1993 to 14 percent of operating disbursements; education expenses grew by 15 percent to 4 percent of the operating expenses; and professional fees climbed 60 percent to almost 5 percent of the operational budget.

DISAGGREGATE UNION INCOME AND OPERATING SURPLUSES

The disaggregated data on operating income and surpluses are reported in Table 5.3. Clearly, the overwhelming proportion of aggregate operating income loss occurred among unions in the private sector. Fourteen of the

Table 5.2
Twenty-Eight Unions' Aggregate Real Member-Based Income and Selected Disbursements (1979–1993)

	Member-Based Income		Salary and Administration Expenditures			
			Salary		Administration	
Year	Receipts (in millions)	Percentage of Operating Income	Disbursements (in millions)	Percentage of Total Operating Disbursements	Disbursements (in millions)	Percentage of Total Operating Disbursements
1979	$1263	.78	$427	.30	$220	.16
1980	1190	.77	422	.30	231	.16
1981	1159	.74	403	.32	227	.18
1982	1099	.70	395	.30	226	.17
1983	1071	.72	397	.30	237	.18
1984	1078	.71	376	.29	257	.19
1985	1055	.71	386	.30	286	.22

1986	1052	.68	392	.26	311	.20
1987	1031	.71	386	.27	303	.21
1988	1027	.73	412	.31	309	.23
1989	1030	.69	386	.27	316	.22
1990	1019	.72	380	.29	328	.25
1991	975	.71	363	.29	309	.25
1992	999	.72	374	.28	312	.24
1993	958	.76	363	.31	298	.26
Percentage Change 1979-1993	-.24		15		.35	
Average 1979-1993	1,067	.72	391	.29	278	.21

Source: Unions' LM-2 financial disclosure forms.
Note: Members rounded to nearest million; percentages should be multiplied by 100 for conventional interpretation.

Table 5.3
Disaggregate Union Real Income and Operating Surpluses

	Operating Income (in millions)[1]				Per-Member Operating Income				Operating Surpluses (in millions)[1]	
Union	1993	1979	Percentage Change 1979-1993[2]	1979-1993 Average	1993	1979	Percentage Change 1979-1993[2]	1979-1993 Average	1979-1993 Average	# Deficits[3]
Private Sector										
IBT	$53	$119	-.55	$82	$40.11	$62.08	-.35	$49.27	$2	5
UFCW	83	87	-.05	92	82.96	80.74	.03	90.95	2	6
UAW	181	360	-.50	325	234.71	234.36	.00	331.29	48	1
IBEW	56	122	-.54	86	79.23	148.53	-.47	108.95	15	0
IAM	70	102	-.31	86	147.94	153.82	-.04	154.42	12	2
CWA	67	47	.42	63	142.65	97.65	.46	123.94	4	3
CJA	43	65	-.33	56	106.45	104.56	.02	97.41	6	4
USW	98	204	-.52	132	231.99	211.32	.10	214.80	5	5
LIU	32	33	-.03	32	78.60	69.90	.12	75.91	7	0
IUOE	27	20	.33	25	88.69	64.85	.37	76.64	3	4
HERE	20	17	.19	18	77.90	45.41	.71	59.00	.6	4
PPI	28	33	-.13	27	128.33	142.85	-.10	120.73	.7	8

UPIU	18	24	-.25	23	98.18	90.61	.08	100.29	1	4
ACTWU	16	35	-.54	24	111.54	114.82	-.03	112.75	-.7	9
IUE	15	24	-.39	20	104.00	95.13	.09	103.57	2	3
ILGWU	48	64	-.25	56	360.85	202.95	.78	280.54	9	0
'RWDSU	6	7	-.21	7	70.10	58.49	.20	63.26	.9	3
Public Sector										
NEA	130	102	.28	113	61.98	60.00	.03	61.95	6	1
AFSCME	65	49	.32	54	55.69	55.33	.01	51.87	4	1
SEIU	42	20	1.13	31	46.23	37.72	.22	42.60	2	1
AFT	55	27	1.05	38	96.59	64.01	.51	75.46	2	4
APWU	27	16	.67	24	108.46	65.84	.65	101.33	2	1
NALC	20	12	.69	18	96.29	78.96	.22	97.82	2	1
IAFF	11	6	.73	8	70.17	40.72	.72	54.47	.4	2
AFGE	16	18	-.12	18	108.04	77.55	.39	102.72	.2	4
NRLCA	3	2	1.14	3	42.75	26.81	.59	45.15	.1	8
NTEU	8	5	.43	7	105.17	77.99	.35	105.95	.3	4
NFFE[4]	3	2	.10	3	88.94	48.14	.85	70.74	0	5

Source: Unions' LM-2 financial disclosure forms.

1. Totals and averages in these columns are rounded to nearest million or one-hundred thousand for some unions with less than $1 million in average surpluses in the average surplus column.
2. Percentages should be multiplied by 100 for conventional interpretation.
3. Deficits refer to the number of years in which operating disbursements exceeded operating revenues.
4. NFFE's average surplus was actually $26,270.

seventeen unions in that group ended the period with less income on an annual basis. In fact, five (the IBT, UAW, IBEW, USW, and ACTWU) had only one-half, or even less, of the income in 1993 they had generated in 1979. Another five (ILGWU, IUE, UPIU, CJA, and IAM) suffered at least a 25-percent reduction. On a per-member basis, however, only five (IBT, IBEW, IAM, PPI, and ACTWU) lost revenue, comparing 1993 to 1979. In this regard, the IBT and IBEW suffered relatively sizable losses.[3]

In contrast, the public sector unions' revenue situations, with the exception of the AFGE, improved in these fifteen years. Six of the eleven public sector unions ended the period with 50 percent or more in operating income than they generated in 1979. This includes each of the postal unions (APWU, NALC, and NRLCA) and three state and local unions (AFT, IAFF, and SEIU). While the AFGE ended the period with 12 percent less in operating income, its per-member revenues actually rose by almost 40 percent. On a per-member basis, in fact, four unions (AFT, APWU, NFFE, and NRLCA) gained 50 percent or more in revenue. Because of their combined growth, the public sector unions accounted for 31 percent of the twenty-eight unions' total operating income in 1993, compared to 16 percent in 1979.

As was the case with regard to disaggregate union wealth and assets, considerable interunion variation exists in operating income between and within sectors. Among private sector unions, average operating income ranged from $7 million (RWDSU) to $325 million (the UAW). In the public sector, it extended from $3 million (NFFE and NRLCA) to $113 million (the NEA). Only three unions, however, across both sectors averaged more than $100 million in annual operating income (i.e., the UAW, USW, and NEA). In 1993, only two unions (UAW and NEA) fell in this category. Ten of the private sector unions, in fact, raised less than $50 million per year in 1993, as was the case with eight of the public sector unions.

Comparing sectors, the private sector unions appear, once again, substantially better financed. Averaged over the 1979–1993 period, the public sector unions raised $29 million compared to the private sector unions' $68 million. Nine of the private sector unions averaged more than $50 million in operating income, while only two of the eleven public sector unions had a similar intake. Also, on a per-member basis, private sector unions' operating income averaged $126 vis-à-vis the public sector unions' $74.

While the aggregate union data show that the unions have been able to avoid an operating deficit, the disaggregate data present a more complicated picture. Only three of the private sector unions and none of the public sector unions avoided a deficit year between 1979 and 1993 (see last column of Table 5.3). Five private sector unions (IBT, UFCW, USW, PPI, and ACTWU) had operating deficits for a third or more of the years observed. The ACTWU, in fact, had such deficits in almost two-thirds of the years, and its operating "surplus" averaged about $700,000 in the red. Two public sector unions (NFFE and NRLCA) had deficits in at least five years, but neither of these had a negative average surplus. Parenthetically, it would seem that the operating surplus observed in the aggregate is heavily attributable to one union. The UAW's average surplus ($48 million) comprises 35 percent of the overall $136 million average. Notwithstanding their sizable income losses, the UAW, IBEW, and IAM had a combined average surplus ($75 million) that accounts for more than 50 percent of the unions' overall average.

Member-Based Income and Selected Expenditures

Disaggregated data on the unions' reliance on member-based income and their salary and administration disbursements appear in Table 5.4. They reveal that private sector unions vary widely in their dependence on dues and other member-based income. While the ILGWU, on average, received just slightly more than a quarter of its operating income from member-based sources, HERE was dependent at the 90 percent level. Twelve private sector unions received, again on average, roughly three-quarters or more of their operating income from their members (IBT, UFCW, IBEW, IAM, CWA, USW, IUOE, HERE, PPI, UPIU, IUE, and RWDSU); another three (CJA, LIU, and ACTWU) received more than two-thirds of their income from member-based sources. The UAW, in contrast, received only 55 percent of its operating income, on average, from its rank and file during the 1979–1993 period. However, in 1993, it received 70 percent from member-based resources.

As a whole, the public sector unions seemed slightly more dependent on member-based income. Their member-based income, on average, constituted 82 percent of operating revenues, compared to about 75 percent among the private sector unions.[4] Over the fifteen-year period, all of the public sector unions received almost three-quarters or more of their operating income from member-based sources, and eight of the eleven averaged more than 80 percent dependence on such income. The 1993 data further illustrate the point, as three unions (SEIU, NFFE, and NTEU) received 90 percent or more of their income from the membership.

In terms of expenditures on salaries and administration, the unions also varied widely. Salary expenses ranged from 21 to 53 percent, on average, of operating disbursements among the private sector unions. Only one (ACTWU) union spent more than 50 percent of its budget on salaries, but three others (USW, UPIU, and IUE) spent more than 40 percent. On average, the IBT and UAW spent the least amount (i.e., 21 percent). Thus, it would appear that unions differ widely regardless of their industrial sector (e.g., manufacturing) or size. In other words, size does not

Table 5.4
Disaggregate Union Member-Based Income and Selected Expenditures as Percent of Operating Income and Disbursements

Union	Member-Based Income as Percentage of Operating Income			Expenditures as Percentage of Operating Disbursements Salaries			Administration		
Private Sector	1993	1979	Average	1993	1979	Average	1993	1979	Average
IBT	.85	.86	.83	.25	.14	.21	.31	.20	.29
UFCW	.88	.62	.81	.27	.31	.25	.17	.10	.09
UAW	.70	.72	.55	.32	.24	.21	.49	.18	.27
IBEW	.80	.68	.74	.42	.19	.34	.20	.08	.16
IAM	.84	.87	.83	.29	.26	.27	.19	.11	.16
CWA	.91	.89	.88	.33	.40	.37	.33	.26	.28
CJA	.63	.86	.69	.30	.30	.27	.14	.07	.12
USW	.82	.88	.81	.42	.41	.40	.27	.14	.22
LIU	.71	.80	.71	.37	.36	.33	.17	.15	.16
IUOE	.70	.78	.74	.43	.36	.35	.14	.15	.14
HERE	.87	.88	.91	.40	.40	.35	.20	.19	.21
PPI	.90	.86	.81	.24	.26	.25	.25	.21	.23
UPIU	.93	.94	.89	.57	.47	.45	.22	.18	.18
ACTWU	.71	.68	.70	.42	.57	.53	.13	.16	.16
IUE	.79	.86	.77	.39	.46	.42	.20	.15	.19
ILGWU	.15	.36	.26	.35	.44	.39	.37	.29	.31
RWDSU	.69	.80	.75	.27	.34	.31	.15	.21	.22
Public Sector									
NEA	.88	.76	.81	.24	.24	.25	.13	.06	.09
AFSCME	.82	.92	.88	.35	.32	.34	.25	.32	.32
SEIU	.90	.90	.88	.29	.20	.23	.23	.25	.25
AFT	.77	.81	.79	.26	.29	.26	.26	.13	.19
APWU	.83	.94	.89	.35	.39	.41	.29	.02	.18
NALC	.86	.84	.86	.33	.42	.42	.49	.30	.46
IAFF	.78	.89	.83	.40	.35	.40	.28	.28	.27
AFGE	.85	.79	.73	.40	.54	.43	.24	.22	.22
NRLCA	.72	.83	.73	.23	.35	.28	.42	.46	.41
NTEU	.98	.62	.84	.56	.50	.53	.36	.24	.29
NFFE	.96	.93	.81	.57	.64	.59	.32	.16	.21

Source: Unions' LM-2 financial disclosure forms.
Note: Percentages should be multiplied by 100 for conventional interpretation.

necessarily lead to proportionately greater expenditures on salaries; if this were the case, one would expect the IBT to have led the private sector pack. Relatedly, the sector differences appear to be rather minor. Specifically, the private sector unions allocated an average of 33 percent of their spending on salaries, compared to 37 percent among unions in the public sector.

With regard to administrative-related disbursements, on average, all of the private sector unions spent less than a third of their expenditures on such items. Nine unions allocated less than 20 percent to administration over the fifteen years. The leading spenders in this category were the ILGWU, IBT, CWA, and UAW, each of which reported spending close to 30 percent of their budget on administration.

Among the public sector unions, three organizations spent close to a third or more of their budget on administration (AFSCME, NALC, and NRLCA). The NALC actually devoted the most, proportionately, to this area, having spent 46 percent of its budget from 1979–1993 for this purpose. On average, the gap between private and public sector unions was greater in spending on administration than on salaries. Public sector unions averaged 27 percent in administrative-related expenses compared to the slightly less than 20 percent the private sector unions allocated.

With regard to spending on both salaries and administrative items, the private sector unions, on average, allocated 54 percent of their budget to these two areas. The public sector unions allocated, again on average, 64 percent of their operating disbursements to salaries and administration over the course of the fifteen years. Thus, these two items comprise the bulk of the twenty-eight unions' spending.

What do these data inform us about the unions' capacity to provide goods and services to their members? This issue is addressed more directly in Table 5.5, which reports the per-member expenditures unions have devoted to salaries and administration.

The data indicate that most of the private and public sector unions have noticeably increased their per-member spending on salaries and administration, comparing 1993 to 1979. With regard to salary expenditures, fifteen of the private sector unions ended the period spending more per member than they had at the beginning, as did eight of the public sector organizations. Five of the private sector unions (IBT, CJA, HERE, ILGWU, and RDWSU) actually spent 50 percent more, as did three public sector unions (SEIU, IAFF, and NTEU).

UNION DUES INCREASES

One way for unions to offset the revenue impacts of a declining membership is by raising dues rates. While dues hikes might often be quite necessary in order to maintain important union services, they are just as likely to provoke controversy among the rank and file. As noted earlier,

Table 5.5
Real Per-Member Union Expenditures on Salaries and Administration

Union	Salaries			Administration		
Private Sector	1993	Percentage Change 1979-1993	Average	1993	Percentage Change 1979-1993	Average
IBT	$13.81	.87	$10.41	$17.49	.65	$14.46
UFCW	21.20	-.08	21.73	13.41	.82	8.03
UAW	60.94	.42	58.19	92.20	1.90	75.52
IBEW	27.02	.01	27.16	13.02	.20	12.28
IAM	35.50	.07	34.81	23.52	.76	22.05
CWA	41.58	.18	41.95	41.28	.85	31.66
CJA	32.51	.76	23.40	15.32	2.40	10.76
USW	93.60	.21	83.30	59.61	1.27	46.26
LIU	23.98	.23	19.64	11.15	.34	9.26
IUOE	29.01	.15	24.17	9.38	-.11	9.42
HERE	26.33	.56	19.78	13.11	.67	11.90
PPI	31.80	.10	28.85	33.17	.38	26.35
UPIU	48.79	.24	42.39	18.54	.22	17.01
ACTWU	57.31	-.20	61.38	18.00	-.09	18.75
IUE	43.23	.28	39.40	22.11	1.01	17.68
ILGWU	117.85	.63	90.84	126.34	1.68	76.36
RWDSU	29.93	.80	17.57	16.47	.59	12.20
Public Sector						
NEA	14.38	.02	14.25	8.02	1.37	5.24
AFSCME	16.54	.00	15.99	12.09	-.27	15.45
SEIU	13.57	.95	9.31	10.63	.24	10.04
AFT	19.97	-.05	18.31	19.75	1.11	13.84
APWU	34.87	.40	41.01	29.13	25.83	19.23
NALC	28.12	-.22	35.32	41.59	.57	39.79
IAFF	25.60	.71	20.94	18.02	.51	14.27
AFGE	41.09	-.01	41.56	25.03	.49	21.39
NRLCA	11.85	.26	11.67	21.38	.71	18.08
NTEU	59.77	.71	54.05	38.02	1.24	29.74
NFFE	47.20	.24	41.03	26.41	1.76	14.75

Source: Unions' LM-2 financial disclosure forms.
Note: Percentages should be multiplied by 100 for conventional interpretation.

the LMRDA guarantees direct or indirect membership approval of dues rates and other fees assessed on membership by requiring that such decisions be approved by a majority vote of delegates attending a regular union convention, a majority vote of union members in a secret-ballot referendum, or a majority vote of the union's executive board. Raises approved by an executive board, however, are effective only until the next regularly scheduled union convention. Union leaders have often incurred considerable wrath in recommending dues increases, inviting criticism of their tutelage as well as union priorities. As Bok and Dunlop (1970: 81) observe: "The process of increasing dues and per capita payments also serves to give the [convention] delegates and members an opportunity to review the overall performance of the union and to express dissatisfactions. An increase in dues often provides an attractive issue to coalesce opposition against incumbent officials, as David McDonald, the president of the Steelworkers, discovered with the formation of the Dues Protest Committee in 1957. This protest culminated in a bitter election challenge that almost unseated McDonald; it also helped to lay the groundwork for the subsequent defeat that McDonald suffered in 1965."

Economic factors per se also may severely constrain the possibility of dues increases. In a period of waning power at the bargaining table and relative wage stagnation, union members may face a financial pinch which would make raising dues quite burdensome and, hence, objectionable.

In any event, unions face continual pressure to raise dues rates, not only to offset revenue losses (from membership shrinkage) but also to keep pace with inflation. Therefore, it is worthwhile to examine what actions the unions took between 1979–1993 with regard to dues rates. Unfortunately, while the LM-2 provides a standard format for reporting dues, unions vary in how they disclose relevant information. Some report single rates, while others may report minimum or maximum rates. Further, a few unions only report such information on appended schedules which were not available for this study, and some have changed how they reported dues rates over the time period. Nonetheless, with these caveats in mind, it is possible to construct a body of evidence showing general trends in dues (see Table 5.6).[5]

The data provide clear evidence that most of the unions raised their dues during this period. The IBT, for example, raised its single rate from $3.15 to $3.90 per month, but this represents a sizable drop in real dues rates (from $4.34 in 1979 to $2.70 in 1993). Even the ACTWU, which raised its single rate from $4.50 to $9.25 per month, noticed only a minimal gain in real dues rates, from $6.20 to $6.40.

Several unions, however, had real increases. NALC's real rate rose from $58 to $82 per year; AFT's from $47 to $67 per year; NTEU's (maximum rate) from almost $99 per year to $129; NRLCA's maximum rate jumped

Table 5.6
Union Dues Rates (1979 and 1993)

Union	Single Rate		Minimum Rate		Maximum Rate	
Private Sector	1979 -	1993	1979 -	1993	1979 -	1993
IBT	$3.15/M	$3.90/M	$--	$--	$--	$--
UFCW	3.90/M	7.04/M	--	--	--	--
UAW	--	--	--	--	--	--
IBEW	--	--	3/M	--	14.30/M	--
IAM	14.10/M	29.55/M	--	--	--	--
CWA	5/M	--	--	--	--	--
CJA	--	--	2.85/M	4/M	4.70/M	7.45/M
USW	--	--	5.00/M	--	2 hrs pay/M	--
LIU	2.75/M	6.50/M	--	--	--	--
IUOE	1.90/M	--	--	13/M	--	--
HERE	--	22.06/M	--	--	--	--
PPI	--	--	4/M	9/M	5/M	10/M
UPIU	5/M	10.17/M	--	--	--	--
ACTWU	4.50/M	9.25/M	--	--	--	--
IUE	5.38/M	10.55/M	--	--	--	--
ILGWU	--	--	--	--	--	--
RWDSU	2.35/M	--	--	4.25/M	--	16/M
Public Sector						
NEA	--	--	--	--	--	--
AFSCME	--	--	--	--	--	--
SEIU	1.80/M	5.10/M	--	--	--	--
AFT	34.30/yr.	97.30/yr.	--	--	--	--
APWU	3.56/M	9.64/M	--	--	--	--
NALC	42/yr	118.82/yr.	--	--	--	--
IAFF	--	--	1.04/M	--	2.07/M	--
AFGE	--	--	--	.50/M	5.65/M	11.05/M
NRLCA	--	--	6/yr.	14/yr.	27/yr.	78/yr.
NTEU	--	--	10/yr.	28/yr.	71.50/yr.	186.16/yr.

Source: Unions' annual LM-2 financial disclosure reports. Data include only the information reported on page one of the LM-2 form for the unions' 1979 and 1993 fiscal years.
Note: M refers to month; yr. refers to year; data are not adjusted for inflation.

from $37 to $54 year; SEIU's single rate climbed to $3.50 per month from $2.50; and APWU's single rate was $6.67 per month in 1993 compared to $4.91 in 1979 (again, in real dollars).

CONCLUSIONS

The data regarding union income reveal a vastly different picture from assets and wealth, but testify to prudent fiscal management with an emphasis on improving membership services. First, while the twenty-eight unions' total receipts were nearly as high in 1993 as in 1979, they significantly overstate the revenues unions have for general-purpose or nominally unrestricted use. Deleting transmittals and major sales income, the unions' revenues declined at a rate in excess of membership losses. This decline forced unions to cut their operating disbursements in order to avoid budget deficits. As a whole, the unions maintained an operating surplus in each of the years observed, but their per-member disbursements decreased.

Second, sizable interunion differences exist both within and between sectors. The public sector national unions averaged much less income than their private sector counterparts. In this vein, they also appeared somewhat more dependent on member-based income. At the same time, public sector union income grew between 1979 and 1993, while the private sector unions' operating revenues shrank. This, no doubt, is attributable in substantial part to public sector membership growth (and dues increases). Within the private sector, however, enormous variation exists in operating income in absolute and per-member terms. Several unions, in fact, suffered major income losses. While some, like the UAW, could shelter their wealth from membership setbacks, they were not so able with regard to income.

Third, member-based income constitutes a relatively small part of total receipts but constitutes the bulk of operating income. Thus, a direct link exists between membership (plus dues rates, obviously) and a union's capacity to serve the rank and file. In fact, member-based income, excluding transmittals, was nearly a fourth lower in 1993 than in 1979. Yet, the unions increased the proportion of their budgets allocated to administrative-related items. More specifically, all but two of the private sector unions spent relatively more on administration on a per-member basis in 1993 than in 1979, as did ten of the public sector unions. To the extent that these spending adjustments reflect intensified efforts to expand services, most unions would have appeared to have increased their capacity to service their members by upgrading their institutional infrastructure without expanding their salary budgets. This increase suggests that unions in general attempted to upgrade the level of services they can provide by increasing education and acquiring more outside professional expertise. Overall, salaries and administration have accounted for the bulk of regular union operating expenditures.

NOTES

1. Title V of the LMRDA establishes "Safeguards for Labor Organizations," establishing strong fiduciary responsibilities. Section 501(a) holds that "officers, agents, shop stewards, and other representatives of a labor organization occupy positions of trust in relation to such organization and its members . . . It is, therefore, the duty of each such person . . . to hold its money and property solely for the benefit of the organization and its members . . . and to account to the organization for any profit received by him in whatever capacity in connection with transactions conducted by him under his direction on behalf of the organization." Thus, the LMRDA, plus attendant fiduciary regulations, essentially "equated union leaders with civil servants who manage the union for the benefit of its members" (Soffer 1964: 100).

2. According to guidelines defining the LM-2 form terms, direct taxes include "all taxes assessed against and paid by . . . [the labor] organization, including . . . FICA taxes as an employer" (U.S. DOL, Office of Labor–Management Standards 1994: 14). It does not include indirect sales and excise taxes for purchases reported as disbursements in other categories.

3. In 1993, the IBEW reported a total income (in current dollars) of $358 million, $241 million of which was derived from the sale of investments and fixed assets and $35 million from transmittals to affiliates. Their dues income was roughly $65.2 million. In 1979, in then current dollars, $60.1 million was from dues out of a total of $130.6 million, $38.8 million of which was from sales and $4.8 million from transmittals to affiliates. Thus, the IBEW's real dues income was $45 million in 1993, compared to $82.5 million in 1979. For the IBT, dues income was $44.7 million (in real terms) in 1993, compared to $102.9 million in 1979.

4. These percentages represent the average of the unions' averages between 1979 and 1993.

5. Although some unions did not report dues data on the first page of their LM-2 forms for the two years observed in Table 5.6 (1979 and 1993), they may nonetheless have raised dues. Certain unions, in fact, reported dues increases during selected years between 1979 and 1993. For instance, the RWDSU reported a single rate of $2.35 per month in 1979 and $3.50 in 1987.

Chapter 6

The Financial Performance of Unions

The data on assets, wealth, and income provide useful information on the overall amounts of financial capital unions have at their disposal. Thus, a union such as the UAW emerges as comparatively munificent, while the ACTWU would seem to have been struggling for some time. However, these data do not address the issue of how well unions have managed their money, given whatever amounts they may have had available to spend or invest. A union, for example, with seemingly small amounts of total assets and wealth may actually have performed better, from a financial standpoint, than a nominally wealthier one, simply because its liabilities are also relatively much smaller. Further, a union's annual surpluses, while again apparently meager on the surface, may be relatively large when compared to regular operating expenses.

More specifically, the data previously presented do not speak directly to three important questions regarding the status of union finances: (1) How large are union surpluses or deficits relative to operating expenditures?; (2) to what extent do unions' current (i.e., liquid) assets exceed their current liabilities?; and (3) how great are their current net assets in comparison to their operating expenditures? To address these questions, this chapter presents data on the twenty-eight unions' aggregate and disaggregate solvency, liquidity, and reserve ratios.

As mentioned previously, solvency is the ratio between operating income and operating expenditures. It indicates the relative extent to which income exceeds expenditures. Liquidity is the ratio between current assets (cash, Treasury securities, and accounts receivable) and current liabilities (accounts payable plus other liabilities). Again, it provides a relative measure—assets above or below liabilities—that can be compared across unions, whereas absolute measures of net liabilities or assets may be somewhat misleading because of the sheer volume of financial transactions involved. Finally, the reserve ratio is the relationship between working capital, as measured by current net assets, and operating expenditures. It indicates the extent to which a union may fund its operations at a prior year's level of services from comparatively liquid financial reserves.[1] This calculation is particularly relevant to assessing the extent to which unions may withstand a strike that would disrupt the flow of regular income from a striking rank-and-file group.

AGGREGATE UNION FINANCIAL PERFORMANCE

The twenty-eight unions' solvency, liquidity, and reserve ratios are reported in Table 6.1, which also breaks down the data between private and public sector unions. The solvency ratios reiterate the aggregate annual surpluses the unions ran during the 1979–1993 period. As a whole, the unions' surpluses ranged from approximately 2 percent (1986) to almost 22 percent (1981) of their operating expenditures. A marked drop occurred in surpluses, however, between 1985 and 1986, and since then the unions have not performed nearly as well as they did during the preceding seven years (1979–1985), when their surpluses averaged close to 16 percent of operating disbursements. Between 1986 and 1993, the surplus averaged slightly less than 6 percent of the operating expenditures. Over the entire fifteen years, the solvency ratio averaged 1.104, meaning that the surpluses exceeded expenses by 10 percent. As will be discussed later in this chapter, however, significant intersector differences exist on this level, which somewhat reflect a reversal of financial performance in both the private and public sectors.

The unions also remained substantially liquid throughout the entire period. Aggregate liquidity ratios indicate that their combined current assets were anywhere from four to thirteen times as large as current liabilities in any given year. A noticeable shift, however, occurred in the mid-1980s, as the ratio fell more or less continually since 1985, with the exception of 1989, when it rose approximately one point to 9.38 from 8.48 in 1988. The downturn is attributable to a rise in current liabilities rather than a decline in current assets. Between 1986 and 1993, these liabilities nearly tripled, climbing from $98 million (in real dollars) to $290 million. They jumped by more than $120 million between 1992 and 1993 alone, precipitating the sharpest year-to-year decline in the liquidity ratio observed over the fifteen years reported. In contrast, current assets, as a whole, rose from roughly $1.18 billion in 1986 to $1.21 billion in 1993,

Table 6.1
Aggregate Union Financial Performance

	Ratios								
	Solvency			Liquidity			Reserve		
Year	Total	Private	Public	Total	Private	Public	Total	Private	Public
1979	1.160	1.194	1.011	12.38	17.41	2.31	.554	0.653	.116
1980	1.084	1.094	1.038	10.77	15.56	2.13	.509	0.587	.124
1981	1.219	1.252	1.073	12.36	18.78	2.15	.646	0.760	.137
1982	1.209	1.241	1.067	12.99	20.03	2.32	.719	0.845	.169
1983	1.134	1.150	1.069	10.50	16.31	1.91	.702	0.837	.141
1984	1.156	1.168	1.105	11.26	18.33	1.90	.697	0.828	.139
1985	1.144	1.162	1.079	12.80	21.45	1.91	.847	1.036	.138
1986	1.018	1.011	1.045	12.04	19.49	2.05	.713	0.864	.140
1987	1.027	1.021	1.046	10.92	17.50	2.14	.735	0.898	.163
1988	1.064	1.082	1.013	8.48	12.33	1.82	.761	0.977	.122
1989	1.033	1.023	1.066	9.38	14.59	1.95	.732	0.905	.149
1990	1.073	1.078	1.061	8.83	14.44	1.68	.793	1.040	.114
1991	1.106	1.091	1.143	7.71	12.64	1.66	.851	1.124	.136
1992	1.048	1.036	1.075	7.18	10.55	1.86	.779	1.042	.143
1993	1.087	1.088	1.083	4.18	4.85	1.85	.823	1.091	.171
Average 1979-1993	1.104	1.113	1.065	10.12	15.62	1.98	.722	.899	.140

Source: Unions' LM-2 financial disclosure forms.

but the climb was uneven. Parenthetically, the bulk of the increase in union liabilities occurred in the catchall other liabilities item reported on the LM-2 form. These separately lumped debts rose from $64 million in 1986 to $250 million in 1993, when they accounted for about 85 percent of the unions' combined current liabilities.

Collectively, the unions not only maintained solvency and liquidity but also improved their reserve ratios. Throughout the fifteen-year period, their reserves or working capital never fell below 50 percent of their operating disbursements (during the year immediately preceding the calculation of the reserve ratio). In fact, since 1981, union reserves have amounted to roughly two-thirds to four-fifths of prior-year operating expenditures. Between 1985 and 1993, the ratio exceeded 80 percent in three different years and continually remained above 70 percent. The average over the 1979–1993 interval was 72 percent. In effect, the unions, on an aggregated basis, have had the capacity to provide nearly three-quarters of prior-year services by drawing upon their working capital.

As mentioned, sizable intersector variation emerges from these data, which is unsurprising given the previously reported data on income, wealth, and the liquidity of asset holdings. A noteworthy common theme, however, emerges between sectors. Specifically, both sectors remained (as shown to some extent in the data in Chapter 5) solvent and liquid, thus holding positive reserve ratios. Beyond this point, the story diverges. The private sector unions averaged approximately 5 percentage points more in surpluses relative to disbursements than their public sector counterparts. Yet, the situation changed in the early to mid-1980s. Between 1979 and 1985, the private sector unions' surpluses—in terms relative to operating expenditures—dwarfed those held among public-employee organizations. As the extreme case in point, the former's surpluses amounted to 19.5 percent of expenditures in 1979, compared to only 1 percent retained by the public sector unions. In contrast, the public sector unions' solvency ratios have exceeded the private sector unions' ratios in five years since 1986. This change no doubt reflects the continual rise in their aggregate income during a period in which the private sector unions experienced a significant decline in operating revenues.

The situation with regard to the liquidity and reserve ratios is even more divergent. On average, the private sector unions' liquidity ratio was nearly eight times (15.62 to 1.98) that maintained by the public sector unions. While the gap most definitely narrowed, particularly in the early 1990s, it still remained sizable. In 1993, for instance, the private sector unions had a liquidity ratio more than two-and-a-half times as large as that which existed among public sector unions. Further, the sheer narrowing of the disparity in liquidity ratios reflects another intersector difference, namely, the relative instability of this measure in the private sector. In this regard, it is important to caution that this volatility may be somewhat related to the significantly greater volume of financial transactions occurring at the national union level among the private sector organizations. As a consequence, these unions' umbrella other liabilities may increase rather steeply in a given year but not be offset by assets reported in the cash, securities, or accounts receivable categories. If these liabilities are not truly current in the basic sense of the term, then the unions' liquidity position will not have diminished over the past several years.

The private sector unions also maintained much larger amounts of reserves in relation to operating requirements, and their superior position in this regard did not diminish. The private sector unions' reserve ratios show that they have had sufficient working capital to fund all prior-year's expenses since 1990, and then some. Indeed, given the low rates of inflation in this decade, these unions probably have been in a position to fund a current services budget (prior-year obligations plus inflation).[2] On average, their reserves amounted to almost 90 percent of the prior-year operating expenditures. In contrast, the public sector unions' reserve ratios reflect a comparatively small capacity to fund such expenses without depleting working capital. The unions' reserves ranged from 11 to 17 percent of operating expenditures. In essence, they have had the capacity, at best, to carry on operations for only two months at previous-year levels, without depleting other nominally less current assets or spending present income. In other words, their financial cushion is simply less luxurious—at least at this level of union organization—than the one maintained among private sector unions.

DISAGGREGATE UNION FINANCIAL PERFORMANCE

All but one union (ACTWU) maintained solvency, averaged over the fifteen years (see Table 6.2). Seven unions, (UAW, IBEW, IAM, CJA, LIU, ILGWU, and RWDSU) had surpluses that averaged at least 15 percent or more of operating expenditures. The public sector unions tended to be bunched relatively close together, with eight averaging surpluses in the 4 to 9 percent range of disbursements. Two federal-service unions, the AFGE and NFFE, emerged as the poorest performers, while the NALC appeared to be the outlier at the opposite extreme.

While, on average, the unions, with the one noted exception, remained solvent during this period, a majority also had more than one deficit year. Seven unions (IBT, UFCW, USW, PPI, ACTWU, NRLCA, and NFFE) recorded operating deficits in one-third or more of the fifteen-year interval. Another twelve unions had deficits in two to four of the years, leaving nine that experienced deficits in only one year at most (UAW, IBEW, LIU, ILGWU, NEA, AFSCME, SEIU, APWU, and NALC).

In terms of liquidity ratios, the data reveal that seven unions (IBT, UFCW, PPI, UPIU, NALC, NRLCA, and NTEU) had current liabilities in excess of current assets in 1993. On average, however, only two unions (NALC and NFFE) had negative current net assets. The NFFE, in particular, while liquid in 1993, had current assets that averaged only slightly above 40 percent of current liabilities. It also experienced negative current net assets in fourteen of the fifteen observed years. Clearly, it is an illiquid case. Indeed, only three other unions had more than two years in which current assets fell short of liabilities (NALC, AFGE, and NRLCA). Six of the ten unions that had such deficit years are in the public sector. While no private sector union had current assets fall short of liabilities for more than two years between 1979 and 1993, their liquidity ratios differed extensively. Among the seventeen unions in that sector, the average ratio extended from roughly 2.00 (ACTWU) to an amazing 308 (an enormous figure reflecting the UAW's huge, by "labor standards," debt-free assets).[3]

Table 6.2
Disaggregate Union Financial Performance

	Ratio								
	Solvency 1979-1993			Liquidity 1979-1993			Reserve 1979-1993		
Union	1993	Avg.	# <1.00[1]	1993	Avg.	# <1.00[1]	1993	Avg.	# <.00[1]
Private Sector									
IBT	.721	1.032	5	.66	8.52	1	-.150	.340	1
UFCW	1.078	1.034	6	.22	2.82	1	-1.104	.094	1
UAW[2]	1.243	1.185	1	390.45	308.80	0	4.856	2.212	0
IBEW	1.228	1.232	0	3.50	44.23	0	.484	.583	0
IAM	1.211	1.183	2	29.96	13.02	0	.285	.503	0
CWA	1.152	1.084	3	3.18	2.57	0	.470	.233	0
USW	1.044	1.039	5	2.52	7.71	0	.476	.572	0
CJA	1.00	1.181	4	5.14	35.63	0	1.264	1.330	0
LIU	1.219	1.291	0	2.86	7.98	0	.280	.270	0
IUOE	1.325	1.125	4	52.37	25.42	0	2.763	1.228	0
HERE	1.178	1.038	4	94.62	67.35	0	.393	.424	0
PPI	.987	1.060	8	.20	4.13	2	-.051	.234	2

UPIU	1.158	1.070	4	.95	10.31	1	-.011	.202	1
ACTWU	.824	.973	9	1.87	2.03	0	.095	.093	0
IUE	.951	1.107	3	1.76	15.74	0	.122	.802	0
ILGWU	1.068	1.186	0	6.48	62.82	0	.123	.275	0
RWDSU	.632	1.161	3	229.06	218.88	0	.995	1.138	0
Public Sector									
NEA	1.024	1.057	1	1.20	1.72	0	.041	.099	0
AFSCME	1.165	1.089	1	1.30	1.37	2	.072	.052	2
SEIU	1.004	1.066	1	4.71	634.96	0	.296	.328	0
AFT	1.259	1.065	4	2.68	2.51	0	.485	.231	0
APWU	1.078	1.082	1	9.92	14.03	0	.573	.424	0
NALC	1.139	1.140	1	.91	.98	10	-.027	-.008	10
IAFF	1.086	1.045	2	2.52	1.89	0	.310	.121	0
AFGE	1.043	1.025	3	1.83	1.11	6	.081	.005	6
NRLCA	.832	1.069	8	.75	1.28	4	-.136	.174	4
NTEU	.994	1.051	4	.83	2.28	2	-.047	.194	2
NFFE	1.072	1.011	5	1.01	.43	14	.002	-.105	14

Source: Unions' LM-2 financial disclosure forms.

1. The numbers in these columns refer to the number of years between 1979 and 1993 in which the solvency and liquidity ratios were less than 1.00 and the reserve ratio was negative.
2. The UAW's liquidity ratio was above 1,000 in eight of the years covered. Technically, its liquidity average is 27, 312. Since 1989, its average ratio is 308.80.

More generally, the unions seem to fall into three liquidity categories. Category one includes those unions with current assets at least twenty-five times the amount, on average, of current liabilities. They include, in addition to the UAW as a patent outlier, the CJA, IBEW, IUOE, HERE, ILGWU, RWDSU, and SEIU. The second category includes those with current assets that averaged between five to fifteen times as much as current liabilities: IBT, IAM, USW, LIU, UPIU, IUE, and the APWU. Nine of the remaining thirteen unions with ratios below 5.00 are found in the public sector.

The unions' reserve ratios also varied widely. Two unions, as would be expected given their liquidity holdings, had average negative reserve ratios (NALC and NFFE). The NFFE's ratio indicated that its net liabilities averaged 10 percent of its operating expenditures over the fifteen years. Among all public sector unions, the APWU, AFT, and SEIU had the highest average ratios, though no union in particular averaged more than 1.00 or recorded close to that performance in 1993. In the private sector, the UAW, CJA, IUOE, and RWDSU had reserve ratios that averaged above 1.00, while only the UFCW and ACTWU had current net assets that averaged less than 10 percent of operating disbursements. According to these data, the UAW maintained, on average, sufficient current assets to fund prior-year level services for well over two years. In 1993, it had the reserve capacity to provide such funding for nearly five years.

CONCLUSIONS

Although unions may possess nominally large amounts of assets and wealth, while also generating impressive sums of revenue, their financial performance may be lacking. As a whole, however, the unions have maintained their solvency and liquidity, though performance on both indicators declined in the latter half of the 1979–1993 period. Perhaps more important, the unions' working-capital situation improved, as reflected in the increase in aggregate reserve ratios. Presumably, the twenty-eight unions' overall capacity to withstand disruptions in income, due to a major strike or other exigencies, has actually increased during a period in which, ironically, strike activity has plummeted.

Private and public sector unions, however, diverge in their financial performance. Reflecting their vastly greater liquid holdings and working capital, the private sector unions have a superior capacity to withstand a strike, which may be due to the relative absence of striker rights in the public sector. However, the tremendous loss in income these unions suffered in the 1980s reversed their solvency situation vis-à-vis the public sector cadre. Both sets of unions have spent 90 percent or more of their operating income since the mid-1980s. While the private sector unions may have diminished leeway to save or invest money, the public sector unions' budgets may be stretched in order to serve a growing membership.

Within each sector, the unions also differ substantially. The data indicate that some unions have been in serious financial trouble. In particular, the ACTWU had deficits in most of the time period reported, as its spending, on average, has exceeded its income. It also has had a relatively low reserve ratio, a condition which has also plagued the IBT.

NOTES

1. Because the reserve ratio is calculated from the assets, liabilities, and disbursements that cover a fiscal year that has just closed, it indicates only the situation for that preceding year. To forecast what it might mean for a union for its current fiscal year, it would be necessary to adjust for inflation and other developments which might affect the availability of current assets and the expenditure of funds.

2. A current services budget assumes no systematic changes in levels of services or the composition of services provided, with a shift in composition implying potentially significant cost increases or decreases.

3. In 1993, the UAW had $1,023,839,237 in current assets and only $2,622,197 in current liabilities, yielding a liquidity ratio of 390.

Chapter 7

Union Political Capital and the Legal Enactment Strategy

While contemporary unions have emphasized collective bargaining and related activities, such as contract administration and the litigation of labor–management controversies, as the means of representing employees, they also have relied upon political action to protect their institutional interests and serve their members' needs (Greenstone 1977). Since the New Deal, union political action has arguably grown in importance (Delaney and Masters 1991b), in substantial part because of the greater role that governments at all levels (federal, state, and local) have played in economic and employment-related matters (U.S. Commission on the Future of Worker-Management Relations 1994a; 1994b). As Bok and Dunlop (1970: 384) note, "Political action is a major item of business for unions in the United States."

Labor unions engage in political action to influence the enactment, administration, and interpretation of laws that affect a wide range of employee concerns and promote their own institutional interests. Representing diverse employee-related concerns, which arguably may be inadequately or inefficiently served through collective bargaining, and promoting institutional power are clearly not mutually exclusive objectives. By advancing fair labor standards regarding wages, hours, and overtime pay, plus securing widely applicable occupational safety and health laws, unions level the economic playing field between nonunion and union employers. In so doing, they may well advance their own interest as bargaining representatives. Similarly, by adopting labor laws which promote the right to organize and negotiate collectively, as public sector unions did successfully in most states in the 1960s, 1970s, and 1980s, unions further serve their ability to organize and bargain more effectively than would be the case without these protections (Aaron, Najita, and Stern 1988). In this regard, proposals to reform labor laws to (1) expedite the process of certifying bargaining units, (2) extend the coverage of worker rights to the "contingent" workforce, and (3) disallow the permanent replacement of economic strikers would all serve to benefit organized labor per se.

The linkages between union political action and organizing and bargaining strength are explicitly and increasingly recognized. Many unions have accelerated their efforts to influence lawmakers at various levels of government. The CWA, for example, refers to organizing, community/political action, and representation (via bargaining) as "The CWA Triangle." In a glossy brochure, the union argues the inseparability of the three sides of this figurative triangle:

> The triangle symbolizes the three major programs of the union. None can stand alone. If the triangle is broken on any side, sooner or later it will be broken on every side. Representation, day to day contract administration and collective bargaining, is the base of the triangle. Yet the other two sides—organizing and community and political action—are just as critical to our strength. Unless we build the labor movement through effective organizing inside existing bargaining units, and by organizing unorganized workers, and adding new units, we will continue to be disappointed at the bargaining table. Similarly, unless we have effective community and political action programs, we will not have the kind of popular and legislative support we need to bargain effectively. (CWA undated brochure)

Illustrative of organized labor's intensified grassroots political action, District 6 of the CWA held CWA Political Mobilization Schools in which "attendees gave up their weekends to . . . discuss . . . an economic presentation, a 'Clinton on the Issues' video, local races, how to involve retirees in the [electoral] process, and get-out-the-vote activities" (CWA 1993: 43). In this regard, a premium is placed on one-on-one efforts to educate local union leaders and the rank and file of the union on the essential role of political action to the future of working people and trade unionism. Obviously, then, the increased political mobilization of union rank and file is critical to this effort.

More generally, unions engage in a variety of political activities in order to influence lawmakers. While these activities in the main complement each other, they may be distinguished in terms of whether they are immediately involved in affecting elections or lobbying lawmakers. Union electoral activities involve direct financial assistance to candidates for office and a myriad of in-kind campaign assistance. Such assistance takes the form of voter education, phone banks, get-out-the-vote drives, voter registration initiatives, and holding rallies. In the realm of voter education, unions sponsor media advertisements, hold special workshops, and distribute literature through door-to-door canvassing or direct mail. As a case in point, the AFL-CIO's $35 million political campaign in 1996 was eventually devoted in substantial measure to political advertisements against forty-five Republican congressional incumbents, eighteen of whom were defeated according to a statement made by AFL-CIO head John Sweeney on November 6, 1996.

With regard to lobbying lawmakers, unions rely on various traditional practices, such as giving testimony before legislative hearings, providing lawmakers with technical background information, and hosting legislative conferences. In addition, unions may mobilize grassroots lobbying efforts in which rank and file are encouraged to contact their legislators (by direct mail or telephone) to voice their opinion on a pending public-policy initiative. Throughout this process, unions are ever mindful that their electoral support for officials is something that facilitates access to these key figures and may be at least implicitly reciprocated by legislators and other policy makers who feel somewhat, if not greatly, indebted to labor for its political backing (Herndon 1982).

While organized labor's involvement in politics has grown considerably in recent decades, it nonetheless has continually provoked controversy. In this vein, it is misguided to view union members as a politically homogeneous group. Research has continually revealed ideological schisms within union ranks as to the propriety of labor's political involvement (e.g., Hudson and Rosen 1954; Blume 1970; Sheppard and Masters 1959; Fields, Masters, and Thacker 1987). Put differently, union leaders do not have a politically homogeneous bank of members that can be delivered to the doorsteps of anxiously waiting politicians. Instead, they must continually seek to extol the relevance of political action and supporting public policies which genuinely serve the best interest of union rank and file. A premium rests on political education at the grass roots.

Nonetheless, union members have shown distinctive bloc voting in elections, backing Democratic candidates more often than the voting population as a whole (Axelrod 1982). Further, union PACs have been heavily tilted to Democrats' advantage. Given that PAC contributions have been shown to influence lawmakers, it became increasingly important that unions generate additional grassroots support for related fundraising efforts. Indeed, PAC fundraising grows in importance as union membership dwindles. According to Moore et al. (1995: 218), "Union PAC contributions to [U.S.] senators and the percent of union membership in the state have significant effects on pro-union COPE [i.e., AFL-CIO Committee on Political Education] votes in the Senate. The rising contributions of union PACs, however, have more than offset the effects of declining membership."

Historically, "the concept of a PAC in fact originated with labor . . . . In July 1943, the CIO went on to form CIO-PAC, the first modern political action committee, to collect and disburse the voluntary political contributions of union members" (Sabato 1985: 5). While federal law, as mentioned earlier, explicitly bans the use of regular union income to help finance congressional and presidential campaigns, it allows the formation of PACs to raise money from the rank and file on a strictly voluntary basis (Epstein 1976; 1980; U.S. FEC 1992). In fact, the Federal Election Campaign Act of 1971, as amended, was designed in large measure to facilitate the role of PACs in order to offset the influence of very wealthy individuals in financing electoral campaigns. PACs among unions and various other member-based organizations raise money in relatively small amounts from many participants and allocate these combined resources to generate a more powerful impact than otherwise would occur. According to research by Sabato (1985), the average amount of money donated by union members to their PACs in the 1981–1982 election cycle was $14 (which amounts to more than $21 today in real dollar terms). Parenthetically, one must note that this is the average amount among *donors*, not all union members. Most rank-and-file members probably do not donate any money to their unions' PACs in the first place. Thus, unions may expand their PAC coffers by raising the average typical donation and increasing participation among the ranks.

This chapter examines the political capital that the twenty-eight unions have raised since the 1980 federal election cycle. It focuses on PAC receipts because the FEC collects and reports data on the money that union PACs raise in conjunction with financing congressional and presidential campaigns or otherwise influencing these elections.[1] Unfortunately, comparable data are unavailable at the state and local levels, where many unions are bound to be quite politically active (Gerhart 1974; Gely and Chandler 1995). As noted, the focus is on each union's principal national PAC. If anything, then, the data understate the overall political efforts unions have made through PACs.[2] Further, union in-kind assistance to campaigns is probably of greater monetary value to candidates than direct donations per se. Nonetheless, PAC receipts provide a key piece of information about the grassroots political mobilization of a union, particularly to the extent that PAC contributions may influence the outcome of elections and legislators' subsequent votes.

Three PAC measures are examined as alternative indicators of a union's capacity to raise political capital. The first is real total PAC receipts. Second, PAC receipts per union member are reported. Finally, PAC receipts as a percentage of member-based income are presented. This last measure in particular provides an indication of union political effort vis-à-vis regular financial activities. In this regard, the donations that union members make to their PAC may be viewed as a "voluntary tax" in contrast to mandatory dues and other assessments. As suggested, although PAC receipts may not capture the full gamut of union political action, which includes lobbying and other forms of electoral participation, they nonetheless provide an estimate of relative political activism among unions' members that may be positively correlated with other political indexes (e.g., lobbying staff; see Delaney and Masters 1991a; 1991b; Masters and Delaney 1987b).[3]

More precisely, this specific measure of political activism is calculated as the ratio between (1) total PAC receipts collected by a union's national PAC in a given two-year election cycle; and (2) the average amount of member-based income collected during the same two-year period. By using the average rather than the sum of the union's member-based income during the relevant two years, the ratio allows for the fact that many unions undoubtedly provide considerable in-kind assistance to candidates that are not necessarily captured in PAC funds per se and that PAC fundraising occurs on a more sporadic basis than dues collections.[4] Thus, the ratio, as calculated, is probably more proximate to general union political capital (PAC and otherwise) than it would be if it represented the percentage of the sum of member-based income over the two-year election cycle.

AGGREGATE UNION PAC RECEIPTS

Just as unions face stiff resistance in trying to organize employees and negotiate higher wage and benefit packages, they encounter keen competition in the political arena (Berry 1989). A multitude of interest groups with widely disparate and often intensely opposite positions seeks to influence electoral outcomes and public-policy decisions on a more or less regular basis (Moe 1981; Salisbury 1969). Such competition occurs routinely in the PAC "business" as unions compete with other groups to raise and spend money in ways that will most effectively serve their interests. Thus, it is worthwhile to compare union PAC receipts with general patterns in interest-group fundraising during the eight federal election cycles between 1980 and 1994.

Table 7.1 reports the total amount of PAC receipts (both unadjusted and adjusted for inflation) collected by all interest groups (union and nonunion) filing with the FEC; by all labor unions; by the twenty-eight major unions' PACs; and by corporate and trade association and related types of PACs.[5] The data reveal significant growth in overall PAC activity during these seven election cycles, as real total PAC receipts were 48 percent higher in 1994 than 1980. Union PAC receipts in particular, however, exceeded this growth by a substantial margin. All union PACs generated nearly $62 million in 1994, or 76 percent more than they did in 1980, and this increase occurred notwithstanding a noticeable downturn in PAC

Table 7.1
Trends in Aggregate Union and Corporate PAC Fundraising (in thousands)

				Major Twenty-Eight as a Percentage of PAC Receipts			
Election Cycle	Total PAC Receipts[1]	Total Union PAC Receipts[1]	Major 28 PAC Receipts[1]	Percentage Total Union PAC Receipts	Percentage Total PAC Receipts	Corporate PAC Receipts[1]	Trade/ Membership/ Health PAC Receipts[1]
1980	$140,159 (181,201)	$27,194 (35,157)	$11,549 (14,932)	.42	.08	$33,960 (43,904)	34,612 (44,747)
1982	199,452 (212,862)	37,474 (39,993)	17,286 (18,449)	.46	.09	47,117 (50,285)	43,357 (46,272)
1984	288,690 (283,725)	51,117 (50,238)	25,077 (24,646)	.49	.09	66,331 (65,190)	59,346 (58,325)
1986	353,429 (325,441)	65,311 (60,139)	32,383 (29,818)	.50	.09	81,960 (75,470)	75,431 (69,458)
1988	384,617 (331,709)	78,509 (67,709)	43,350 (37,387)	.55	.11	96,917 (83,585)	89,539 (77,222)
1990	372,358 (292,389)	88,957 (69,852)	48,596 (38,159)	.55	.13	106,311 (83,479)	92,065 (72,293)
1992	385,316 (279,823)	89,863 (65,260)	50,966 (37,013)	.57	.13	112,360 (81,598)	95,730 (69,521)
1994	391,760 (267,778)	90,303 (61,724)	50,313 (34,390)	.56	.13	114,996 (78,603)	96,372 (65,873)
Percentage Change 1980-1994 Real PAC Receipts	.48	.76	1.303			.79	.47

Sources: U.S. FEC (1982; 1983; 1985; 1988; 1989; 1991; 1993; 1995a; 1995b).
Note: Percentages should be multiplied by 100 for conventional interpretation.
1. Numbers in this column are (a) the nominal (unadjusted for inflation) PAC receipts and (b), in parentheses, the inflation-adjusted figures corresponding to the two-year election cycles.

fundraising since the 1990 peak, when $70 million was raised. The major unions' PACs performed even better, ending the period with 130 percent more PAC funds than they generated at the start of this period. This increase would appear to reflect some combination of stepped-up fundraising efforts (of which there is ample anecdotal evidence) and the consolidation of PAC activity among unions.[6] In this regard, the percentage of total union PAC receipts accounted for by the twenty-eight unions' principal national PACs rose from 42 percent in 1980 to 56 percent in

1994. Further, the twenty-eight unions' principal national PACs grew as a percentage of overall PAC fundraising (labor and nonlabor), climbing from 8 percent in 1980 to 13 percent in 1994. Thus, union PAC activity, at least at the federal level, would seem to have become more concentrated during these eight election cycles covering sixteen years.

At the same time, however, corporate PACs and trade associations also accelerated their fundraising, both of which were substantially greater than organized labor's at the beginning of this period. Corporate PACs, as a whole, raised 27 percent more money (in real terms) than all labor PACs combined in 1994, and 128 percent more than the top 28 unions' PACs. Trade/member/health association PACs increased their receipts by 47 percent between 1980 and 1994, and they raised more money than labor as a whole in each cycle. Moreover, labor PACs in total accounted for only 13 percent of all reported interest group receipts in the 1994 cycle.

Several caveats, however, are noteworthy before one dismisses labor unions as being swamped in the political den. First, union PACs have grown faster than PACs in general, despite sizable membership losses. Second, labor unions have tended to contribute their PAC money in a relatively more homogeneous fashion than many business groups. As an illustration, unions gave $40 million of the $42 million they made in PAC contributions to *Democratic* congressional and presidential candidates in 1994, compared to corporations that split their $68 million largesse almost evenly between Republicans and Democrats.[7] In other words, unions have behaved in a much more ideologically consistent manner in terms of how they allocate PAC money. Further, PAC contributions are associated with other forms of political support, such as get-out-the-vote and voter-registration drives that unions conduct on behalf of party candidates (Masters 1962; Masters and Delaney 1987a; 1987b). Finally, as member-based organizations with a long tradition of grassroots political activism, unions are far better positioned than most corporations and many other interest groups to orchestrate such political activities in a potentially pivotal or decisive manner (Delaney, Masters, and Schwochau 1988; 1990; Juravich and Shergold 1988; Masters, Atkin, and Schoenfeld 1990). In fact, the AFL-CIO can legitimately claim to have mobilized volunteers in the numerous congressional districts they targeted in the 1996 elections. Each political organizer the federation planned to deploy in these various districts was expected "to sign up 100 to 150 activists . . . [who] will be asked to work at least 30 hours before the election, writing letters, making phone calls and arranging meetings to push the labor agenda" (Seib 1996: A16). Few businesses or business groups could make a similar claim. However, it is worth mentioning that certain ideologically conservative groups (such as the Christian Coalition or the National Rifle Association [NRA]) have considerable grassroots appeal (Clark and Masters 1996). In reality, a sizable segment of the labor rank and file support the NRA's political agenda, which may effectively undercut the economic policies of unions (Clark and Masters 1996).[8] However, the AFL-CIO estimates that 62 percent of union households voted for Democratic congressional candidates in 1996.

Table 7.2 presents the twenty-eight unions' aggregate PAC receipts (1) per member and (2) as a percentage of member-based income. The data portray a trend similar to the one associated with the unions' total PAC receipts. That is, per-member PAC receipts increased significantly over the eight election cycles, rising steeply between 1980 and 1988 and leveling off in 1990, and thereafter declining. Yet, despite the drop in the 1990s, these unions have nearly tripled the amount of money raised per union member by their principal PACs since 1980, which has enabled them to offset what would otherwise be the negative consequences of a declining membership base. Similarly, PAC receipts have grown as a percentage of member-based income. The percentage tripled between 1980 and 1988, to 3.6 percent of such income, and has remained more or less steady since. These data strongly suggest that unions became much more politically active in the 1980s.

DISAGGREGATE UNION PAC RECEIPTS

Table 7.3 disaggregates the unions' PAC receipts for the 1994 and 1980 cycles, and reports the percentage change in receipts collected between these two cycles and the average receipts over the eight election periods.

Table 7.2
Twenty-Eight Major Unions' Real PAC Receipts (1980–1994)

Election Cycle	Real Total PAC Receipts (in thousands)	PAC Receipts Per Member	PAC Receipts as a Percentage of Member-Based Income
1980	$14,932	$0.99	0.012
1982	18,449	1.27	0.016
1984	24,646	1.73	0.023
1986	29,818	2.14	0.028
1988	37,387	2.78	0.036
1990	38,159	2.86	0.037
1992	37,013	2.75	0.037
1994	34,390	2.61	0.036

Source: U.S. FEC (1982; 1983; 1985; 1988; 1989; 1991; 1993; 1995a; 1995b).
Note: Percentages should be multiplied by 100 for conventional interpretation.

Table 7.3
Major Unions' Real PAC Receipts

Union	PAC Receipts 1994	PAC Receipts 1980	Percentage Change 1980-1994	Average PAC Receipts
Private Sector				
IBT	$6,282	$316	18.89	$4,488
UFCW	1,558	1,023	.52	1,464
UAW	2,963	2,317	.28	2,702
IBEW	1,653	331	3.99	1,301
IAM	2,398	1,339	.79	2,089
CWA	1,490	910	.64	1,494
USW	938	1,266	-.26	1,151
CJA	1,129	752	.50	1,177
LIU	965	501	.93	715
IUOE	557	615	-.09	830
HERE	206	275	-.25	208
PPI	589	216	1.73	470
UPIU	83	122	-.32	82
ACTWU	166	253	-.34	271
IUE	302	83	2.64	244
ILGWU	528	1,623	-.67	949
RWDSU	27	39[1]	-.30[2]	27[3]
Public Sector				
NEA	3,076	813	2.78	2,611
AFSCME	3,892	680	4.72	2,204
SEIU	809	168	3.81	460
AFT	1,586	368	3.31	1,109
APWU	837	129	5.47	716
NALC	1,094	47	22.43	1,363
IAFF	519	23	21.68	202
AFGE	214	335	-.36	328
NRLCA	383	129	1.97	410
NTEU	142	224	-.36	245
NFFE	2	73	-.97	46

Sources: U.S. FEC (1982; 1983; 1985; 1988; 1989; 1991; 1993).
Note: Percentages should be multiplied by 100 for conventional interpretation.
1. Applies to 1984, the first cycle for which RWDSU receipts could be identified from FEC reports.
2. Compares changes between 1984 and 1994.
3. Averages receipts from 1984 to 1994.

The data reveal vast differences in the amount of money that unions have raised, both in any given cycle and over time. In contrast to wealth, PAC fundraising would seem to be relatively dispersed among unions. In 1994, eleven of the twenty-eight unions raised more than $1 million in PAC money. Still, a few unions accounted for the majority of the twenty-eight majors' overall PAC receipts. The top five (IBT, AFSCME, UAW, NEA, and IAM) fundraisers, in fact, amassed 54 percent of the total receipts. While these unions (e.g., the IBT and NEA) have relatively sizable memberships from which to raise money, their PACs have exhibited quite different rates of growth. For example, the IBT's PAC grew exponentially. Starting off with a paltry $300,000 PAC in 1980, its receipts ballooned to peak at well over $8 million (again in real dollar terms). The IBT's average PAC receipts during these seven cycles was almost $1.8 million greater than the second highest average (cf. $4.5 million to the UAW's $2.7 million).

The NALC is another union that has greatly expanded its PAC fundraising. Its PAC receipts rose nearly twenty-two-fold, from less than $50,000 in 1980 to almost $1.1 million in 1994. Overall, most of the unions, as would be expected given the aggregate trends, raised more PAC money in 1994 than they did in 1980, regardless of whether they lost members. However, each of the major federal-service unions (AFGE, NFFE, and NTEU) raised remarkably less, which may seem somewhat curious given that this drop coincided with the highly challenging and threatening politics of the Reagan presidency.[9]

The data in Table 7.4 provide another indication of the considerable variability in union PAC fundraising. The range in PAC receipts extended from less than 10 cents (NFFE) per member to approximately $5.21 (NALC) in 1994. Only two unions raised more than $5.00 per member in that cycle, while eleven raised less than $2. Interestingly, the postal unions as a group raised relatively large amounts on a per member basis: NALC ranked first, NRLCA ranked fourth, and APWU was eighth (sixth excluding its postal kindred). AFGE, NFFE, and NTEU fell dramatically on the per-member scale. They ranked among the top ten per-member PAC fundraisers in 1980 (NTEU actually ranked second) but fell to twenty-second, twenty-eighth, and eighteenth positions, respectively, in 1994.

In terms of PAC receipts as a percentage of member-based income, unions varied from less than one-tenth of a percent (NFFE) to almost 16 percent (NRLCA) in 1994 (see Table 7.5). Only two unions (IBT and NRLCA) had PAC receipts greater than 10 percent of member-based income in that cycle. The NRLCA was the only union, in fact, that had PAC receipts that averaged more than 10 percent of member-based revenues between 1980 and 1994. Only three other unions averaged more than 5 percent (IBT, ILGWU, and NALC). While the postal unions would appear relatively strong in this respect (NALC's PAC receipts relative to member-based income was sixteen times its 1980 level in 1994), the AFGE, NFFE, and NTEU, once again, presented a much different

Table 7.4
Major Unions' Real Per-Member PAC Receipts

Union	Per-Member PAC Receipts 1994	1980	Percentage Change 1980-1994	Average Per-Member PAC Receipts 1980-1994
Private Sector				
IBT	$4.77	$ .16	27.95	$3.16
UFCW	1.56	.96	.63	1.46
UAW	3.84	1.66	1.31	2.88
IBEW	2.33	.40	4.81	1.72
IAM	5.06	2.00	1.52	3.88
CWA	3.16	1.84	.72	2.94
USW	2.23	1.33	.67	2.05
CJA	2.77	1.22	1.27	2.14
LIU	2.36	1.06	1.24	1.73
IUOE	1.82	1.91	-.04	2.51
HERE	.80	.74	.07	.69
PPI	2.68	.94	1.83	2.12
UPIU	.44	.47	-.05	.37
ACTWU	1.16	.89	.30	1.35
IUE	2.11	.33	5.29	1.40
ILGWU	3.97	5.24	-.24	4.57
RWDSU	.34	.36[1]	-.05[2]	.25[3]
Public Sector				
NEA	1.46	.48	2.05	1.41
AFSCME	3.33	.75	3.44	2.03
SEIU	.88	.31	1.83	.60
AFT	2.76	.85	2.25	2.13
APWU	3.36	.53	5.39	3.09
NALC	5.21	.31	15.85	7.07
IAFF	3.44	.15	21.31	1.36
AFGE	1.44	1.44	-.00	1.74
NRLCA	4.76	2.12	1.24	6.19
NTEU	1.91	3.40	-.44	3.88
NFFE	.07	1.50	-.95	1.02

Sources: U.S. FEC (1982; 1983; 1985; 1988; 1989; 1991; 1993; 1995).
Note: Percentages should be multiplied by 100 for conventional interpretation.
1. Number is based on 1984 election cycle.
2. Percentage compares 1984 to 1994.
3. Number is based on cycles between 1984 and 1994.

Table 7.5
Major Unions' PAC Receipts as a Percentage of Member-Based Income (MBI)

Union	1994	1980	Percentage Change 1980-1994	Average PAC Receipts/MBI
Private Sector				
IBT	.142	.003	42.05	.080
UFCW	.021	.017	.26	.020
UAW	.024	.010	1.44	.016
IBEW	.037	.004	8.58	.025
IAM	.041	.015	1.73	.030
CWA	.025	.021	.19	.027
USW	.012	.007	.64	.012
CJA	.042	.014	2.03	.033
LIU	.043	.020	1.14	.032
IUOE	.030	.038	-.21	.045
HERE	.012	.020	-.40	.013
PPI	.023	.008	1.86	.023
UPIU	.005	.006	-.16	.004
ACTWU	.015	.011	.34	.017
IUE	.026	.004	5.37	.017
ILGWU	.072	.079	-.07	.068
RWDSU	.007	.008[1]	-.07[2]	.005[3]
Public Sector				
NEA	.027	.010	1.62	.028
AFSCME	.074	.016	3.71	.044
SEIU	.021	.009	1.26	.016
AFT	.038	.018	1.05	.034
APWU	.038	.008	3.55	.032
NALC	.063	.004	13.86	.082
IAFF	.063	.004	13.83	.028
AFGE	.016	.024	-.34	.025
NRLCA	.156	.100	.55	.190
NTEU	.019	.058	-.68	.045
NFFE	.001	.032	-.97	.020

Sources: U.S. FEC (1982; 1993; 1995a; 1995b); unions' LM-2 reports.
Note: Percentages should be multiplied by 100 for conventional interpretation.
1. This number pertains to the 1984 election cycle.
2. Percentage change compares 1984 to 1994.
3. Average is based on 1984–1994 data.

picture. AFGE's proportionate intake fell by 34 percent; NTEU's dropped by more than 67 percent. NFFE's PAC receipts as a percentage of member-based income declined by 97 percent, reflecting a veritable standstill in PAC fundraising.

PUBLIC-PRIVATE SECTOR COMPARISONS

Comparisons between private and public sector unions on these PAC dimensions reveal divergent trends, consistent with the membership and financial data (see Table 7.6). Public sector union PAC receipts were 320 percent higher in 1994 than in 1980, despite having leveled off since the late 1980s. While the private sector unions' PACs enjoyed about $400,000 more in absolute PAC growth (comparing 1994 to 1980), their rate of growth was comparatively anemic at 83 percent. Given their much greater rate of PAC expansion, the public sector unions also grew faster in terms of per-member PAC receipts, which were nearly three-and-a-half times greater in 1994 than in 1980.

Nonetheless, it is important to note that, despite sizable membership losses, the private sector unions raised almost $10 million more in PAC money in 1994 than in 1980. In fact, if one were to compare 1990 to 1980, the increase was almost $14 million, after adjusting for inflation. With their significant membership losses, the private sectors raised between two and three times as much PAC money per-member in the 1990s as compared to 1980. In addition, they have roughly tripled in the amount of their PAC intake relative to overall member-based income during this period. In some respects, then, the interesting picture is the remarkable resistance (to membership decline) and tenacity these unions have shown in raising PAC money.

Despite the PAC growth in both sectors, even with the leveling off of the late 1980s, the scope of this political activity has remained minor relative to broader union finances. PAC receipts in both sectors amounted to less than 4 percent of the unions' *average* member-based income over the two years in the 1994 election cycle; in 1980, the unions' PACs raised considerably less than 2 percent of such income. While PACs do not capture the full gamut of union political action, they are nonetheless a widely publicized and potentially effective pursuit. At the very least, these data help to put PAC fundraising into a broader context of union activity. Thus, they shed light on the extent to which there might be the potential for expansion in this aspect of political action.

CONCLUSIONS

Union PAC activity has increased significantly in several respects in the 1980s. Absolute growth, in real dollars, is complemented by substantially higher per-member donations and PAC receipts as a percentage of member-

Table 7.6
Private–Public Sector Union PAC Data

Union Sector	Election Cycle	Real PAC Receipts (in thousands)	Per-Member PAC Receipts	PAC Receipts/Income Percentage
	1980			
Private		$11,943	$1.13	.012
Public		2,989	.66	.014
	1982			
Private		12,884	1.30	.014
Public		5,565	1.21	.026
	1984			
Private		15,894	1.65	.019
Public		8,752	1.88	.038
	1986			
Private		19,129	2.10	.024
Public		10,690	2.23	.042
	1988			
Private		25,614	3.03	.034
Public		11,774	2.36	.042
	1990			
Private		25,659	3.21	.035
Public		12,500	2.33	.042
	1992			
Private		24,291	3.11	.036
Public		12,722	2.27	.040
	1994			
Private		21,834	2.93	.034
Public		12,556	2.20	.039

Sources: U.S. FEC (1982; 1983; 1985; 1988; 1989; 1991; 1993; 1995a; 1995b).
Note: Percentages should be multiplied by 100 for conventional interpretation.

based income. Also, growth occurred in both the public and private sectors, and it outpaced the climb in corporate and overall interest group PAC activity.

Still, union PAC fundraising must be viewed as having failed to tap its full potential. In real dollars, the unions raised less than $3 per-member over a two-year period encompassing the 1994 election cycle. Interestingly, a $3-per-member political "tax" would raise slightly more ($39 million-plus) than the $35 million the AFL-CIO budgeted to influence the 1996 elections. It would, therefore, seem that unions might benefit from extended efforts to extol the need to expand PAC participation by increasing the number of union members who actually donate and encouraging donors to give more. A rather modest increase in per-member donations, as will be shown in Chapter 9, would materially raise organized labor's political presence.

NOTES

1. As noted earlier, PAC receipts and contributions raised and made in the context of federal elections constitute only part of the realm of union political action. Unions, under federal election law, may use their treasury money to (1) make partisan political communications to their membership; (2) make nonpartisan political communications to the general public; and (3) aid state and local political organizations (to the extent permitted by state law). Also, unions may engage in an extensive array of lobbying activities which are financed with treasury money.

2. For example, the IBEW had at least seventeen PACs registered with the FEC, in addition to its principal national PAC, the IBEW Committee on Political Education. The largest of these seventeen (IBEW Local 349 Electro-PAC) raised $103,944 in the 1994 cycle, or $71,048 in real dollars.

3. Indeed, given the $5,000 cap on PAC donations that a candidate may receive in federal elections, coupled with the high cost of running for office, PAC money alone may not trigger the the kind of impact unions want. Most congressional candidates, in fact, receive much less than the $5,000 maximum from union PACs. Thus, to maximize the PAC impact, unions, particularly those with an extensive grassroots apparatus, will provide other support in tandem with PAC dollars. As Bok and Dunlop (1970: 416) observe: "According to many politicians, labor has its greatest political impact, not by offering money, but by providing services: campaign workers to canvass, address envelopes, or drive reluctant voters to the polls." To some extent, however, these activities, if they are given directly to a candidate, may count as a contribution against the ceiling. According to the FEC (U.S. FEC 1992: 7), a contribution "is anything of value given to influence a federal election," including "Gifts of money; Gifts of goods and services . . . , and Loans and guarantees or endorsements of loans."

4. In 1989, the author conducted a survey of unions' PAC fundraising efforts during the 1987–1988 election cycle. Eighteen unions, ranging widely in size and industry, responded through their legislative or political directors on a strictly

confidential basis. Ten of these unions indicated that they solicited their membership once a year; six solicited rank and file more than three times a year; one had an "ongoing" solicitation conducted by local unions; and one union indicated that it had no formal solicitation mechanism. Average donations to their PACs ranged from $2 or $3 to $26 dollars. The number of donors ranged from 20 to more than 60,000.

5. Among the major corporations in terms of PAC fundraising are the United Parcel Service ($2,854,404 in PAC receipts in 1993–1994); American Telephone & Telegraph ($2,556,703); and Ameritech ($1,389,291). Altogether, corporations sponsored 1,468 PACs that registered with the FEC in the 1994 cycle. Trade/membership/health organizations sponsored 633 such PACs in that cycle. The top three PAC fundraisers in this category were sponsored by the National Rifle Association ($6,831,712); the Association of Trial Lawyers ($5,409,066); and the American Medical Association ($4,465,815).

6. For example, in a document celebrating its fiftieth anniversary, the USW (1986: 129) highlighted certain political recommendations emanating from a 1984 convention report entitled *Forging a Future:* "The Report urged the strengthening of PAC committees at the national, district, and particularly within the local union. In addition to broadening the PAC channels at all levels, the Committee pointed out the growing value of a central data bank, the use of polling and similar surveys, and direct mail. Cited also was the need for more training, fund raising seminars, and a greater cultivation of retiree participation."

7. Corporate PACs doled out $34 million to Democratic congressional candidates in 1994 and almost $35.5 million to Republicans. Trade/membership/health PACs gave $28.3 million to Democrats and $24.5 million to Republicans. All PACs (corporate, labor, nonconnected, trade/membership/health, cooperative, and corporations without stock) contributed $189.6 million to federal candidates, with $117.7 going to Democrats and $71.6 to Republicans.

8. In a survey of approximately 1,150 union rank and file conducted in fall 1995, Clark and Masters (1996) found that almost 34 percent of the members were supportive or very supportive of the political goals of the NRA. Twenty percent indicated that they would vote for a candidate for office endorsed by the NRA even if the opposing candidate were endorsed by their union. Among those rank and file who supported the NRA, a sizable majority (60 percent) voted for the 1994 Republican gubernatorial candidate who was opposed by labor. Less than 30 percent voted for the union-backed Democratic candidate, who lost by a fairly narrow margin.

9. President Ronald Reagan campaigned on antigovernment themes. His efforts to hold down spending posed threats to federal employees' jobs and pay increases. Ironically, however, PATCO was one of the few unions to endorse Reagan in the 1980 elections.

Chapter 8

Union Profiles

The data on union membership, finances, and political capital reveal vast interunion and intersector differences. Given that all three sets of measures arguably are relevant to assessing organized labor's institutional strength and capacity to effect change, it is useful to develop a composite picture of how well the unions have fared. This chapter depicts the top and bottom union "performers" on each set of measures. More specifically, it identifies the top five and bottom five unions on several of the key membership, financial, and political indicators, and within each set derives a "composite" top and bottom ranking. Finally, the composite classifications within each set of measures are compared.

This is a relatively simplistic but straightforward approach to constructing union profiles. The profiles graphically show the extent to which there are unions that might have fared consistently well or poorly across these multiple indicators. Further, it reveals the extent to which unions might exhibit divergent levels of performance in different categories of institutional strength.

With these caveats in mind, five union profiles, plus a grand composite, are presented. One includes measures on union membership, three pertain to union finances (wealth, operating income, and financial performance), and the last portrays selected PAC measures. Again, the objective here is not to provide precise distinctions among unions but rather to reveal patterns that may exist among the top and bottom performers. The decision to present only the five highest and lowest ranked unions is purely arbitrary. However, the specific measures chosen within each profile are intended to differentiate among unions in terms of their position at the end of the 1979–1993 period (i.e., those which appeared strongest at the of the period); over the fifteen years; and, where appropriate, at the end and over time on a per-member basis.

MEMBERSHIP PROFILE

Figure 8.1 presents profiles on three union membership indicators: 1993 levels, percentage change between 1979 and 1993, and the 1979–1993 average level. The fourth overall category includes those unions that appeared in at least two of the preceding three categories. The figure shows that public sector unions dominated the top five on two membership indicators: 1993 level and growth, as reflected in the percentage change between 1979 and 1993. Overall, AFSCME and the SEIU appeared in two of the three categories, indicating that they have ranked high in terms of both size and growth. The SEIU emerged in the composite category because of its enormous growth during this time period, which catapulted it into the top five in terms of total membership. In contrast, the IBT and UFCW ended up in this composite ranking as a result of their residually high membership levels rather than growth per se. In fact, the IBT, which was the largest among all twenty-eight unions in 1979, saw its membership slide to well below the NEA's by the mid-1980s.

While the public sector unions dominated the top performers, they also comprised a majority in the bottom rankings on absolute and average membership levels. Thus, the NFFE, NTEU, and NRLCA also ended up in the composite bottom five classification, as did the RWDSU and ILGWU, the latter of which, along with four other manufacturing-based unions, suffered the relatively largest membership losses during this fifteen-year period. In fact, four of the five bottom-ranked unions in terms of average membership are in the public sector.

Figure 8.1
Membership Dimension

	1993	Percentage Change 1979 - 1993	Average 1979 - 1993	Overall
Top 5	NEA IBT AFSCME UFCW SEIU	SEIU NALC AFT NRLCA AFSCME	NEA IBT AFSCME UFCW UAW	AFSCME NEA IBT UFCW SEIU
Bottom 5	ILGWU NRLCA RWDSU NTEU NFFE	IUE UAW ACTWU USW ILGWU	IAFF RWDSU NRLCA NTEU NFFE	ILGWU NRLCA RWDSU NTEU NFFE

On the surface, these profiles suggest that the NFFE, NRLCA, and NTEU, plus the IAFF (over the fifteen years), are relatively weak performers on this dimension. However, none appeared in the bottom set on membership change (i.e., loss), and the NRLCA actually was among the top five in this specific indicator. Moreover, it is important to distinguish among these unions on the basis of the occupational and industrial sectors in which they operate. The NRLCA and IAFF organize within narrow occupational jurisdictions—rural letter carriers in the U.S. Postal Service and fire fighters. Within these restrictions, these two unions have achieved comparatively high levels of penetration. The IAFF "has little competition for the right to represent firefighters" (Stern 1988: 82), and the NRLCA has organized the bulk of the U.S. Postal Service's rural letter carriers. Only 7 percent of the approximately 87,000 employees the NRLCA represent do not actually belong to the union as dues-paying members (Masters and Atkin 1993b; 1995).

Conversely, the NFFE and NTEU are multi-occupational unions that organize broadly within the federal service (Masters and Atkin 1989; 1990; 1993b; 1995; 1996c). The NFFE in particular organizes among both blue-collar and white-collar employees. In 1991, it represented 146,000 employees in 370 bargaining units scattered among twenty-three federal agencies (Masters and Atkin 1995). NTEU represented 152,000 employees in forty-eight units located in ten different agencies. Each union, however, had far fewer actual members than their bargaining unit representation levels would suggest. Approximately three-fourths of the employees represented by the NFFE did not actually belong to the unions. The comparable free-riding figure for NTEU in the early 1990s was slightly above 50 percent. Thus, their organizing challenges are literally wide open, even among units for which they have secured formal representational rights. Across the federal government as a whole, while 60 percent of the workforce is nominally represented by unions, most of these represented employees are nonunion. Of the 940,000 federal employees represented by the AFGE, NFFE, and NTEU in 1991, less than 30 percent had actually joined ranks as dues-payers (Masters and Atkin 1995; 1996c). Thus, given the potential base from which they have chosen to represent and should be able (ideally) to organize members, the NFFE and NTEU (plus the AFGE) have performed disappointingly.

FINANCIAL PROFILES

Six dimensions of union wealth are profiled (see Figure 8.2). Two federal service unions (AFGE and NFFE) appeared in four of six of the bottom rankings and hence the overall bottom category. As just noted, these unions have had extraordinarily large free-riding rates, which undoubtedly have hindered their financial capacity (Masters and Atkin 1993b; 1995;

Figure 8.2
Wealth Dimension

	1993 Total	Percentage Change 1979 - 1993	Average 1979 - 1993	Per-Member 1993	Per-Member Percentage Change 1979 - 1993	Average Per-Member 1979 - 1993	Overall
Top 5	UAW ILGWU IBEW USW LIU	NALC AFT APWU NRLCA IAFF	UAW USW IBT ILGWU CJA	ILGWU UAW USW LIU PPI	NALC AFT APWU IBEW IAFF	ILGWU UAW USW PPI CJA	UAW ILGWU USW
Bottom 5	AFGE NRLCA NTEU NFFE UFCW	HERE USW ACTWU IBT UFCW	NTEU IAFF NRLCA AFGE NFFE	AFGE NFFE NEA AFSCME UFCW	SEIU ACTWU AFSCME IBT UFCW	NFFE IAFF NEA AFSCME AFGE	AFGE NFFE UFCW

1996a, 1996c). The UFCW appears in this category because of its negative wealth recorded in 1993, which caused it to rank at the very bottom on three of the measures. More generally, the public sector unions comprise the full bottom sets in average total and per-member wealth between 1979 and 1993. They also comprise four-fifths of the bottom five in terms of total and per-member wealth recorded in 1993. At the same time, public sector unions ranked at the top in terms of wealth gain, in percentage terms, comparing 1993 to 1979. Further, they constituted four-fifths of the top set on per-member percentage change, 1979–1993.

Private sector unions, particularly within the manufacturing and construction sectors, emerged as the top performers, despite the fact that some experienced the largest losses in total wealth (USW, ACTWU, IBT, and UFCW) and per-member wealth (ACTWU, IBT, and UFCW). The UAW, ILGWU, and USW earned rank among the top composite performers, appearing in at least two-thirds of the six top categories. Each had high levels of total wealth and per-member wealth, and maintained those positions, on average, during these fifteen years. In terms of losses, comparing 1979 to 1993 on a percentage basis, the ACTWU, IBT, and UFCW would appear to be the big private sector losers—in terms of total and per-member wealth (the UFCW, again, because of its negative wealth in 1993). In short, the UAW, ILGWU, and USW emerged as the top union performers on this wealth dimension, despite being the bottom performers on the membership change indicator. The ACTWU, however, was not so classified.

Figure 8.3 reports the unions' income profiles. Again, the split between private and public sector unions regarding those which gained or lost most but remained relatively small or large appears vividly. The public sector unions dominate the bottom five in terms of total and per-member income in 1993 and averaged over the fifteen years. Yet, they are the leaders

Figure 8.3
Income Dimension

	1993 Total	Percentage Change 1979 - 1993	Average 1979 - 1993	Per-Member 1993	Per-Member Percentage Change 1979 - 1993	Average Per-Member 1979 - 1993	Overall
Top 5	UAW NEA USW UFCW IAM	NRLCA SEIU AFT IAFF NALC	UAW USW NEA UFCW IAM	ILGWU UAW USW IAM CWA	NFFE ILGWU IAFF HERE APWU	UAW ILGWU USW IAM CWA	UAW USW IAM
Bottom 5	IAFF NTEU RWDSU NRLCA NFFE	UAW USW ACTWU IBEW IBT	IAFF NTEU RWDSU NRLCA NFFE	NEA AFSCME SEIU NRLCA IBT	ACTWU IAM PPI IBT IBEW	IAFF AFSCME IBT NRLCA SEIU	NRLCA IBT

in percentage change in total income. The private sector unions dominate the 1993 totals, average totals, and per-member totals (in 1993 and on average). The story this seems to tell is that private sector unions retained their dominant position because they had relatively high income levels at the beginning.

While the private sector unions dominate the top performers across the six indicators, they also comprise the full set of losers on a percentage basis. The ACTWU, IBEW, and IBT are among the bottom five in percentage change in total and per-member operating income. The NRLCA appears in the overall bottom box because its absolute levels in total and per-member income have been comparatively low.

The financial performance profiles appear in Figure 8.4, which reports the top and bottom ranked unions in terms of solvency, liquidity, and reserve ratios in 1993 and average ratios during the 1979–1993 period. The UAW,

Figure 8.4
Financial Performance Division

	Solvency 1993	Average Solvency 1979 - 1993	Liquidity 1993	Average Liquidity 1979 - 1993	Reserve 1993	Average Reserve 1993 - 1979	Overall
Top 5	IUOE AFT UAW IBEW LIU	LIU IBEW ILGWU UAW IAM	UAW RWDU HERE IUOE IAM	UAW SEIU RWDS HERE ILGWU	UAW IUOE CJA RWDSU APWU	UAW CJA IUOE RWDSU IUE	UAW IUOE RWDSU
Bottom 5	IUE NRLCA ACTWU IBT RWDSU	UFCW IBT AFGE NFFE ACTWU	NTEU NRLCA IBT UFCW PPI	AFSCME NRLCA AFGE NALC NFFE	NTEU PPI NRLCA IBT UFCW	ACTWU AFSCME AFGE NALC NFFE	NRLCA IBT

ratios in 1993 and average ratios during the 1979–1993 period. The UAW, IUOE, and RWDSU emerge on the top of the heap, appearing in four or more of the six specific financial performance categories. IBT and NRLCA, in contrast, appear in the composite bottom set. What emerges as a somewhat related trend is the relatively poor performance of the AFGE and NFFE on the average solvency, liquidity, and reserve dimensions. These unions thus have been weak not only on the membership and wealth dimensions, but also on two key financial performance indicators. In 1993, ACTWU was among the bottom in terms of solvency, average solvency levels, and average reserve ratios, reflecting its more or less consistently disappointing performance (relative to other unions).

POLITICAL CAPITAL

The unions' profiles on six PAC-receipt dimensions are included in Figure 8.5. Several patterns emerge. First, the public sector unions dominated in terms of percentage change in total and per-member PAC receipts. Second, federal-employee unions dominated the bottom performers in percentage change in total PAC receipts. NFFE ranks at the bottom in all six categories, and UPIU and RWDSU fall into five of the bottom sets.

Third, the postal unions appear to be relatively strong PAC performers. APWU and NALC rank among the top in percentage change in total and per-member PAC receipts. The NALC and NRLCA, the latter of which has ranked comparatively low on several other non-PAC dimensions, rank high in terms of per-member receipts in 1994 and average PAC receipts. NALC, in fact, ranked among the top five in four of the six categories and, thus, overall. Curiously, the NTEU, while ranked low in the PAC receipts (1994) and percentage change (total and per member)

Figure 8.5
PAC Receipt Dimension

	PAC Receipts 1994	Percentage Change PAC Receipts 1980 - 1994	Average PAC Receipts 1980 - 1994	Per-Member PAC Receipts 1994	Percentage Change Per-Member PAC Receipts 1980 - 1994	Average Per-Member PAC Receipts 1980 - 1994	Overall
Top 5	IBT AFSCME NEA UAW IAM	NALC IAFF IBT APWU AFSCME	IBT UAW NEA AFSCME IAM	NALC IAM IBT NRLCA ILGWU	IBT IAFF NALC APWU IUE	NALC NRLCA ILGWU NTEU IAM	IBT IAM NALC
Bottom 5	HERE NTEU UPIU RWDSU NFFE	ACTWU AFGE NTEU ILGWU NFFE	HERE IAFF UPIU NFFE RWDSU	SEIU HERE UPIU RWDSU NFFE	RWDSU UPIU ILGWU NTEU NFFE	NFFE HERE SEIU UPIU RWDSU	NFFE UPIU RWDSU HERE

categories, ranked among the top in average per-member receipts during the eight election cycles between 1980 and 1994.

Conversely, the IBT scored massive gains. It led the unions in three areas: PAC receipts in 1994, average total PAC receipts, and percentage change in per-member PAC receipts. It also ranked among the top five in every PAC dimension but average per-member receipts. Thus, a union which lost ground on the membership front, and especially on the financial playing field, gained enormously on this other capital dimension, which requires an extensive grassroots mobilization of the rank and file.

CONCLUSIONS

Figure 8.6 summarizes the composite top and bottom set for each of the five major categories. The figure graphically demonstrates the usefulness of looking at diverse measures of union strength. Despite its loss in membership, for instance, the IBT is still among the largest unions in the United States, ranked only second behind the NEA. While it has suffered financially, its political profile has skyrocketed. Similarly, the ILGWU and UAW, both of which lost many of their members in the 1980s, ranked high on several financial dimensions. The former ranked high on the composite wealth dimension, in particular, and the UAW achieved similar status on each financial dimension. The USW, which also saw its membership halved, remained strong on multiple measures of wealth and income, despite numerous reports of its financial woes. The IAM, which joins the UAW and USW in the year 2000, is strong on both the income and PAC-receipt dimensions.

In contrast, the NFFE and NRLCA are more or less consistently weak on at least three dimensions. NFFE has ranked poorly in terms of membership, wealth, and PAC activity, while the NRLCA is weak in membership,

Figure 8.6
Composite Dimensions

		Financial			
	Membership	Wealth	Income	Performance	PAC Receipt
Top 5	AFSCME NEA IBT UFCW SEIU	UAW ILGWU USW	UAW USW IAM	UAW IUOE RWDSU	IBT IAM NALC
Bottom 5	ILGWU NRLCA RWDSU NTEU NFFE	AFGE NFFE UFCW	NRLCA IBT	NRLCA IBT	NFFE UPIU RWDSU HERE

income, and financial performance. It, however, has a comparatively strong PAC, at least in terms of per-member receipts. Also, as noted earlier, it is a fundamentally craft-type union with a decidedly restricted occupational jurisdiction, thus limiting its potential membership base. The NFFE is perhaps the most consistently weak performer to emerge in this analysis.

In sum, the unions that emerge among the top composite categories in Figure 8.6, of which there are twelve, have maintained a strong position on at least one of the three broad dimensions of union strength: human, financial, and political capital. They thus have had the capacity to mobilize considerable resources to attack the problems which confront them, even if their performance may appear weak on another front. The UFCW, for instance, has a large membership base, and its losses in the 1980s were minimal, despite the tumultuous forces of change in the industries in which it operates (Craypo 1994). As a case in opposite point, the ILGWU, which lost a big portion of its membership, has remained strong on several financial dimensions. Thus, in merging with the financially pressed ACTWU, it brought "plenty of money, buildings, and other resources" (Greenhouse 1995b: A16), each of which is an incentive for amalgamation.

Chapter 9

Baseline Union Budgets: Implications for Representational Services and Bargaining Clout

The strategic framework presented in Chapter 2 suggests that unions pursue at least three broad sets of strategies to represent their members. They provide services as bargaining representatives, negotiate agreements, administer contractual protections, litigate unfair employer practices, and resolve impasses through strikes or alternative dispute resolution procedures, such as arbitration. On the political front, they help to elect politicians and lobby them once in office. Further, to preserve or expand their institutional base, unions organize new members, which also redounds to their advantage in collective bargaining and politics (Rose and Chaison 1996).

Indisputably, each of these pursuits costs money, and the amount a union spends on any particular strategy is one clear measure of its organizational commitment. Ideally, then, it would be desirable to examine union expenditures on bargaining, political, and organizing activities over time to assess current levels of and trends in commitment to these strategic approaches. Unfortunately, the LM-2 forms do not permit such a breakdown of expenditures. In essence, no programmatic or functional breakdown of spending priorities is required or, for all practical purposes, attainable from the data reported on these forms. In contrast, Canadian unions, for example, are required to break down expenditures into certain functional categories, such as organizing expenses (Arrowsmith 1992). While an attempt was made to impose new programmatic spending requirements on unions during the Bush administration and has been advocated elsewhere

(Masters, Atkin and Florkowski 1989; Atkin and Masters 1995), it was rejected under the Clinton administration. Further, while a few attempts have been made to estimate expenditures, using selected proxies, such as the number and compensation of employees allocated to specific functions (e.g., political action and organizing; see Masters 1983; 1984; 1985; Voos 1987), they are bound to be limited in their inclusivity of expenditures. They also require detailed inspections of cumbersome union financial schedules, a task beyond the scope of this endeavor.[1]

Nonetheless, it is possible to adopt certain assumptions in order to construct rough estimates of a union's budgetary allocations. While these estimates will not be accurate with respect to any particular union's allocation of expenditures (each union is bound to differ at least somewhat in terms of how much it spends on a given set of representation functions), they provide baselines from which it is possible to examine relative union expenditures, given certain assumptions, and estimate the spending impacts of a reallocation of organizational priorities, to which the AFL-CIO and various individual unions have committed in order to expand organizing and political activities. For example, the ACTWU has doubled its organizing budget since 1990; the IBT's "reformer president, Ronald Carey, put an extra $25 million into organizing, even though he inherited a nearly bankrupt union" (Bernstein 1995a: 87), and the LIU, which had no organizing budget per se a few years ago, "is spending $5 million [in 1995] . . . to sign up poultry-plant, golf-course, and other workers outside its traditional domain" (Zachary 1995: A1).

Therefore, three assumptions are made in calculating baseline budgets for the unions, on aggregate and disaggregate bases. First, given that it is widely accepted that unions devote the bulk of their efforts to collective bargaining (e.g., Fiorito, Gramm, and Hendricks 1991) and related activities, it is assumed that they allocate, on average, at least 50 percent of their operating disbursements to this strategic function. Second, according to a previously cited report (Bernstein 1995a), which indicates that unions in the main allocate between 2 and 4 percent of the budgets to organizing, it is estimated that most unions allocate 3 percent of their budgets to this effort, although it is known that vast interunion differences currently exist.[2] Third, given that union PAC activity is correlated with other forms of political action (as shown in work by Masters and Delaney 1985; and Delaney, Fiorito, and Masters 1988), it is assumed that unions, on average, will spend that portion of their budget which is equal to the ratio between their PAC receipts and their member-based income, averaged over the election cycle. For instance, if a union's PAC receipts in 1991–1992 equaled 1 percent of its average member-based income for those two years, it is assumed that its overall political budget (for PAC fundraising, political education, lobbying, etc.) in 1993 would equal 1 percent of operating expenditures in that same year.[3] The unions' aggregate political budget assumes that spending each year is equal to the average ratio (over seven election cycles 1980–1992) between PAC receipts and member-based income.[4] Based on these assumptions, total and per-member union expenditures on bargaining, organizing, and political activities are estimated. Aggregate estimates are provided over time (1979–1993), and thus adjusted for inflation. The disaggregate data are reported only for 1993 (in current 1993 dollars) to show the unions' most recent estimated budget allocations. The estimated political budget is equal to the same percentage of disbursements as the ratio between 1991–1992 PAC receipts and the 1991–1992 average in member-based income for each union.

In addition, an attempt is also made to estimate the unions' relative capacities to fund a strike. Such a capacity is arguably an important consideration in assessing a union's ability and willingness to sustain a prolonged strike (Weil 1994). Although many other factors, including striker solidarity, the extent of union penetration of an industry workforce, an employer's product market competition and its ability to pay, and the favorableness of public opinion, will affect a union's effectiveness in striking (as well as its willingness to initiate a strike in the first place), its financial capacity to pay striker benefits and withstand the resulting disruption in dues-based income is bound to exert some impact on its institutional resolve (Weil 1994; Troy 1995; Bennett 1991). As a case in point, the USW, under the leadership of George Becker, has recently undergone significant restructuring to improve its financial situation, in part to better equip itself to withstand strikes. In this regard, it created a "Corporate Campaigns Department designed to deal with corporations perceived by the union to be deliberately avoiding contract settlements" (DaParma 1994: H6). The USW's aggressive international secretary-treasurer, Leo W. Gerard, is quoted as saying that "'98 percent of our contracts are settled without lockouts or strikes . . . But for that small percentage where employers are determined not to reach a settlement, we just want them to know we are as determined as they are'" (DaParma 1994: H6).

A union's capacity to fund a strike is estimated as follows. The cost of a strike is assumed to include two major components: (1) striker benefit payments and (2) dues-related revenue losses. Strike benefits are assumed to equal $175 per week (a hypothetical midpoint range), and the number of strikers is assumed to equal one-third of a union's membership.[5] This is equivalent to the size of some unions' major bargaining units (U.S. DOL, BLS 1995). The UAW, for example, negotiates for units of 240,000 and 95,000 at General Motors and Ford, respectively. Strikers are further assumed to be out for three weeks, slightly longer than the typical striker in 1994 (U.S. DOL, BLS 1995).[6] Income loss is calculated to be the equivalent of one-third of total member-based revenue for a full month. Thus, it includes the loss of one-third of the members' revenues for three weeks, plus one more week, which should cover at least some of the additional charges (public relations, litigation, political action) for which a union might have to divert revenue in the course of any major strike. Unfortunately, as suggested previously, these ancillary costs cannot be directly ascertained from the LM-2 breakdown of union expenditures.

The ratios between union wealth and working capital (current assets minus current liabilities), on the one hand, and the sum of striker benefits payments and income loss, on the other hand, are calculated as relative indicators of a union's capacity to fund a strike. Aggregate estimates of strike fund capacity are provided for the 1979–1993 period, and adjusted for inflation. Disaggregate union capacities are estimated for 1993 in current dollars.

AGGREGATE UNION BUDGET ESTIMATES

The unions' aggregate real budget estimates on bargaining, organizing, and political disbursements, based on the aforementioned assumptions, are reported in Table 9.1, along with their total operating expenditures. Bear in mind that these estimated allocations are not intended to be precise estimates of how much any set of these unions actually devoted to these selected activities, but rather to establish baseline trends from which it is possible to assess the financial implications of unions' placing more emphasis on organizing and political action. The data show, as mentioned in Chapter 5, that aggregate disbursements decreased significantly between 1979 and 1993, reflecting the sharp drop in income, particularly since the mid-1980s. Consequently, the amount of money the unions had to spend per member on the various goods and services they provided dropped to $87, from $92 in 1979 and a peak of $109 in 1986.

Given the decline in total operating expenditures, the unions' spending estimates in the selected representational areas fell commensurately. Bargaining representation disbursements fell from a peak of $756 million, or $54.58 per member, to approximately $577 million in 1993, or just above $43 per union member. What is particularly impressive about the data, however, is the seemingly paltry amounts the unions have devoted to organizing and political activities in view of the stipulated budget allocations. In real dollars, organizing disbursements reached their maximum at just $45 million in 1980, or only $3.27 per member. Since then, estimated disbursements fell to $35 million, or about $2.60 per member (assuming, of course, a constant 3 percent budget allocation), due, obviously, to the drop in union revenue available for this particular, or any other, purpose.

Political spending, under the assumed rate of 2.7 percent, fell to just above $30 million in 1993, or only $2.37 per member. In real terms, the

Table 9.1
Aggregate Real Union Bargaining, Organizing, and Political Budget Estimates

	Operating Disbursements		Bargaining Disbursements		Organizing Disbursements		Political Disbursements	
Year	Total (in millions)[1]	Per-Member	Total (in millions)[1]	Per-Member	Total (in millions)[1]	Per-Member	Total (in millions)[1]	Per-Member
1979	$1,399	$91.80	$699	$45.90	$42	$2.75	$38	$2.50
1980	1,417	95.00	708	47.50	42	2.85	39	2.59
1981	1,276	87.45	638	43.73	38	2.62	35	2.38
1982	1,296	89.53	648	44.77	39	2.69	35	2.44
1983	1,309	91.11	655	45.56	39	2.73	37	2.48
1984	1,312	92.58	656	46.29	39	2.78	36	2.52
1985	1,300	92.84	650	46.42	39	2.78	35	2.53
1986	1,513	109.15	756	54.58	45	3.27	41	2.97
1987	1,413	104.51	706	52.27	42	3.14	38	2.85
1988	1,321	98.62	661	49.31	39	2.96	36	2.69
1989	1,441	108.34	721	54.17	43	3.25	39	2.95
1990	1,314	98.09	657	49.04	39	2.94	36	2.67
1991	1,233	91.30	617	45.65	37	2.74	34	2.49
1992	1,321	99.07	660	49.53	40	2.97	36	2.70
1993	1,154	87.73	577	43.86	35	2.63	31	2.37

Source: Unions' LM-2 financial disclosure forms.
Note: Estimates are based on 50 percent of total disbursements for bargaining; 3 percent of total disbursements for organizing; and 2.7 percent of total disbursements for political spending.
1. Totals are rounded to the nearest million.

unions as a whole spent a seemingly meager $65 million, or only $5.00 per member, on their combined organizing and political functions in 1993, down from $86 million in 1986 and $80 million in 1979. On all counts, then, given the general drop in operating disbursements, the unions' financial commitments to these areas fell between 1979 and 1993. This drop is particularly disturbing to the extent that organizing and political functions may have been relatively minor to begin with, as has been suggested by others (Block 1980; Masters 1983; 1985). Regardless of whether these spending assumptions are accurate, they demonstrate the very real importance of making appropriate allocations across union functional activities and understanding how to gain additional efficiencies with an allotted expenditure level. Furthermore, the need to raise additional income, either by increasing dues or diversifying revenue portfolios, becomes more obvious, if the objective is to maintain given levels of service across representational areas while still embarking upon new programmatic efforts.

DISAGGREGATE UNION BUDGET ESTIMATES, 1993

Table 9.2 presents the individual unions' budget estimates for 1993 (in constant dollars). As would be expected, given their widely disparate operating totals, the unions' functional disbursements also varied significantly under the various allocation assumptions. On a per-member basis, estimated bargaining disbursements among private sector unions ranged from $40 (IBT) to $244 (ILGWU). In the public sector, the range was more restricted yet still substantively meaningful, extending from a low of $33 (SEIU) to a high of more than $76 (NTEU). Only three unions, however, spent more than $100 per member on bargaining (the USW and UAW, plus the top-spending ILGWU). Eight unions, all but one (NTEU) of which is in the private sector, spent somewhere between $75 to $100 per member on this function (ACTWU, PPI, CWA, IAM, RWDSU, IUE, and CJA).

Reflecting their comparatively low spending levels, most of the public sector unions spent less than $75 per member on negotiating-related activities. Five of them, in fact, spent less than $50 on per-member bases (IAFF, NEA, NRLCA, AFSCME, and SEIU). Interestingly, the SEIU, which gained the most among all of the unions in terms of its membership growth rate between 1979 and 1993, spent the least per member on bargaining. Indeed, its very growth may have severely stretched its per capita financial capacity, revealing in a real sense the potential tradeoffs between fulfilling the role of representing current employees versus adding new members via an aggressive organizing strategy, which, as mentioned earlier, the SEIU has pursued in terms of both recruiting new members and amalgamating with other unions.

To the extent that the 3 percent allocation to organizing is generally on target, the data vividly show the degree to which unions may have minimized their commitment of resources to this function. (As will be demonstrated in Chapter 10, this baseline assumption may be adjusted upward in order to calculate the additional money unions would be able to spend organizing new members even within their current budget or revenue constraints). Under the 3-percent assumption, the ILGWU, USW, UAW, ACTWU, PPI, CWA, and IAM led the private sector unions—and the public sector ones as well—in per-member organizing disbursements, devoting more than $5 in 1993 dollars. Still, the maximum expenditure per member is less than $15, and the second highest organizing allocation (the USW's $9.63) is $5 below the ILGWU's spending. The fact that these unions lost many members during the 1980s (their combined ranks shrank by 724,000 between 1979 and 1993) does not necessarily mean that their relatively greater financial capacity to pursue organizing is meaningless. These unions have operated in industries

Table 9.2
Disaggregate Union Bargaining, Organizing, and Political Budget Estimates (1993)

	Actual Operating Disbursements		Bargaining Disbursement Estimates		Organizing Disbursement Estimates		Political Disbursement Estimates	
Union	Total (in millions)	Per-Member	Total (in millions)	Per-Member	Total (in millions)	Per-Member	Total (in millions)	Per-Member
Private Sector								
IBT	$105.86	$80.44	$52.93	$40.22	$3.17	$2.41	$14.60	$11.09
UFCW	110.85	111.18	55.42	55.59	3.32	3.33	2.26	2.27
UAW	210.29	272.75	105.15	136.38	6.31	8.18	4.84	6.28
IBEW	62.21	93.25	33.10	46.63	1.99	2.80	2.40	3.38
IAM	83.67	176.52	41.83	88.26	2.51	5.29	3.45	7.27
CWA	84.44	178.90	42.22	89.45	2.53	5.37	2.63	5.58
USW	135.19	321.11	67.59	160.55	4.06	9.63	2.04	4.85
CJA	62.74	153.78	31.37	76.89	1.88	4.61	2.76	6.75
LIU	38.03	93.20	19.01	46.60	1.14	2.80	2.26	5.54
IUOE	29.50	96.73	14.75	48.37	.88	2.90	1.06	3.49
HERE	24.66	95.58	12.33	47.79	.74	2.87	.36	1.41
PPI	41.31	187.80	20.66	93.90	1.24	5.63	1.75	7.96
UPIU	23.03	122.50	11.51	61.25	.69	3.67	.08	.43
ACTWU	27.98	195.66	13.99	97.83	.84	5.87	.59	4.17
IUE	22.60	158.02	11.30	79.01	.68	4.74	.50	3.50
ILGWU	64.96	488.45	32.48	244.22	1.95	14.65	4.55	34.19
RWDSU	12.82	160.22	6.41	80.11	.38	4.81	.06	.72
Public Sector								
NEA	183.65	87.45	91.82	43.73	5.51	2.62	5.45	2.59
AFSCME	80.62	69.08	40.31	34.54	2.42	2.07	5.07	4.34
SEIU	61.16	66.56	30.58	33.28	1.83	2.00	1.16	1.26
AFT	63.62	110.84	31.81	55.42	1.91	3.32	2.83	4.92
APWU	36.20	145.39	18.10	72.70	1.09	4.36	1.45	5.83
NALC	25.65	122.15	12.83	61.08	.77	3.66	1.82	8.65
IAFF	14.10	93.36	7.05	46.68	.42	2.80	.78	5.18
AFGE	22.81	149.71	11.15	74.85	.67	4.49	.33	2.21
NRLCA	5.99	74.27	2.99	37.14	.18	2.23	1.19	14.71
NTEU	11.37	152.86	5.69	76.43	.34	4.59	.28	3.80
NFFE	3.64	119.85	1.82	59.93	.11	3.60	.03	.86

Source: Unions' LM-2 financial disclosure forms.

Note: Estimates are based on the assumption that bargaining comprises 50 percent of the unions' operating budget, organizing comprises 3 percent of the budget, and political action comprises the percentage of the budget equal to the ratio between PAC receipts and the average member-based income for the union during the 1991–1992 election cycle. Data are based on actual 1993 dollars, unadjusted for inflation.

which have undergone downsizing and in which employers have faced almost irresistible economic pressures to operate with a nonunion workforce (Arthur and Smith 1994; Katz and MacDuffie 1994; Chaykowski, Thomason, and Zwerling 1994; Goldfield 1987; Kochan, Katz, and McKersie 1986; Dertouzos, Lester, and Solow 1989). In any event, even these unions spent seemingly small sums in an absolute sense, especially in comparison to their estimated expenditures on bargaining-related activities.

Given the 3-percent assumption as to organizing allocations, the public sector unions would seem to have a bare-bones commitment to this activity, at least at the national level of organization. None of these unions spent more than $5 per member, and five actually allocated less than $3 per member. The NTEU, AFGE, APWU, NALC, and NFFE are the leading per-member spenders, and it may thus seem curious that the AFGE and NFFE are the only two public sector unions which suffered sizable losses in membership in the 1980s.

It is important to emphasize, however, that unions among state and local government employees tend to be relatively decentralized in terms of bargaining and organizational structure. Thus, their financial commitments to organizing may occur primarily at lower organizational levels (e.g., state affiliates of the NEA). Also, it is known that at least one of these unions—the SEIU—devotes a much larger portion of its international union budget to organizing. If its reported one-third allocation is accurate, then the SEIU would have spent $20 million on organizing, or three times the total amount spent by the UAW, which, according to the 3-percent estimate, devoted only $6.3 million to organizing in 1993. On a per-member basis, the SEIU would have spent almost $67, or four-and-a-half times as much as the ILGWU, which stands as an outlier. In other words, SEIU's reported organizing budget testifies to the relatively huge gains that unions might achieve in organizing expenditures if they were to give this function a much higher organizational priority. As a final observation, some public sector unions may encounter comparatively weaker employer resistance to union organizing efforts, therefore lessening the costs of expanding their membership bases relative to those incurred trying to organize private sector workers (Freeman 1993). Obviously, most public sector employers are not motivated to attain profits (Wellington and Winter 1971; Feuille 1991), but some may nonetheless aggressively resist unions in order to maintain managerial prerogatives. Also, many public sector unions organize in the for-profit and non-profit private sector. In this regard, SEIU has a nontrivial private sector membership and thus often faces employers with strong financial incentives to resist unions. Employer opposition, in fact, accounts for the union's aggressive "Justice for Janitors" initiative, which has brought 35,000 additional members to the SEIU (*The Kiplinger Washington Letter*, August 25, 1995: 1).

As noted above, the unions' political spending levels in 1993 are estimated to be equivalent to the ratio between their PAC receipts in 1991–1992 and the average member-based income they generated in those two years. Among the private sector unions, the IBT had a commanding lead in estimated political spending. Assuming that it allocated nearly 14 percent of its overall budget to this function, it spent more than $14 million on political activities, or $11 per member. Only the ILGWU spent more per member ($34), but its total overall spending was estimated to be less than $5 million. In fact, except for the IBT, no other union in the private sector was estimated to spend more than $5 million on political activities in 1993. The UAW, ILGWU, and IAM spent more than $3 million, and they were joined by the NEA and AFSCME from the public sector, where eight unions spent less than $2 million, as was the case with seven private sector unions.

On a per-member basis, the ILGWU, NRLCA, IBT, NALC, and PPI ranked as the top five union political spenders. The IAM, CJA, UAW, APWU, CWA, LIU, and IAFF joined these five in spending more than $5 per member. In other words, less than half of the unions represented here spent an estimated $5 or more per member on political action in 1993. Given their comparatively large PACs, especially on a per-member basis, each of the postal unions is among this group.

In sum, the unions as a whole are estimated to spend modest amounts, in both absolute terms and on a per-member basis, on organizing and political activities. Altogether, the unions spent less than $35 million ($50 million unadjusted for inflation) on organizing in 1993, according to this estimate. They spent less than $45 million on political action. These totals amount to less than $3.50 compared to the $44 per person spent on bargaining-related activities. If union spending at the local level is assumed to be roughly comparable to what occurs on a national scale (Troy 1975; Sheflin and Troy 1983; Masters and Atkin 1996c), then it may be estimated that total organizing and political action amounted to about $225 million in 1993 dollars, assuming, of course, a similar functional allocation of money.

BARGAINING CLOUT

Strikes constitute perhaps the most controversial and publicized weapon in organized labor's economic arsenal (Gramm 1992). Unions threaten or actually engage in strikes in order to apply economic pressure on employers (LeRoy 1995). Conversely, employers may on occasion precipitate a strike for the strategic or tactical purpose of weakening a union by, perhaps, replacing the strikers (LeRoy 1995; McCallion 1990). Regardless of whether a strike is ultimately effective, its viability is arguably essential to union bargaining leverage. If, for whatever reasons, strikes should become largely infeasible or unsustainable, unions would lose a genuine source of influence at the negotiating table.

From a union's standpoint, strikes may become less appealing if they threaten financial stability or viability itself. Strikes interrupt the flow of income because strikers do not pay dues. Also, unions may pay benefits to strikers in order to provide some income security and, hence, greater economic willpower to sustain a work stoppage. While these benefits may be nominally modest, they can aggregate to very large sums if spread among thousands of members over a long period of time. In addition, unions may incur nontrivial legal, public relations, and other costs in conjunction with a strike. Thus, a union's capacity to endure the financial consequences of a strike is a potentially important factor in assessing bargaining power. While it is clearly not the sole or perhaps even one of the key elements of a strike outcome, the financial drain a union suffers may at some point become relevant in determining whether to continue a work stoppage. As Weil (1994: 154) observes, "a strike fund is a well-known device to indicate [to management] a union's preparation for tough negotiations." Further, the financial capacity to sustain a strike may grow in importance, even when the absolute number of the strikes is declining, as some strikes in the recent past, such as the UAW's against Caterpillar, "have become much longer and possibly more bitter" (Goldfield 1987: 46).

Clearly, the sustainability of a strike is more relevant to unions in the private sector, where strikes are permissible, than the public sector, where work stoppages are generally banned. Yet, striker payments constitute only one type of emergency expenditure. Thus, the estimates given (in Table 9.3) may be viewed as a relative indication of the unions' capacities to fund equivalently large activities. Further, strikes are permitted among selected public employees in several states, and they sometimes may occur where they are prohibited (Schneider 1988).

Table 9.3 reports the unions' overall strike costs and financial capacities to sustain a major work stoppage (i.e., one that includes a third of their members and lasts for three weeks). The data reveal the enormous cost that may be incurred in the course of a strike, particularly if even modest benefits are paid to those walking the picket line. Assuming that striker benefits average $175 per week (which is admittedly larger than the $50 Holley and Jennings [1994] report most unions may offer but still much less than the $300 per week the UAW recently paid to striking Caterpillar workers and on par with what has been proposed for IBT strikers in the Detroit newspapers' dispute), the union's real aggregate benefit payments would have amounted to almost $1.6 billion in 1993 during a full three-week strike. In 1993 dollars, the amount would have exceeded $2.3 billion.

Table 9.3
Unions' Aggregate Real Strike Fund Capacity Estimates

Year	Strike Benefits (in millions)[1]	Income Loss (in millions)[1]	Strike Cost (in millions)[1]	Real-Wealth-to Strike-Cost Ratio	Real-Working-Capital-to-Strike-Cost Ratio
1979	$3,677	$35.1	$3,712	.479	.209
1980	3,175	33.1	3,208	.530	.225
1981	2,809	32.2	3,841	.635	.290
1982	2,626	30.5	2,656	.724	.351
1983	2,525	29.7	2,554	.791	.360
1984	2,387	29.9	2,417	.868	.379
1985	2,778	29.3	2,307	.907	.478
1986	2,213	29.2	2,242	.945	.481
1987	2,082	28.6	2,110	.997	.492
1988	1,982	28.5	2,010	1.030	.500
1989	1,877	28.6	1,906	1.057	.553
1990	1,794	28.3	1,823	1.096	.572
1991	1,736	27.1	1,763	1.132	.596
1992	1,663	27.7	1,690	1.157	.608
1993	1,593	26.6	1,619	1.161	.569

Source: Unions' LM-2 financial reports.
Note: These numbers are rounded to the nearest million.

The unions' income loss is comparatively quite modest. In real dollars, they would have lost under $27 million in member-based income with one third of their strikers not paying dues or other assessments or fees for one month. In 1993 dollars, the union loss was under $39 million, or just 1.7 percent of the total striker payments. The estimated inflation-adjusted cost of the major work stoppage involving one-third of the unionized workforce is roughly $1.62 billion.

To what extent can unions afford such a financial hit? A partial glimpse of the answer to this question lies in the ratio between their wealth (real net assets) and the estimated cost of the strike. This ratio, as reported in Table 9.3, shows the extent to which the unions have improved their financial capacity over time. Since 1979, their wealth-to-strike-cost ratio has more than doubled, rising consistently from less than 50 percent to 116 percent.

While not all of a union's net assets may be readily convertible to cash and spent to sustain a strike, they may nonetheless be used as leverage to secure loans. Also, a union may seek to liquidate some of its assets to preserve a strike. Such a willingness was evidenced during the UMWA's prolonged strike against Pittston Coal Company. According to Weil (1994: 154), "the leadership of the United Mine Workers of America (UMWA) indicated at several points during the Pittston strike their willingness to devote virtually the union's entire resources to winning the strike." Admittedly, unions would only make such bold pronouncements when losing a strike itself might render its future meaningfulness as a bargaining power highly dubious. Accordingly, the working-capital-to-strike-cost ratio is calculated to show a union's financial capacity when relying more or less upon liquid wealth (cash, U.S. Treasury securities, and accounts receivable).

The working-capital ratio has steadily improved since 1979, although it declined somewhat in 1993. While it was less than .21 at the beginning of this period, indicating that unions' working capital amounted to under 21 percent of their aggregate strike costs, the ratio rose to almost .61 in 1992. Since 1985, the unions have had roughly 50 percent or more of the working capital needed to fund these major work stoppages. Unmistakably, regardless of whether the wealth or working-capital ratio is used, the unions' combined strike fund capacity has grown considerably over the past decade and a half.

Given the demonstrated disparities in union membership, income, wealth, and working capital, these aggregate data clearly mask wide differences among individual unions. Such interunion variation in strike-fund capacity is portrayed vividly in Table 9.4, which reports the various estimates for 1993 in current dollars. Focusing on the two ratios, the data show that the ILGWU and UAW are standouts when it comes to having sufficient wealth to sustain a major strike. The ILGWU has nine times the wealth it would need to pay the estimated more than $23 million its strike action would cost. The UAW has eight times its imputed strike cost. Interestingly, however, the ILGWU does not have a working-capital-to-strike-cost ratio greater than 1.00. Because its assets are mostly nonliquid, as defined in this context, its working-capital ratio is a modest 34 percent.[7]

More generally, the unions fall into three distinguishable categories regarding working capital. The first, which includes the UAW, IUOE, and CJA, has working capital in excess of their estimated strike costs. A second set consists of those unions with somewhere between 25 and 99 percent of the reserves needed to fund a major strike (RWDSU, USW, CWA, APWU, ILGWU, AFT, IAM, and IBEW). The remaining unions have working capital reserves of less than 25 percent of their estimated strike costs. Nine of these unions are in the public sector, including the NALC, NRLCA, and NTEU, each of which has a negative working-capital ratio. Of the eight private sector unions in this category, four have negative ratios (UFCW, IBT, PPI, and UPIU).

In short, only three unions had working-capital ratios greater than 1.00, even though twelve had wealth-to-strike-cost ratios that showed excess funding capacity. Thirteen unions had working-capital ratios at or

Table 9.4
Disaggregate Union Strike Fund Capacity Estimates (1993)

Union	Strike Benefits (in millions)	Income Loss (in millions)	Strike Cost (in millions)	Wealth to Strike Cost Ratio	Working Capital to Strike Cost Ratio
Private Sector					
IBT	$230.30	$ 1.79	$232.09	.276	-.069
UFCW	174.75	2.92	177.39	-.213	-.690
UAW	134.92	5.11	140.04	7.825	7.292
IBEW	124.25	1.81	126.06	1.481	.254
IAM	82.95	2.37	85.32	1.780	.280
CWA	82.60	2.46	85.06	1.000	.466
USW	73.67	3.21	76.88	2.188	.837
CJA	71.40	1.09	72.49	1.788	1.094
LIU	71.40	.91	72.31	2.137	.147
IUOE	53.37	.76	54.14	1.739	1.506
HERE	45.15	.71	45.86	.356	.211
PPI	38.50	1.01	39.15	1.862	-.053
UPIU	32.90	.69	33.59	.912	-.008
ACTWU	25.02	.46	25.48	.413	.104
IUE	25.02	.47	25.50	1.719	.108
ILGWU	23.27	.30	23.57	8.836	.338
RWDSU	14.00	.15	14.15	1.980	.900
Public Sector					
NEA	367.50	4.56	372.01	.105	.020
AFSCME	204.22	2.14	206.37	.072	.028
SEIU	160.82	1.53	162.36	.250	.111
AFT	100.45	1.71	102.16	.377	.302
APWU	43.57	.90	44.48	.525	.466
NALC	36.75	.70	37.45	1.110	-.018
IAFF	26.42	.33	26.76	.266	.163
AFGE	26.07	.55	26.63	.153	.068
NRLCA	14.10	.10	14.20	.173	-.057
NTEU	13.02	.31	13.33	.172	-.040
NFFE	5.31	.10	5.42	.120	.001

Source: Unions' LM-2 financial disclosure forms.
Note: Calculations are based on actual 1993 dollars.

below .10, and seven of these were actually in the red, so to speak. Thus, at least some of these unions would appear to face at least modest difficulty in funding a prolonged strike action involving a sizable number of their members, particularly without liquidating assets that are otherwise available. On this last point, fifteen unions (ten of which are in the public sector) have insufficient wealth to fund the estimated strike costs. In the private sector, the UFCW, IBT, HERE, and ACTWU (at least before its merger) could be expected to have financial problems if faced with a work stoppage of the magnitude assumed here.

CONCLUSIONS

As unions face the future, they will make important choices on how to allocate resources. With membership and density declining, organized labor can be expected to respond by spending more on recruiting new members. SEIU, for example, has set a goal of increasing its new recruits by three to four times the current level (Bernstein 1996). Accordingly, it is imploring its local units to spend 20 percent of their budgets on organizing by the year 1998. To appreciate the resource allocation implications of such increases, this chapter examined the budget allocations of the twenty-eight unions—aggregated and disaggregated—based on certain assumptions. It also assessed the bargaining-clout implications of the unions' financial conditions by estimating their relative capacities to fund a major strike.

Given certain baseline assumptions, the data show that the unions as a whole have devoted remarkably little to organizing and political activity. It is estimated that they spent less than six dollars per member on such functions in 1993. Furthermore, as the unions' operating disbursements have fallen, because of declining revenues, their overall spending on bargaining, organizing, and political action have similarly decreased. With a shrinking resource base to fund important activities, the choices unions make in the future will become even more difficult.

Although these spending estimates are only as good as the reported assumptions behind them, they nonetheless show the clear possibility that unions could make a noticeably increased effort in this area with a modest shift in organizational priorities. In this regard, SEIU's commitment of one-third of its national budget to organizing becomes a target toward which unions might be expected to move (albeit not with some considerable internal resistance). While a diminution in bargaining service might be expected from such a general shift in union priorities, this may not necessarily be the case. Unless unions can organize more workers, their bargaining power can be expected to continue to wane. This logic is clearly behind the SEIU's push to triple or quadruple its recruiting levels.

The new head of SEIU, Andy Stern (who succeeded John Sweeney), says that his union needs "to make our local leaders see that because of lower-wage competition, they must represent more of their industries to bargain effectively for existing members" (Bernstein 1996: 73).

With respect to bargaining clout in terms of capacities to fund a strike, the data show that the major unions have improved their position between 1979 and 1993. Since 1988, in fact, they have had sufficient working capital to fund anywhere from 50 to 60 percent of the estimated costs of a major strike. Their aggregate wealth has exceeded the projected strike costs in terms of lost dues and striker-benefit payments. Yet, there is considerable interunion variation. At least four private sector unions had a negative working-capital-to-strike-cost ratio. Most public sector unions at the national level have only a marginal capacity to fund strikers, a reality perhaps dictated in part by the relative absence of strike protections in much of the government at all levels, as well as by their decentralized bargaining structures, especially among state and local employees.

NOTES

1. Masters (1983; 1985), for example, estimated the political expenditures made by federal-employee unions (AFGE, NFFE, and NTEU) based on the gross expenditures allocated to professional political employees itemized on the unions' LM-2 schedules. Voos (1983; 1984a, 1984b; 1987) estimates the organizing expenditures of manufacturing unions over the 1954–1977 period. In so doing, she relied upon the unions' financial statements, other documentary evidence, and interviews with union staff. Organizing expenditures included (1983: 579) "organizers' salaries . . . ; reimbursements to organizers for expenses . . . , and miscellaneous direct organizing expenditures (such as leaflets and hall rentals)." The union sample included the IBT, USW, UAW, CJA, IAM, URW, ILGWU, IBEW, SEIU, CWA, and the Clothing Workers and Textile Workers (which were separate unions for most of the period she examined).

2. For example, SEIU, as reported earlier, supposedly allocates about one-third of its national operating budget to organizing. Voos (1984b) estimated that the manufacturing unions allocated about 20 percent of their budgets to organizing in the 1970s. Interviews with union staff suggested that the 2-to-4 percent range (across unions generally) is probably a good ballpark figure, notwithstanding interunion differences.

3. Seven rather than eight election cycles are used because complete member-based income was unavailable for 1994 at the time this study was initiated.

4. Again, the 1993–1994 cycle estimate is not used to compute the overall average because 1994 data on member-based income were not available when this study began. As a practical matter, however, the seventh and eighth election cycle average ratios are literally indistinguishable: .027 (1980–1992 average ratio of PAC receipts to member-based income) versus .028 (1980–1994 average, with 1994 member-based income computed from 1993 data, adjusted for inflation).

5. The UAW paid $300 per week in strike benefits in the walkout against Caterpillar. Holley and Jennings (1994: 223) report that such benefits are "usually $50 or less per week." The level of benefits is often a source of controversy within unions. James Hoffa, Jr., who is challenging incumbent Ronald Carey for the IBT's presidency, has proposed to increase benefits to strikers against the Detroit newspapers from the current $55 per week to $160 per week (Newsday 1996: A12).

6. In 1994, slightly more than five million days were idle due to strikes involving 322,000 workers. This amounts to 15.6 days per worker (U.S. DOL, BLS 1995).

7. In 1993, the ILGWU reported approximately $210 million in total assets, $170 million of which was categorized as "other investments." Another $15 million was listed in the "fixed assets" category, and $14 million were "other assets."

Chapter 10

Strategic Union Resource Allocations

A fundamentally strategic issue facing major U.S.-based unions is how they might mobilize and allocate human, financial, and political capital—amid a declining membership—in order to launch an unparalleled organizing effort to reverse a four-decade-long drop in aggregate union density that has involved extremely steep declines among several major unions. The need for such a commitment, which evidently is gaining wide acceptance on a tangible scale in the labor movement among both leaders and rank and file, is dictated by unfavorable structural economic forces, increased employer resolve and sophistication in opposing unions, political and public-policy barriers, and the low organizational priority unions have evidently given to organizing for much of the time since their halcyon years of the 1950s. Unions made such a massive effort in the 1930s, when faced with profoundly destabilizing economic and political challenges. They mobilized workers at the grassroots and displayed a willingness to use bold militant tactics. They also, as previously shown, spent relatively large sums of money to initiate and support organizing. Furthermore, unions also activated workers on the political front, forging deep ties with the Democratic party (especially within the metropolitan areas of the Midwest and Northeast) that they cemented in substantial measure with cash and in-kind campaign assistance (Greenstone 1977).

Unions cannot be expected to make strategic realignments of organizational priorities and resource allocations either rashly or blindly. As Voos

(1983: 591) states, "unions are complex institutions with political as well as economic dimensions. If so, unions will not expand organizing programs unless internal political pressure builds for such an expansion or unless union officers are convinced that such an expansion would be desirable." The election of John Sweeney to the AFL-CIO helm, plus growing evidence of new investment (e.g., the Teamsters' commitment of $25 million to expand organizing) and initiative (the UAW, USW, and IAM merger), indicate that unions have recognized the need for strategic change.

Sweeney campaigned successfully on the twin themes of expanded organizing and political activism. Organizing serves workers' self-interests by preserving and raising real wages (Voos 1983; 1987). Political action levels the public-policy playing field, thereby reducing the costs of organizing, at least to the extent it both eases the process of representing workers and takes wages and benefits out of competition. In more specific terms, Sweeney ran on a platform that promised "creating a political training center to train political campaign organizers and campaign managers" (Nomani and Rose 1995: C13). He also pledged to deploy an additional 1,000 new organizers and infuse an extra $10 million into the AFL-CIO's former Organizing Institute. Also, in fulfillment of his pledge, President Sweeney named Richard Bensinger, formerly head of the federation's organizing institute, chief organizer for the AFL-CIO. Bensinger is well known for his aggressive grassroots organizing style and "wants to use much of that money and clout to adapt some tactics of the 1960s civil-rights movement to today's labor movement" (Zachary 1996c: B1). Even before the AFL-CIO's $35 million campaign to oust the Republican control of Congress, Sweeney had poised organized labor at the forefront of the upcoming 1996 elections (Marcus and Edsall 1995: A12): "The AFL-CIO has targeted 55 GOP House incumbents whose constituencies include a high percentage of union members or union retirees . . . The campaign which Sweeney said would cost at least $1 million, involves critical radio and television ads aimed at 22 members of the [U.S.] House, and a direct mail campaign to union members and retirees in the remaining 33 congressional districts. The effort is part of Sweeney's larger commitment to rebuild the political strength of organized labor."

This initiative explicitly recognizes the strategic importance of mobilizing organized labor's multifaceted sources of institutional strength. It entails activating human capital politically—members and retirees—and commits nontrivial sums of money—financial and political capital—to the effort. Thus it illustrates the broader need to mobilize human, financial, and political capital on an unprecedented scale and target these resources so as to maximize gains, particularly, in the ultimate analysis, on the organizing battleground. While organizing new members is the paramount need of labor today (and into the foreseeable future), it also may be pursued effectively by deploying resources into bargaining and political strategies, which, if translated into favorable public policies and regulatory actions, may reduce the cost of organizing additional ranks.

Indeed, faced with declining memberships and regular income, unions must creatively tap all three dimensions of power and expand them wherever feasible in order to conduct the kind of economic and political warfare that is called for by current circumstances. First, especially with declining income, unions will need to pay even more attention to allocating financial capital in ways that maximize efficiencies and coordinate activities toward central missions such as organizing. Altering investment policies so as to gain more return on their wealth and to expand income—either by diversified investment portfolios or increased dues that may be earmarked specifically for demonstrably urgent priorities—also may be strategically crucial decisions.

Second, unions must focus more systematically on mobilizing human capital—their reserves of current and retired members. Although they may, in absolute terms, possess what appears to be a lot of wealth and regular income, unions clearly cannot compete with business on this dimension. As a whole, corporations clearly have the financial capacity to overpower labor unions. According to the CWA (undated brochure: 19), AT&T's computing subsidiary, NCR, spent $1 million to fight an effort to organize 150 field engineers in Dayton, Ohio and Indianapolis, Indiana. (The CWA lost the NLRB certification election in Dayton by only three votes.) More generally, Levitt (1993: 5) estimates that U.S. businesses fund "more than seven thousand attorneys and consultants across the nation who make their living busting unions . . . [thus making] the war on organized labor a $1 billion-plus industry," an estimate which may be conservative. Given their comparatively enormous wealth, the Fortune 500 alone could explode that particular industry with little felt pain.[1] And this says nothing about the sheer financial power corporations wield by exercising well established managerial prerogatives, such as plant closures or relocations, which have dire consequences for union members.

Corporations, however, do not operate as a cohesive employment or economic force. Their economic and political needs and objectives often compete or conflict. Thus, unions possess a distinct advantage when they can mobilize their members (and retirees). Although they have declined in workforce representation, unions, with well over sixteen million members, still constitute one of the largest single organized economic and political interest groups in the United States—a potential human capital force that can be allied with other grassroots organizations to pursue common objectives. Goldfield (1987: 243) pointedly expresses the imperative of coalescing union members and others with similar interests in the pursuit of a successful labor struggle:

> Massive employer offensives against workers' organizations and standards of living have historically been met and defeated by massive working-class counteroffensives and insurgencies . . . . It is most likely that union gains and large-scale growth in

union membership will only be won in the foreseeable future on the basis of broad class struggle and innovative disruptions of production (as happened during the 1930s). The defeat of PATCO, Phelps-Dodge, and Hormel were not due to a lack of corporate campaigns and innovative tactics. All these struggles lost because they did not receive timely solidarity from workers and unions around the country.

Given the labor intensiveness of the organizing (e.g., cost of paid organizers) and political participation (e.g., paid lobbyists, campaign workers, media consultants), the financial implications of energizing a sizable bloc of union members should not in any way be understated.

Third, because they are member-based organizations with a core ideology, especially among the leadership, unions have the potential to compete aggressively on the political front, even under the current climate of membership decline and conservative public opinion. They have the potential to deploy thousands of campaign workers to do the unglorified but all-important work of politics, namely, registering voters, getting out the vote, orchestrating rallies, and raising money. While corporations employ tens of millions more than unions have as members, their PAC fundraising is typically restricted to the more elite managerial or executive ranks (U.S. FEC 1992).[2] Further, their PAC-giving habits have tended to be more diffused and ideologically imbalanced (Sabato 1985). In sharp contrast, unions raise their money from the grass roots and allocate it with much more of an apparent ideological bias (Masters and Delaney 1985; Masters and Zardkoohi 1987; Delaney and Masters 1991). To the extent labor unions can increase the coordinated political participation of their members, they are capable of exerting power beyond what their sheer numbers would indicate possible (Bok and Dunlop 1970; Bennett 1991). What Hudson and Rosen (1954: 404) observed more than forty years ago still rings largely true today: "Sixteen million workers with their . . . [spouses] and families are a political potential that no politician can afford to overlook," especially, it might be added, if they are highly involved and committed to a particular cause.

The objective of this chapter is to estimate the additional resources that unions can bring to bear on organizing and political activities by reallocating current budgets and mobilizing their rank and file. Specifically, it estimates the additional money that unions would spend if they increased their current budget estimate allocation (3 percent) to 10, 33, and 50 percent of their operating disbursements. The chapter also estimates the number of organizing (or, alternatively, political) volunteers they might assemble if just 10 percent of their rank and file devoted one day a month to relevant pursuits. The imputed financial costs of having paid staff do the same as this "reserve" squad are also calculated. Finally, the incremental PAC receipts unions would generate if each member gave $5 or $10 per election cycle are estimated. In Chapter 11, the organizing increments in particular are used to estimate the additional members unions might gain if they increase their budget allocations to this function.

ORGANIZING BUDGET INCREMENTS

Unions may incur substantial expense in organizing new members. In a study on the costs and benefits of organizing workers in twenty major manufacturing industries, Voos (1984a: 44) estimated that the "cost of each additional union member ranged from $580 to $1,568" in 1980 dollars. The most significant costs unions incur in this effort are direct expenses, which "include organizers' salaries . . . ; reimbursements to organizers . . . ; and miscellaneous direct organizing expenditures (such as leaflets and hall rentals)" (Voos 1983: 579). Indirect costs may include members' volunteer efforts. Parenthetically, Voos (1983: 577) estimates that these indirect costs are "small in most instances," but expanded union efforts to use current members as recruiters might substantially elevate these implied financial costs. Obviously, the opportunity costs of spending less on other union functions is something that will implicitly or explicitly weigh on union policy makers in allocating scarce financial resources (Block 1980; Voos 1983; 1987).

In contrast, the potential benefits of organizing new members include increased wages due to expanded bargaining power, higher dues intake relative to servicing costs, and greater political clout via a bigger union voting bloc, inter alia. According to Voos's (1983: 590) analyses, "it would appear that, on average, the expenditures of internationals on organizing programs can be justified by the monetary benefits [i.e., higher wages] directly received by their members."

Thus, from the standpoint of setting union priorities, it is important for unions to appreciate fully the financial implications of increasing the proportion of their disbursements allocated to organizing related activities. Table 10.1 reports the aggregate real amounts the twenty-eight unions would have spent on organizing between 1979 and 1993 under four budget allocation baseline assumptions: (1) current 3 percent; (2) 10 percent; (3) one-third; and (4) one-half. The data attest powerfully to the additional resources unions would have brought to bear on their organizing efforts under these different scenarios and, by implication, the additional members they might have recruited over this otherwise dismal time period for organizing.

According to the 3-percent baseline estimate, these twenty-eight national unions' spending on organizing ranged from a low of $35 million (in 1993) to a high of $45 million in 1986 (again, in inflation-adjusted dollars). Over the entire fifteen-year period, the unions spent an estimated

Table 10.1
Unions' Aggregate Real Organizing Budget Increments (1979–1993, in millions)

Year	Current Budget Estimate[1]	Ten-Percent Budget Estimate[1]	One-Third Budget Estimate[1]	One-Half Budget Estimate[1]
1979	$42	$140	$461	$699
1980	42	142	467	708
1981	38	128	421	638
1982	39	130	428	648
1983	39	131	432	654
1984	39	131	433	656
1985	39	130	429	650
1986	45	151	499	756
1987	42	141	466	706
1988	40	132	436	661
1989	43	144	476	721
1990	39	131	434	657
1991	37	123	407	617
1992	40	132	436	660
1993	35	115	381	577
Total	601	2,002	6,607	10,010
Percent Increase Between Estimates[2]		2.331	10.00	15.655

Source: Unions' LM-2 financial disclosure forms.
1. Estimates are rounded to the nearest million.
2. Percentages should be multiplied by 100 for conventional interpretation.

$600 million. Assuming that their combined spending on organizing had been at the level of 10 percent of operating disbursements, the unions' expenditures would have risen by 233 percent to slightly above $2 billion between 1979 and 1993.

Taking the estimate a step further, the sum expended on organizing would have risen tenfold, to $6.6 billion, if the unions had allocated one-third of their budget toward this end. In 1986 alone they would have spent $500 million, or nearly as much as was spent over the entire decade and a half under the 3-percent baseline estimate. Obviously, the incremental expenditures would be even more impressive if the unions had allocated a full half of their budgets to organizing. Under this scenario, union organizing expenditures would have been more than sixteen times the amount spent under the 3-percent estimate. Totaling more than $10 billion between 1979 and 1993, the unions' organizing budgets would have exceeded the grand total in the current budget estimate in each individual year except 1993, when expenditures were an estimated $577 million.

Bear in mind that these expenditure increments are somewhat conservative given that they are based on the unions' actual budgets, which do not reflect the financial implications of union growth. Assuming that additional expenditures would have added new members, union income and, hence, disbursements would have risen accordingly. Thus, their organizing allocations would have been larger than those assumed here. In any event, the data reveal a powerful story.

Table 10.2 indicates the various levels of expenditure unions would have made (in 1993 dollars) to organize under the four scenarios. These estimates should help put current reports regarding union investments into organizing into a broader context as well as show the potential contributions individual unions could make to the overall organizing picture. The data also imply the extent to which these incremental expenditures might be squandered if unions invest them in competition for the same organizing base, with the caveat that additional competition might beget intensified effort, as was the case in the 1930s when the CIO's organizing aggressiveness intensified AFL efforts on the same front.

The data further attest to the dramatic gains the unions would have made in allocating money under these incremental estimates. By raising their budget allocations to 10 percent, the unions' organizing spending in 1993 would have risen by more than $100 million to approximately $167 million. Under the one-third estimate, spending jumps up nearly another $400 million. An additional $284 million is allocated under the one-half scenario. Thus, if the UAW and NEA nationals had spent one-third of their total operating budget in 1993 on organizing, then they each would have spent more than all twenty-eight unions under the 3-percent estimate. In contrast, if the SEIU had spent what the 3-percent unions on average reportedly allocate, then their organizing expenditures would have dropped from an estimated $20 million (one-third) to less than $2 million.

ORGANIZING RESERVE SQUADS

Assuming, for the sake of argument, that these unions had in fact spent one-half, or $833 million, of their operating budgets on organizing, they would still have been outspent by Levitt's (1993) estimate of the union-busting industry in a comparable time period (circa 1993). Although it should not be assumed that unions and businesses are equally efficient or effective in spending such allocations, it still cannot be denied that

Table 10.2
Union Organizing Budget Increments (1993, in millions)

Union	Current Budget Estimate[1]	Ten-Percent Budget Estimate[1]	One-Third Budget Estimate[1]	One-Half Budget Estimate[1]
Private Sector				
IBT	$3.17	$10.58	$34.93	$52.93
UFCW	3.32	11.08	36.58	55.42
UAW	6.31	21.03	69.40	105.15
IBEW	1.99	6.62	21.85	33.10
IAM	2.51	8.37	27.61	41.83
CWA	2.53	8.44	27.86	42.22
USW	4.06	13.52	44.61	67.59
CJA	1.88	6.27	20.70	31.37
LIU	1.14	3.80	12.55	19.01
IUOE	.88	2.95	9.74	14.75
HERE	.74	2.47	8.14	12.33
PPI	1.24	4.13	13.63	20.66
UPIU	.69	2.30	7.60	11.51
ACTWU	.84	2.80	9.23	13.99
IUE	.68	2.26	7.46	11.30
ILGWU	1.95	6.50	21.44	32.48
RWDSU	.38	1.28	4.23	6.41
Public Sector				
NEA	5.51	18.36	60.60	91.82
AFSCME	2.42	8.06	26.60	40.31
SEIU	1.83	6.12	20.18	30.58
AFT	1.91	6.36	20.99	31.81
APWU	1.09	3.62	11.95	18.10
NALC	.77	2.56	8.46	12.83
IAFF	.42	1.41	4.65	7.05
AFGE	.67	2.23	7.36	11.15
NRLCA	.18	.60	1.97	2.99
NTEU	.34	1.14	3.75	5.69
NFFE	.11	.36	1.20	1.82
TOTAL	50.02	166.74	550.23	833.69

Source: Unions' LM-2 financial disclosure forms.

1. Estimates are rounded to the nearest million. They are in 1993 dollars.

corporations have the distinct financial advantage. Thus, the mobilization of workers or current members into a volunteer organizing reserve is a potential source of capital (in this case human) from which unions can compete. Indeed, the various grassroots, community-based organizing campaigns such as "Justice for Janitors" suggest the concerted recognition and implementation of this possibility. Current members are often the most effective communicators with potential ones, and their systematic mobilization for this purpose is arguably the most powerful tool in labor's organizing arsenal. As the current head of SEIU, Andy Stern observes: "Nonunion workers are ready to join unions . . . The question is whether unions are ready to reach out to them" (Bernstein 1996: 73).

Table 10.3 provides an estimate of human (and imputed financial) resources the unions, as a whole, might have mobilized for organizing purposes. The organizing reserve squad (which also could be equated with a political action reserve) is estimated to be the equivalent of paid organizers under these assumptions: (1) 10 percent of the 28 unions' combined

Table 10.3
Unions' Aggregate Organizing Squad Budget Estimates

Year	Organizing Squad	Real Expenditures[1] (in millions)	Current (1993) Expenditures[1] (in millions)
1979	73,124	$7,564	$5,484
1980	71,581	6,531	5,368
1981	70,037	5,779	5,253
1982	69,504	5,402	5,213
1983	68,971	5,193	5,173
1984	68,029	4,911	5,102
1985	67,224	4,686	5,042
1986	66,524	4,552	4,989
1987	64,865	4,282	4,865
1988	64,312	4,077	4,823
1989	63,857	3,862	4,789
1990	64,326	3,691	4,824
1991	64,843	3,571	4,863
1992	63,989	3,421	4,799
1993	63,134	3,277	4,735
TOTAL	1,004,321	75,324	70,800

1. Estimates are rounded to nearest million.

membership; multiplied by (2) 12 working days (or one day a month); divided by (3) 250 days, or one working year. The resulting number of unpaid, year-round volunteers would have ranged from 63,000 to more than 73,000 in each year since 1979, or a 1,000,000-plus reserve of full-time organizers over the fifteen-year period.

The cost of employing full-time organizing staff in equivalent numbers is estimated in the second and third columns, in real and 1993 dollars, respectively. (The estimate is based on assumptions that each full-time organizer, on average, is [1] paid $45,000 per year; with fringes [2] equal to one-third of the annual salary; and [3] expenses and clerical aid equivalent to one-third of the annual salary. Thus, each reserve person, as a fully paid organizer, would cost an estimated $75,000 per year.) In real dollars, the cost of a paid organizing staff of equivalent size (to the reserve squad) would have totaled more than $75 billion. If Voos (1983) is accurate in noting that most unions have made little systematic use of such a volunteer force, then these imputed expenditures, for the most part, would have been above and beyond actual union efforts in this regard. In 1993 dollars, the unions would have spent an estimated $4.7 billion on such a full-time organizing staff. If they had spent one-third of their budgets on "direct" organizing items, their combined organizing expenses would have been in excess of $5.2 billion, or considerably above reported union-busting efforts.

Table 10.4 disaggregates these union organizing reserve squad estimates, reporting the number of full-time organizing reserves (and their implied costs) for each union in 1993. According to this estimate, three unions (NEA, IBT, and AFSCME) would have had more than 5,000 such reservists. Another eight unions (UFCW, SEIU, UAW, IBEW, AFT, IAM, CWA, and USW) would have had more than 2,000, while even relatively small unions like the NTEU, NRLCA, and LIU would have had several hundred. The estimated costs of hiring such a squad are more than $200 million for eight unions (NEA, IBT, AFSCME, UFCW, SEIU, UAW, IBEW, and AFT), and larger than each of their total operating budgets.

PAC RECEIPT INCREMENTS

As reported in Chapter 7, the twenty-eight unions' principal national PACs alone raised more than $34 million in real terms in the 1993–1994 election cycle. Financing congressional and presidential campaigns through PAC money is a longstanding union political activity, one that has been shown to produce results (Moore et al. 1995). If nothing else, it is essential to maintaining a visible presence in national politics and securing access to, if not influence over, lawmakers (Herndon 1982).

While it may seem ironic to push for increased PAC fundraising at a time of emboldened political opposition and a shrinking base from which to raise such money in the first place, it is these very circumstances which have

Table 10.4
Union Organizing Reserves (1993)

Union	Reserve Squad	Budget Estimates[1] (in millions)
Private Sector		
IBT	6,317	$474
UFCW	4,786	359
UAW	3,701	278
IBEW	3,408	256
IAM	2,275	171
CWA	2,266	170
USW	2,021	152
CJA	1,958	147
LIU	1,958	147
IUOE	1,464	110
HERE	1,238	93
PPI	1,056	79
UPIU	902	68
ACTWU	686	51
IUE	686	51
ILGWU	638	48
RWDSU	384	29
Public Sector		
NEA	10,080	756
AFSCME	5,602	420
SEIU	4,411	331
AFT	2,755	207
APWU	1,195	90
NALC	1,008	76
IAFF	725	54
AFGE	715	54
NRLCA	387	29
NTEU	357	27
NFFE	146	11
TOTAL	63,134	4,735

1. Estimates are rounded to nearest million.

occasioned an intensified commitment to political action at the grassroots level. Labor expanded its political efforts largely to protect its prior legislative gains rather than to embark on a bold, new public-policy course of reform (Masters and Delaney 1987b; Masters and Atkin 1992). Thus, to some extent, unions have used these conservative-led threats to stimulate increased political activism among their members. Their ultimate goal, however, is not only to generate sufficient PAC money and other forms of activism to stymie hostile legislative initiatives but also to turn the political tide and press a public-policy agenda more favorable to the institutional vitality of organized labor.

With a shrinking membership base, unions can raise additional PAC money in one or two principal (but not mutually exclusive) ways. As noted, the first is to convince more members that they should donate to the union PAC (i.e., increase participation per se). The second is to encourage larger donations. One argument that unions might use to encourage both is to show the sizable gains in PAC money, hence political clout, unions might gain if their members contributed, on average, $5 or $10 every *two* years to their union PACs.

Table 10.5 reports the twenty-eight unions' aggregate real PAC receipts for each cycle between 1980 and 1994. It also shows the relative increase in real receipts unions might have garnered if the rank and file, on average, had contributed $5 and $10, respectively, to the PAC. With a $5 donation, the unions' principal PACs would have raised nearly $515 million in real

Table 10.5
Unions' Aggregate Real PAC Receipt Increments (in millions)

Election Cycle	Real Total PAC Receipts	Real $5.00/Member Estimate	Real $10.00/Member Estimate
1980	$14.93	$97.44	$194.87
1982	18.45	77.56	155.13
1984	24.65	70.13	140.25
1986	29.82	64.14	128.29
1988	37.39	58.02	116.05
1990	38.16	52.42	104.85
1992	37.01	48.73	97.46
1994	34.39	44.94	89.89
TOTALS	234.80	513.39	1,026.79

Sources: U.S. FEC (1982; 1983; 1985; 1988; 1989; 1991; 1993; 1995a; 1995b).

dollars, or about 120 percent more than the roughly $235 million in actual receipts. At $10 a head, the intake would have ballooned to more than $1 billion, or five times as much as the recorded yield. For the 1994 election cycle, the twenty-eight unions would have raised more than $130 million in current dollars, or 1.6 times as much as they actually did.

The unions' disaggregate PAC gains for 1994 (in constant dollars) under the $5 and $10 scenarios are reported in Table 10.6. By raising $5 per member in PAC money, nine unions would have increased their 1994 PAC receipts by more than 100 percent (RWDSU, UPIU, NFFE, SEIU, HERE, AFGE, NEA, UFCW, and ACTWU) above 1993–1994 levels. Several other unions' receipts would have been at least 50 percent higher (USW, IUOE, IUE, and NTEU). Only seven unions would have raised less PAC money, and they include two postal-employee organizations (NALC and NRLCA).

With PAC funds coming in at the rate of $10 per member, the union intake would have been 160 percent greater than it was in 1992, or $131 million. No major unions' principal national PAC would have raised less money. Eight private sector unions' PACs would have generated at least 200 percent more in income (RWDSU, UPIU, HERE, UFCW, ACTWU, IUE, IBEW, and IUOE), while five public sector unions would have had increases at that level or more (NFFE, NTEU, SEIU, AFGE, and NEA). In short, with seemingly modest amounts of member donations, which amount to about 21 cents ($5 total) or 41 cents ($10 total) per month over a two-year cycle, most unions could have substantially enlarged their PAC coffers. The combined effect would have been quite significant, especially if PAC expenditures were targeted to those races where unions might have the greatest impact, given their membership (and retiree) presence.

CONCLUSIONS

The data presented in this chapter yield several important conclusions. First, if unions had followed SEIU's practice of spending one-third of their budgets on organizing, they would have allocated $6.6 billion dollars on this function between 1979 and 1993, or eleven times as much as they allocated under the 3-percent baseline assumption. In 1993 alone, they would have spent $550 million rather than the 3-percent estimate of $50 million (in actual 1993 dollars).

Second, on the political front, the unions could have become considerably bigger PAC players if they achieved only modest increases in either member donations or fundraising participation. If the rank and file had given $10 per year during the last election cycle, the major unions' PACs would have accounted for more than one-third of overall federal PAC

Table 10.6
Disaggregate Union PAC Receipt Increments (1993–1994)

Union	1 1993-1994 Receipts (in millions)	2 $5.00/Member Receipts (in millions)	Percentage Change (1-2)	3 $10/Member Receipts (in millions)	Percentage Change (1-3)
Private Sector					
IBT	$9.19	6.58	-.28	13.16	.43
UFCW	2.28	4.98	1.19	9.97	3.37
UAW	4.43	3.85	-.11	7.71	.78
IBEW	2.42	3.55	.47	7.10	1.93
IAM	3.51	2.37	-.32	4.70	.35
CWA	2.18	2.36	.08	4.72	1.16
USW	1.37	2.10	.53	4.21	2.07
CJA	1.65	2.04	.23	4.08	1.47
LIU	1.41	2.04	.44	4.08	1.89
IUOE	.81	1.52	.87	3.05	2.74
HERE	.30	1.29	3.27	2.58	7.55
PPI	.86	1.10	.28	2.20	1.55
UPIU	.12	.94	6.75	1.88	14.50
ACTWU	.24	.71	1.95	1.43	4.90
IUE	.44	.71	.62	1.43	2.24
ILGWU	.77	.66	-.14	1.33	.72
RWDSU	.04	.40	8.98	.80	18.95
Public Sector					
NEA	4.50	10.50	1.33	21.00	3.67
AFSCME	5.69	5.83	.02	11.67	1.04
SEIU	1.18	4.95	2.89	9.19	6.76
AFT	2.32	2.87	.24	5.74	1.47
APWU	1.22	1.24	.02	2.49	1.03
NALC	1.60	1.05	-.34	2.10	.31
IAFF	.76	.75	-.01	1.51	.99
AFGE	.31	.74	1.38	1.49	3.76
NRLCA	.56	.40	-.28	.81	.44
NTEU	.21	.37	.79	.74	2.57
NFFE	.03	.15	48.83	.30	98.65
TOTAL	50.31	65.76	.31	131.53	1.614

Source: U.S. FEC (1995).
Note: Data are in actual dollars, unadjusted for inflation. Membership is assumed to be at the 1993 level for the 1993–1994 cycle. Percentages should be multiplied by 100 for convenient interpretation.

PAC fundraising in 1994, which totaled $391.76 million. While such participation would seem to represent a quantum leap forward, it may not be inconceivable. Studies show that more than one-half of union members vote consistently with union endorsements in presidential and congressional elections, suggesting a larger base of political support than has been tapped effectively in the PAC fundraising arena (Axelrod 1982; LeRoy 1990; Delaney, Masters, and Schwochau 1990; Clark and Masters 1996). This potential base might be tapped more fruitfully if unions can tie political participation with work-related matters, such as job security, wages, benefits, and safety and health (Clark and Masters 1996).

Finally, the unions could substantially increase their capacity to organize and participate politically if they were to cultivate a stable cadre of volunteers. The imputed financial costs (benefits) of having 10 percent of their combined memberships devote twelve days a year to either organizing or political action amounted to nearly $5 billion in 1993. This sum is larger than the amount companies reportedly spend on union busting. In other words, the deployment of human capital is probably the only way that unions can ever begin to amass the resources they must in order to meet firms head-on on the organizing front.

NOTES

1. General Motors alone reported nearly $169 billion in revenues in 1995, with $217 billion in assets and $6.9 billion in profits ("The largest industrial and service corporations." 1996: F-1). In total, the Fortune 500 largest firms had $4.7 trillion in revenues, $10.5 trillion in assets, and $244 billion profits.

2. According to Saboto (1985), corporations generally limit their PAC fundraising solicitations to corporate executive personnel, although they are permitted to conduct broader solicitations (e.g., to stockholders) twice a year under federal law.

Chapter 11

Union Growth Scenarios and Mergers

The decline in union density, membership, and organizing activity (at least in terms of formal certification elections conducted by the NLRB) might suggest that these major unions have added no new members in recent years. However, unions do not exist in a static condition. Their membership situation changes continuously. Just to remain stable, unions must replace members who quit, retire, or lose their jobs. To grow in absolute numbers, they must add new members above and beyond this basic level of attrition. Further, to increase density rates, membership growth levels must exceed the expansion in the nation's labor force. At the same time, unions must also weigh the need to serve current members' interests in order to retain them and avoid decertification activity, which grew in the 1980s. While 301 decertification elections were conducted by the NLRB in 1970, there were 816 in the 1980s. Also, the number of employees involved in such elections grew and union success rates declined (i.e., unions failed to defeat a larger percentage of decertification elections).[1]

Without doubt, unions have no choice but to be interested in organizing, if only to replace members lost by attrition, particularly since there is little expansion occurring by virtue of employment growth in already recognized bargaining units. Obviously, the continual decline in union membership and density among the major unions studied here justifies intensified organizing efforts. Interviews with officials of one of the larger unions in this sample revealed that the union espouses a 100-percent commitment to recruiting new members. In other words, all activities presumably must serve the organizing purpose. While this particular union did not grow in absolute numbers between 1979 and 1993 (in fact, it had fewer members at the end of the period), it still has recruited roughly one million new members to its ranks over these years, an impressive figure but nonetheless insufficient to offset losses due to attrition and downsizing in the industries in which it operates. This single union's situation attests to the formidable task unions as a whole face, not only in just trying to keep even but in expanding their density by appreciable levels.

This chapter explores a set of union growth scenarios that demonstrate the scope of recruiting unions need to undertake in order to maintain current levels and to grow at accelerated rates. In so doing, it projects where these major unions might be relative to the workforce (i.e., their aggregate density) in the year 2000 under three different scenarios. In addition, the costs of organizing at these different paces are estimated. Finally, the chapter explores the resource implications of union mergers and the formation of superunions. Mergers, as noted before, have been advocated by some as a means of promoting union growth (Willman and Cave 1994; Stratton-Devine 1992).

UNION GROWTH SCENARIOS

Three growth scenarios are presented for the 1996–2000 period. One is steady-state membership, in which it is assumed that the twenty-eight major unions will merely hold their aggregate current membership level (more than thirteen million) over the next several years. (The base from which these unions start in these scenarios is their 1993 membership, which is the most recent year for which these numbers are available from a common source.) A second scenario is that the unions will grow by one percent each year. The third scenario is a 10-percent-per-year growth rate.

These estimates account for the membership unions must replace to achieve the alternative rates of growth (0 to 10 percent). Specifically, it is assumed that the unions, on average, must replenish 5 percent of their membership each year simply in order to keep even. To put this number into perspective, it has been estimated that turnover rates commonly vary from 2 to 35 percent, depending on industry, occupation, and the seniority distribution of the workforce (Mathis and Jackson 1991).[2] A 1990 Bureau of National Affairs (BNA) survey put average turnover rates at 4.2 percent among organizations, with the high being 38 percent.[3] Obviously, to the extent unions have greater or lesser turnover rates (and one would certainly expect considerable variation in this phenomenon given the diverse demographic, occupational, and industrial compositions of the unions), the estimates could be revised accordingly. Nevertheless, to be realistic, there must be some way to account for attrition, which all unions experience.

Table 11.1 reports the growth needs under the three scenarios. Just to remain at steady state, or more than 13,000,000 members, the twenty-eight unions would have to replace roughly 657,000 members per year, or nearly 3,300,000 members over five years, based on a 5-percent turnover rate per year between 1996 and 2000. To grow at a 1-percent-per-year rate, the unions would have to add an additional 670,000 to the more than 3,300,000 necessary replacements. In total, then, they would have to recruit over 4,000,000 into their ranks to achieve a net gain of 670,000, which would bring their total membership to almost 14,000,000 in the year 2000.

To expand at a 10-percent-per-year clip, the unions would have to achieve a net gain of eight million new recruits and replace four million others. Overall, twelve million new members would have to be recruited, which would raise the total membership to more than twenty-one million in 2000.

Obviously, adding new union recruits cannot be assessed in a vacuum but must be measured against projected growth in the labor force (or, more precisely, the number of employed persons, which is the base from which the BLS estimates density). Membership growth that fails to keep pace with the labor force will merely repeat the union experience of the 1960s and 1970s. Therefore, it is appropriate to examine the impact of these growth scenarios on the twenty-eight unions' workforce penetration. Table 11.2 compares the percentage of the workforce that the twenty-eight unions comprise in 1995 (again, based on their 1993 membership levels) to projections under the three growth scenarios for the year 2000. To compute the density rate, the number of employed persons

Table 11.1
Union Growth Scenarios (1995–2000)

Scenario	1995[1]	1996	1997	1998	1999	2000	Totals Over 5 years
(1) Steady State	13,151	13,151	13,151	13,151	13,151	13,151	
Attrition		657	657	657	657	657	3,288
(2) One Percent	--	13,282	13,415	13,549	13,685	13,822	--
Gain	--	131	133	134	135	137	670
Attrition	--	657	664	671	677	684	3,353
Addition	--	788	797	805	812	821	4,023
(3) Ten Percent	--	14,466	15,911	17,502	19,093	21,102	--
Gain	--	1,315	1,445	1,591	1,750	1,909	8,012
Attrition	--	657	723	796	875	955	4,006
Addition	--	1,972	2,168	2,387	2,625	2,864	12,016

1. The unions' 1993 combined memberships are used as a baseline for calculating subsequent estimates.

Table 11.2
Membership Density Implications of Growth Scenarios

Scenario	Number (in thousands)	2000 Year Density[1]
Steady State	13,151	.11
1-Percent Rate	13,822	.12
10-Percent Rate	21,102	.18

1. Density is calculated from a base of 116,799,000 employed persons. The density rate for 1995 (13,151,000 divided by 110,038,000) is 12 percent for these twenty-eight major unions.

in the U.S. economy is projected to be 116,779,000 in the year 2000, compared to 110,038,000 in 1995.[4] This projection is based on an employment growth rate slightly above 1 percent per year, which is the average rate that occurred between 1990 and 1995.

While at the present time the twenty-eight unions comprise approximately 12 percent of the employed workforce, their density rate would fall to 11 percent under the steady-state scenario. Growing at 1 percent per year, the unions' density rate would essentially remain unchanged, despite the acquisition of four million new recruits. Under the 10-percent projection, however, the unions' density rate would climb sharply, increasing to 18 percent of the employed workforce in 2000. To achieve this goal, the unions would have to add almost as many new recruits as they presently have as members. In other words, they would literally have to double their ranks in only five years.

How much might it cost for the unions to perform at these projected levels? Table 11.3 provides three estimates. The first is based on Voos's (1984a) analysis of organizing costs in selected manufacturing industries among twenty-five unions between 1964 and 1977. As noted, Voos (1984a: 44) found that "the marginal cost of each additional member ranged from $580 to $1,568 (1980 dollars)." Taking the midpoint of this range, the per-member cost is $1,074, or nearly $1,828 in 1995 dollars.[5] While this estimate cannot be presumed to apply to each organizing campaign across industry, occupation, region, and employer, it nonetheless provides one of the few concrete benchmarks on the costs of securing new members. For strictly comparative purposes, the costs of organizing are also estimated on a $1,000- and $500-per-person basis. To the extent that any of these three estimates understate or exaggerate the real costs of organizing, then the projected union expenditure requirements may be revised

Table 11.3
Estimated Costs of Union Growth (1996–2000, in millions)

	Estimated Costs (in millions)		
Membership Growth (in thousands)	$1,828/Member	$1,000/Member	$500/Member
Steady-State 3,288	$6,010	$3,288	$1,644
1-Percent Rate 4,023	7,354	4,023	2,011
10-Percent Rate 12,016	21,965	12,016	6,008

downward or upward. The objective here is not to attach an unassailable price tag to organizing, but rather to show the potential magnitude of investments unions might have to make as they establish strategic organizational priorities in the years to come.

Under any of the per-member estimates, the aggregate costs of organizing are quite steep. With a $1,828-per-new-recruit price tag, unions would have to spend more than $6 billion over the next five years just to stay at their current membership levels (based on the 5 percent annual attrition rate); nearly $7.4 billion to grow at 1 percent per year, which would merely maintain their current density rate; and about $22 billion to attain the 10-percent-per-year growth. The costs obviously drop by nearly one-half under the $1,000-per-recruit estimate, but large absolute sums would still have to be expended. At $500 per member, the cost of maintaining current density is over $2 billion.

To put these figures into perspective, it is instructive to compare them to the unions' total adjusted revenues in 1993. Based on this comparison, more than twenty-eight unions would have had to spend 90 percent of the nearly $1.8 billion they raised in operating income in order to maintain steady state at the cost of $500 per new recruit. The $6-billion price tag attached to growing at the 10-percent rate (again $500 per new member) is more than three times as large as their revenue intake. As the real costs of organizing move closer to the higher per-member estimates, the feasibility of financing organizing at that pace would seem to become almost inconceivable, assuming, of course, that alternative capital could not make up for the financial constraints that unions clearly face.

On this point, it is unsurprising that labor organizations are looking explicitly at creative ways to raise more money, leverage other sources of money to which they have some access, and look for human capital substitutes. Just recently, the AFL-CIO negotiated a contract with Household International Inc. to allow the company to handle the union's $3.4 billion credit card portfolio (Miller 1996: B4). Approximately 2.2 million union members hold credit cards under the Union Privilege program, and the federation should receive "more than $300 million over the next five years . . . [to] be used in part to help finance organizing efforts" (Miller 1996: B4). In addition, unions are aggressively pushing institutional investors and shareholders to use their influence to promote union objectives, including those on the organizing front. The IBT alone, for instance, has 175 pension funds with assets of $48 billion (Lublin 1996: B1). Further, the "Justice for Janitors" campaign, launched by the present head of SEIU, Andy Stern, is looked upon increasingly as the model organizing campaign. In this campaign, as suggested before, SEIU "forged alliances with local church and community groups in large cities to mount campaigns, including mass protests and civil disobedience, against owners of office buildings who subcontracted janitorial work at dirt-cheap wages" (Bernstein 1996: 73).

UNION MERGERS

Historically, unions have pursued mergers for a variety of different reasons. Stratton-Devine (1992) identifies five sets of benefits unions and their leaders might derive from merging. One is increased power at the bargaining table and in the political arena. A second is improved strategic capability to manage their affairs (unions vary widely in their skills at managing their internal operations; see Bok and Dunlop 1970). The third is the leaders' self-interest in their status or salary, which is complemented by another self-interested motivation, namely, enhanced job security. The last type of benefit is the achievement of union growth, by expanding jurisdictions and gaining additional resources and economies of scale in union operations. By merging, unions may avoid squandering precious resources fighting each other in organizing a common set of workers.

The potential or putative benefits of merging were explicitly touted when the UAW, IAM, and USW announced their planned amalgamation. Garland et al. (1995: 42) describe four specific benefits of this "mega-union":

Organizing. Stop the waste of resources and energy expended when the three unions fight each other during membership drives. That should help their efforts to organize more high-tech industries.

Bargaining. Add negotiating muscle, especially at large companies that now deal with multiple unions.

Lobbying. Become a major political force, with a super-PAC and the capacity to organize massive grassroots campaigns.

International Expansion. More effectively coordinate with Mexican, Asian, and other overseas unions to organize offshore U.S. plants.

The expected benefits of mergers no doubt have contributed to the accelerated pace of mergers that began in the 1970s, in comparison to the two prior decades. Indeed, heightened merger activity is a strategy that the AFL-CIO officially sanctioned in its introspective report by a special committee on the evolution of work (1985). In fact, it has been argued that this mega-union "merger will likely speed consolidation among other unions, whittling them down to 20 from 100—much like the mega-unions dominant in Western Europe" (Garland et al. 1995: 42). Since 1987, for example, at least four "superunions" have been formed in the United Kingdom. This wave of mergers represents "a departure from the traditional merger process involving the absorption of small unions by large ones and reflects the use of the merger process by the largest unions to protect their relative membership share" (Willman and Cave 1994: 395).

But there are potential downsides to mergers. As Willman and Cave (1994: 410) note regarding the merger wave that has led to the aforementioned creation of superunions in the United Kingdom: "It is not clear that mergers are the best solution to . . . [union] problems. Mergers eliminate competition, but do not necessarily realize scale economies. In so far as they frequently maintain sections or divisional structures representing previous union affiliations, it is not clear that they sit easily with representational effectiveness . . . Neither collaborative arrangements nor full merger solve the central problem of union growth." A key problem associated with mergers identified by Willman and Cave (1994: 395) is that "merger activity displaces efforts to organize the non-union sector." Thus, mergers that do not increase the commitment of resources to organizing the unorganized miss one of the central putative benefits of amalgamating. In this vein, Chaison (1986) examined the growth implications of union mergers in the cases of AFSCME, SEIU, UFCW, and the Brotherhood of Railway and Airline Clerks. He found, among other things, that about half of AFSCME's growth in the 1975–1984 period was accounted for by mergers, and most of SEIU's growth in 1980–1984 was due to absorptions of other labor organizations. In a broader statement, Chaison (1986: 115,117) echoes Willman and Caves's (1994) warning:

> Absorption can be viewed as a fast, effective, and relatively inexpensive form of organizing which results in the movement of members from one union to another . . . but produces no net gain in aggregate membership unless the absorption is followed by organizing campaigns among unorganized workers. It is also possible that the ability to 'organize unions' through absorption may be counterproductive to the labor movement because it may reduce the incentive to organize in the traditional sense . . . . Accordingly, individual union growth through absorptions could actually result in a decline in aggregate union growth.

Therefore, to succeed in achieving growth, merged unions should expand not only their resource bases but also their resource allocations to organizing-related activities. "Collaborative arrangements which concentrate recruiting expertise may deploy union resources better than merger arrangements founded on other concerns, but the central question—Who pays?—remains paramount" (Willman and Cave 1994: 410).

Ongoing and Superunion Mergers

As suggested, the allocation of additional resources to organizing may even be more of a critical issue among merged unions, which may experience a false sense of institutional security by their mere combination. Therefore, it is relevant to examine the resource implications of union mergers. This analysis proceeds at two levels (see Table 11.4). The first examines selected resources of recent and planned mergers. It involves the UFCW plus RWDSU; ACTWU and ILGWU into UNITE; and the Metals union (UAW, IAM, and USW). The second level constructs a set of superunions, or broad union consolidations around major industries and occupations. The Education superunion includes the AFT and NEA. The State and Local Service giant includes AFSCME, IAFF, and SEIU. The Federal Service consists of the AFGE, NFFE, and NTEU, while the Postal Employees includes APWU, NALC, and NRLCA. TranServe combines the IBT with UFCW, RWDSU, and CWA. Manufacturing is made up of the UAW, IBEW, IAM, USW, UPIU, ACTWU, IUE, and ILGWU. Last, the Building superunion combines CJA, LIU, IUOE, and PPI.

Table 11.4 reports various human, financial, and political capital measures for the merged unions. Among the current or planned mergers, the Mega-Metals union has about 1.7 million members and net assets in excess of $1.4 billion, or $850 per member. Its combined income was almost $430 million in 1993, and its PAC raised nearly $9.2 million in 1994, or more than $5 per member. The Mega-Metals union's organizing reserve includes approximately 8,000 members, which amounts to an imputed $600 million investment in organizers.

Adding the RWDSU modestly increases the UFCW's membership to about 1.1 million and improves its wealth situation, reducing its deficit to $10 million. Compared to UNITE and Mega-Metals, however, the UFCW-Plus has a low income and PAC base, on a per-member basis, but its organizing reserve squad is worth an estimated $388 million. UNITE's reserve value is a more modest $99 million, due to its smaller membership.

The superunion data highlight the financial strength of the manufacturing sector unions. With just about three million members, the Manufacturing superunion's wealth comes close to $2 billion, or $636 per member. Its adjusted income is over $630 million, or $212 per member, and its PAC raised $4.43 per member with an intake of more than $13 million. Its organizing reserve would translate into an imputed $1.1 billion investment.

Table 11.4
Capital Implications of Current Mergers and Superunions (1993)

Merger	Membership	Wealth (in millions)[1]	Wealth Per-Member	Operating Income (in millions)[1]	Income Per-Member	1993-1994 PAC Receipts (in millions)[1]	PAC Per-Member	Organizing Reserve Squad	Imputed Reserve Investment (in millions)[1]
Current									
Food and Commercial Workers-Plus	1,077,000	$-10	($-9.04)	$124	($114.82)	$2.3	($2.15)	5,170	$388
UNITE	276,000	219	(792.78)	93	(336.75)	1.0	(3.65)	1,325	99
Mega-Metals	1,666,000	1,416	(849.91)	429	(257.59)	9.2	(5.53)	7,997	600
Super Union									
Education	2,674,000	78	(29.05)	247	(92.47)	6.8	(2.55)	12,835	963
State and Local Service	2,237,000	62	(27.94)	156	(69.68)	7.6	(3.41)	10,738	805
Federal Service	253,782	7	(27.67)	37	(147.06)	.5	(2.06)	1,218	91
Postal Employees	539,600	67	(124.09)	68	(125.73)	3.4	(6.28)	2,590	194
TranServe	3,123,000	155	(49.76)	339	(108.43)	13.7	(4.38)	14,990	112
Manufacturing	2,983,000	1,896	(635.58)	634	(212.51)	13.2	(4.43)	14,318	1,074
Building	1,341,000	452	(336.96)	171	(127.96)	4.7	(3.53)	6,437	483

Sources: Membership from Gifford (1994); finances from LM-2 annual reports; PAC receipts from U.S. FEC (1995a).
1. Monetary numbers are in actual dollars, unadjusted for inflation. Total monetary numbers are rounded to the nearest million.

TranServe would be the biggest superunion in terms of membership, with more than a $1.1 billion organizing reserve price tag. Financially, however, it pales in comparison to the Manufacturing giant, though TranServe would have the biggest PAC, based on 1994 data. On a per-member basis, the Postal Employees have the largest PAC, while the Federal Service PAC is almost empty. Compared to the Manufacturing and Building superunions, the others appear weak on the wealth dimension, as are the Education and State and Local Service unions in terms of income. However, the latter two have nominally large PACs, and a combined organizing reserve of more than 23,000, with an imputed financial investment of nearly $1.8 billion.

CONCLUSIONS

The data vividly show the formidable challenge unions face in reversing their membership fortunes and the enormous resource commitments they might have to make in order to do so. While total union membership in the United States has declined in all but two years in the past fifteen years or so, this does not imply that unions have gained no new members. Instead, unions as a whole have been unable to (1) offset attrition; and (2) keep pace with employment growth. To increase their density, unions must not only do each of these, but must also exceed the expansion in the number of employed persons. Increased attrition rates and employment growth (in the nonunion sector, where most is anticipated to occur) merely exacerbate this task.

The major twenty-eight unions, given a 5 percent annual attrition rate, must add 657,000 persons per year to stay at steady state. An additional 130,000 must be added per year to achieve a modest one-percent growth rate over the 1996–2000 period. More than twelve million new recruits need to be acquired in these years in order for the major unions to raise their density from 11 percent to 18 percent.

As employers and government (at least at the federal level) generally seem disinclined to enter any bipartite or tripartite pact with labor to facilitate union-organizing efforts, the costs of achieving growth under any of the scenarios are bound to seem intimidating. They range from more than $1.6 billion to maintain steady-state membership at a $500-per-recruit price tag, to more than $22 billion to achieve 10-percent annual growth at $1800-plus per head.

To the extent any of these cost estimates are on target, funding such an organizing program within existing budgeting conditions is unrealistic. While unions could dramatically raise their financial commitment to this effort by spending one-third of their operating disbursements (as shown in the previous chapter), they must look to leverage human capital and other financial resources. Mobilizing a sizable organizing reserve would thus seem imperative, as would leveraging pension funds and other sources of money to which unions have access (Lublin 1996: 31–32). Relatedly, to the extent political capital—coupled with union-based political reserves—can be used to reduce the costs of organizing, or at least increase employers' resistance costs, then it should be directed to that end, especially in targeted localities and states (or congressional districts) likely to yield maximum impact.

As a final conclusion, the advent of union mergers and the possibility of superunions would undoubtedly result in some nominally well-equipped unions. But merging alone does not reverse the membership decline or create an overall bigger pie. Forthcoming mergers or conceivable superunions must still confront the issues of resource allocation and mobilization. Nonetheless, the prospect of bold new mergers suggests that unions are rethinking their positions and looking for ways to harness resources. The ultimate test is whether these mergers can forge the kind of commitment to the labor struggle necessary to attract the volunteers and cement the broad-based alliances to facilitate organizing a changing and increasingly diverse workforce.

NOTES

1. In the 1980s, an average of 816 decertification elections per year were held, compared to 301 in 1970 and 237 in 1960. Unions lost approximately three-fourths of the elections in the 1980s. An average of 37,260 employees were eligible to vote for decertification in that decade. Decertification activity has fallen in the 1990s. In 1994, 493 elections involving 21,933 eligible voters occurred. Unions won only 34 percent of these contests (U.S. NLRB 1996).

2. Mathis and Jackson (1991: 91) report "that normal turnover rates vary among industries . . . . New employees are more likely to leave than employees who have been on the job longer."

3. The *BNA's Quarterly Report on Job Absence and Turnover, 4th Quarter, 1990* (1991) was discussed in Ivancevich (1992: 780).

4. Note that union density rates are based on the number of employed persons, not the size of the labor force, which includes both employed and unemployed ranks.

5. The CPI rate for 1980 is .822, and for 1995 it is 1.524. The midpoint was multiplied by 1.702.

Chapter 12

Strategies for Union Growth

At the crossroads, organized labor faces a series of strategic and tactical decisions on how to reverse its seemingly unstoppable shrinkage in the workforce and set itself on a steady upward path. John Sweeney, upon assuming the AFL-CIO's helm, has energized the federation with a flurry of new activity. Grassroots mobilization is the wind behind the invigorated union sail, copied much after the civil rights movement of the turbulent 1960s. The federation has launched a "Union Summer" campaign to enlist supporters on the nation's college campuses, created a better-financed Organizing Department, stepped up political action, and, at the same time, pushed its affiliate unions to follow suit. The AFL-CIO's highly publicized $35 million campaign to reelect Clinton–Gore and a Democratic U.S. Congress in 1996 underscores organized labor's new-found brass-tacks approach. The unprecedented multimillion-dollar plan, which aroused considerable ire among Republican leaders, evidently produced some successful results, as eighteen of the forty-five principal GOP targets were defeated.

Altogether, these and various other recent developments undertaken by individual unions represent a departure from the traditional "parachute in," reactive approach, in which labor *responded* to events by assigning paid representatives to orchestrate whatever worker support that might exist in local settings. A strategic question facing labor, however, is whether this bolder approach will work better or, more critically, well enough to reverse the downward trend in membership density. This issue raises the need to present a framework to facilitate the systematic analysis of the strategies and tactics available for union growth. No one strategy or tactic can be assessed in isolation from the others available. Inescapably, given present difficulties, unions must think creatively and expansively on how to link strategic and tactical options for maximum effect.

Without dispute, irreversible environmental factors, such as economic globalization and restructuring, will affect the capacity of unions to affect their future. Indeed, some, such as Troy (1995), argue vigorously that these trends are inherently so unfavorable that organized labor's days as a major economic and political player may be decidedly numbered, especially in the case of unions among private sector employees. But the historical ebb and flow of U.S. union membership and density suggests that this fate is not inevitable. The challenge facing unions is not to stop the unavoidable forces of change but rather to exploit or capitalize on them. To succeed, the labor movement must adopt a panoply of strategies and tactics that run in alignment with rather than directly opposite to the economic realities of today and tomorrow. Unions must capture, as they did in the 1930s, the spirit and needs of the time and leverage the political world to expand such opportunities. While the ideological conservativism of the Gingrich–Armey Republican Congress may be hostile to labor's traditional legislative agenda, it may ironically create opportunities to mold a new program that enlivens the rank and file and attracts new members.[1]

At this point, it is important to stress that what follows are *options* from which labor may pick and choose as circumstances warrant. A variety of different combinations of these strategic and tactical alternatives may be both plausible and desirable. Unquestionably, unions will have to be pliable, emphasizing those activities likely to yield the highest benefit/cost ratio at any given time or over whatever horizon seems reasonable. The basic notion, however, is that a systematic, coordinated approach to growth is needed, in which unions maximize the potential for gain by employing their current and future options for the explicit purpose of swelling their ranks on a scale unseen in several decades past. Perhaps more than present memory can recall, unions need to think "outside-of-the-box." They need to explore new approaches toward which their valuable resources might be deployed. It is in this spirit that the following thoughts are offered.

STRATEGIC APPROACHES AND TACTICS

Figure 12.1 elaborates various approaches unions might pursue to promote growth. The ultimate union goal in this context is increased density, which can be facilitated by strategies and tactics that reduce the costs of unionizing and increase the commitment of resources directly or indirectly aimed at growth. Strategies and tactics will be targeted toward specific growth opportunities, depending upon various environmental and

Figure 12.1
Union Growth Strategies

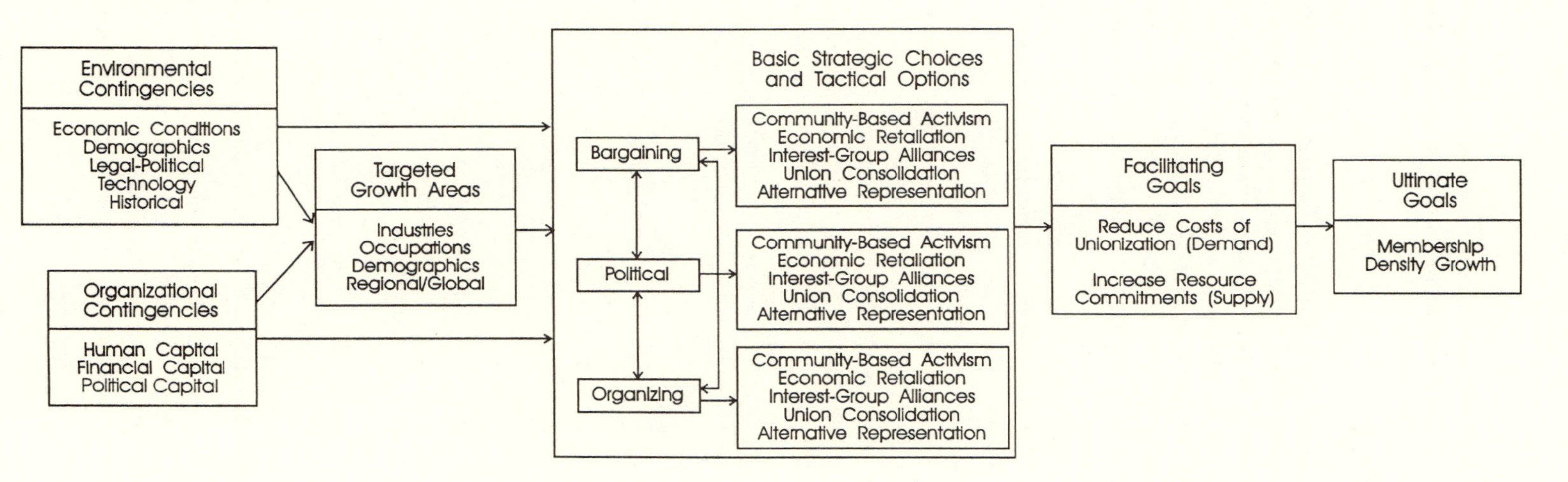

organizational contexts or contingencies, which in turn will affect the relative capacities of unions to exercise certain options.

Ultimate Goals

The framework stresses the willingness of unions to depart from the traditional focus on achieving exclusive bargaining rights via formal certification campaigns. Instead, the organizing goals should be to increase membership and density per se, even if this means avoiding the certification route. The central point is that unions need to grow in ranks if they are to remain economically and politically viable. Exclusive bargaining representation, which requires majority status among workers unions seek to represent, is only one form of serving employees and securing membership. Its attainment, moreover, often comes at a very high price, especially under the current labor-relations framework that allows employers to resist certification aggressively (Rose and Chaison 1995).[2] Along this line, Rogers (1995: 375) has argued that unions should lessen their reliance on achieving majority status and, hence, exclusive representation rights in favor of a more regional (as opposed to firm-specific), coordinated, multi-union organizing strategy that emphasizes a different type of representation that serves the production needs of employers and the job-security (e.g., mobility and transferability) interests of employees:

> At least in today's organizing climate, the preoccupation with *majority status* imposes too demanding a condition on the needed coordination across [employer] sites. It also carries enormous opportunity costs for membership growth, since in virtually all workplaces some significant percentage of workers now wish to belong to unions; to gear organizing only to those sites where such workers are in the majority is to abandon a huge market. Economic restructuring has made employer investment, relocation, technology, and training decisions decisive for member well-being; unions can no longer afford to *ignore the control of production*. (Rogers 1995: 375)

In fact, there is evidence that shows that a sizable portion of real and potential demand for union representation is unfulfilled. In the fall of 1994, Richard Freeman and Joel Rogers conducted a national survey on workers' attitudes toward unions and various other workplace issues. The final report of the U.S. Commission on the Future of Worker–Management Relations (1994b) highlights the findings of their "Worker Representation and Participation Survey" of more than 2,400 workers in the private sector, where, to repeat, union membership is a paltry 10.4 percent. Among the key findings that indicate opportunities for unions to exploit are the following:

- A third of the surveyed workers do not "look forward" to going to work on the average day (U.S. Commission on the Future of Worker–Management Relations 1994b: 64); 41 percent and 42 percent of lower-income and African-American workers, respectively, expressed similar sentiments;

- While 64 percent of the employees feel loyal to their companies, only 38 percent trust their companies to keep promises made to them;
- Almost two-thirds (63 percent) of the workers indicated that they want more influence at work;
- Depending upon the specific question asked, between 43 and 57 percent of the employees "say they would feel more comfortable raising work problems through an employee association or with the help of fellow employees, rather than as an individual" (U.S. Commission on the Future of Worker–Management Relations 1994b: 64); and
- A third of the nonunion employees surveyed would vote for a union, and almost 80 percent of the employees believe that management cooperation is the key to the success of employee organization.

Based on these data, if unions were to succeed in organizing those workers who have expressed support for such representation, they would achieve a density rate comparable to their apex in the 1940s and 1950s. More important, certain forms of more cooperative workplace representation, outside the context of exclusive representation, might receive substantially greater support among workers, and they might also provoke much less employer opposition. In theory, as well as in practice, unions might play a key role in such representation. Organized labor could even consider the heretical step of backing the relaxation of the NLRA's 8(a)(2) ban on certain employee–employer decision-making arrangements so as to encourage employee involvement and, furthermore, promote worker–council types of representation that might provide a springboard for union growth.[3]

The strategies and tactics unions pursue facilitate union growth (or at least intend to do so) by either reducing the costs of unionizing or increasing the commitment of resources (i.e., human, financial, and political capital) toward that end. To organize, employees often incur significant personal cost and risk (McDonald 1987; 1992). They must invest time and energy and may alienate co-workers who hold different views. Also, union supporters may jeopardize their jobs when confronted by hostile employers (Peterson, Lee, and Finnegan 1992). Arguably, these costs and risks escalate as the formal certification process accelerates. In addition, employees that join a union incur a direct financial cost, including initiation charges and regular dues, plus whatever other special assessments and fees may be levied. One approach, then, that unions might take is to pursue strategies that will lower these costs, perhaps either by easing the burden of forming/joining union-type organizations or lessening the incentives for employer opposition. By reducing the costs of unionizing, employee demand for union representation (of various kinds) might be increased or better exploited.

Another approach, which is not by any stretch of logic mutually exclusive, is to increase the commitment of resources to organizing new members. A widespread criticism of labor unions has been the general neglect of such effort. To the extent unions as a whole have placed minimal emphasis on organizing, the potential demand for union membership and representation has probably been undercapitalized. In effect, the result is too few paid organizers, organizing volunteers, and community-based initiatives to serve the demand for union representation. Furthermore, bargaining and political activities may have been too loosely tied to organizing drives. Indeed, the failure to link these activities to organizing is perhaps one reason why there appears to be a trade-off between representing current employees and organizing new ones.

Targeted Growth Areas

The efforts of unions will necessarily be targeted to those areas where maximum gain is both likely and essential. As observed in Chapter 2, union membership levels and trends have varied across industry, occupation, and demographic group. Further, they have also differed across regional areas, being for example, relatively low in density in the southern region of the United States.[4] In determining which specific areas to target, unions need to know at least three key pieces of information: (1) What are the current levels of density? (2) What have been the trends in the recent past?; and (3) What will the level of employment be in these areas over the next several years? In determining targets for growth, unions must balance those areas where they currently have a relative advantage in terms of density, sectors which are likely to grow at high rates and areas which will constitute a large portion of the workforce in the future, regardless of extant density levels, recent density trends, and expected population growth rates.

Table 12.1 reports these key data. Specifically, it presents the 1985 and 1995 density rates in major gender, race, age, industry,and occupation categories, as well as the trend, or percentage change, over the past decade. It also reports the percentage change, according to "moderate" estimates provided by the BLS, in projected labor-force population in these same categories for the 1992–2005 period.[5] Based on these BLS "moderate" rates, projected labor-force and employment levels for the year 2005 are presented.

The data pose a challenging picture for unions. First, unions must do considerably better in organizing among both women and men. Starting with a relatively lower density rate that has nonetheless declined in the past decade, women will increase their presence in the workforce at a much faster pace than men. At the same time, the union density rate among men fell more steeply between 1985 and 1995 than it did among women. Further, the male labor-force population will increase by another 14 percent (1992–2005) to nearly seventy-nine million, or nearly seven million more than the projected female population.

Second, density rates fell most steeply among the racial groups (i.e., Hispanics and African-Americans) that are expected to grow fastest.[6] If current trends continue, the density rates among Hispanics and African-Americans will fall from 13 percent and 20 percent, respectively, to 9 percent and 16 percent. These trends clearly suggest that labor will have to work increasingly harder to attract minorities to their ranks in order to maintain existing density levels, especially given the projected growth in population among these groups. While doing so, however, unions can ill afford to neglect the majority white population, where density fell almost as sharply as it did among African-Americans during 1985–1995. Even if all Hispanics (who in most BLS statistical reports, until recently, may technically fall into any racial category) were classified as nonwhite, whites will still comprise close to 73 percent of the labor force in 2005. To maintain a 14.2 percent density rate among non-Hispanic whites, white union membership would have to grow by nearly 2.4 million members (from 11.7 million in 1995 to 14.1 million) by the year 2005, based on a projected wage and salary workforce of 136.3 million.[7] To put this number into perspective, it is equal to at least 63 percent of the current 3.87 million African-American and Hispanic union members (it is at least this percentage because Hispanics may be double counted to some extent due to their multiple racial classifications).[8]

Third, in terms of age, current density rates are low among the 16–24-year-old group and have fallen the most significantly, in percentage terms, among this group since 1985. Further, population among this group is expected to grow only modestly more than among those in the 25–54-year-old group. Although relative growth (in percentage terms) is expected to be highest among those 55 and older, the overwhelming bulk (almost 70 percent) of the labor-force population will fall into the 25–54 range. Thus, while organized labor clearly has an interest in remaining stable or growing in the 16–24 and (especially) 55-and-over groups, it must make much greater inroads among those who will be between 25 and 54 by the year 2005. Thus, those who are now in their early twenties, thirties, and forties are critical targets.

Fourth, on the industry front, nonagricultural private sector employment growth will be proportionately greater than in the government, rising 24 percent to 111 million jobs. If the union density rate in the private sector were to fall by the same percentage it did between 1985 and 1995 (28.8 percent) over the next ten years, it would stand at 7.4 percent in 2005. This would translate into 8.2 million union members in that year versus 9.4 million in 1995. To keep the density rate at 10.4 percent, an additional two million workers would have to be unionized (11.54 million in 2005 in comparison to 9.4 million in 1995).

Within private industry, employment in the mining, construction, transportation, and finance sectors is expected to stay relatively small, regardless of change rates. In the mining sector, in particular, it is projected

Table 12.1
Union Growth Target Opportunities

	Union Density Trends			Labor Force Growth[1]		
Major Category	(1995) Current	1985	Percentage Change	Percentage Change 1992-2005	Projected Level, 2005 (in millions)[2]	Targeted Area[3]
Gender						
Men	17.2%	22.1%	-22.2%	13.8%	78.7	G
Women	12.3	13.2	-6.8	24.2	71.8	G
Race						
White	14.2	17.3	-17.9	15.0	124.8	G
African-American	19.9	24.3	-18.1	25.2	17.4	G
Hispanic[4]	13.0	18.9	-31.2	63.7	16.6	G
Age						
16-24 yrs.	6.7	9.2	-27.2	18.0	24.1	S
25-54	19.1	25.0	-23.6	15.3	105.0	G
≥ 55	20.3	26.7	-24.0	38.3	21.3	S
Industry						
Private Nonagriculture	10.4	14.6	-28.8	24.3	110.9	G
Mining	13.8	17.3	-20.2	-.10	.6	S
Construction	17.7	22.3	-20.6	26.0	5.6	S
Manufacturing	17.6	24.8	-29.0	-2.9	17.5	G

to be less than 0.5 percent of total nonagricultural private industry employment. Although the transportation sector is the most densely unionized industry outside of government, a 100 percent unionization rate among the 6.5 million employees projected in 2005 would yield less than 6 percent of the total 111 million nonagricultural private sector workers. In contrast, the finance sector has the lowest rate of unionization (just above 2 percent), with the second largest decline in density (after manufacturing) rate between 1985 and 1995.

To achieve a considerable reversal in aggregate density rates, unions must clearly concentrate on services, trade, and manufacturing industries, which will collectively comprise almost 80 percent of all nonagricultural private sector employment in 2005, notwithstanding the projected drop in manufacturing jobs. Employment in the services and trade industries will rise proportionately more than in any other major private sector industry, and

Table 12.1 ***(continued)***

Major Category	Union Density Trends (1995) Current	1985	Percentage Change	Labor Force Growth[1] Percentage Change 1992-2005	Projected Level, 2005 (in millions)[2]	Targeted Area[3]
Industry						
Private Nonagriculture	10.4	14.6	-28.8	24.3	110.9	G
Transportation	27.3	37.0	-26.2	13.8	6.5	S
Trade	6.1	7.2	-15.3	22.0	31.0	G
Finance	2.1	2.9	-27.6	21.3	8.0	S
Services	5.7	6.6	-13.6	47.0	41.8	G
Government	37.8	35.8	5.6	18.1	22.0	G
Occupation						
Managerial/Professional	13.8	15.2	-9.2	32.6	38.0	G
Technical/Sales	9.9	10.8	-8.3	17.9	46.7	G
Service	13.5	14.4	-6.2	33.4	25.8	G
Precision Production	23.3	23.5	-18.2	13.3	15.4	S
Operators/Laborers	23.0	31.8	-27.7	9.5	17.9	S

Source: U.S. DOL, BLS (1986; 1993; 1996b).

1. Based on "moderate growth projections" estimated by the U.S. DOL, BLS (1993b).
2. Gender, race, and age numbers are based on labor force participation; industry and occupation numbers are based on projected employment levels.
3. Targeted area refers to whether unions should emphasize growth (G) or stability (S), depending on the overall number of employees projected in the demographic category and the projected rates of growth.
4. Hispanics may be of any race; hence there is double counting in the white and African-American categories to the extent that Hispanics are classified in either category. The U.S. DOL, BLS (December 1, 1993) estimates that there will be 109.7 million white, non-Hispanics in 2005, or 73 percent of the labor force.

both have had low union density rates. Despite a projected 3-percent fall in manufacturing employment, almost eighteen million jobs will remain there.

The occupational data indicate that unions will have to grow in those three areas where their presence is currently small and their legal standing (to the extent it pertains to supervisors, managers, executives, and administrators) is somewhat problematic.[9] Employment in managerial/professional, technical, and service occupations will comprise nearly 80 percent of the total jobs by the year 2005. Unions must substantially accelerate inroads in these job sectors if their general situation is to improve. Even if 100 percent of the precision production and operator classes of work were organized, which would require sharp departures from density trends between 1985 and 1995, unions would still account for less than 25 percent of the projected 133 million nonagricultural workforce by the year 2005 (the actual percentage may be less given that some of these workers may be self-employed and thus not included in the 133 million nonfarm wage and salary workers).

In sum, these data suggest that unions must adopt a broad-based, multigroup organizing strategy to reverse widespread patterns of decline. They must make impressive gains among men *and* women, whites *and* nonwhites. Unions must focus on making major gains among those employees who will be between 25 and 54 ten years from now. In addition, while holding their own, or perhaps even advancing in the public sector, unions must establish a sizable presence in the service and trade industries. Similarly, they need to arrest their spiraling downfall in the manufacturing sector and recapture the once pivotal position they held in that area. While staving off further shrinkage in density among precision production workers and operators, unions cannot avoid making sizable gains in the professional, technical, and service ranks if density levels are to rise appreciably. Bluntly, there is not much of the workforce—in demographic, occupation, and industry terms—that labor can afford to avoid. To grow, organized labor must literally advance across the board, exploiting common opportunities and needs among these diverse groups of employees. Niche strategies, unless frequent and coordinated enough to have considerable breadth, seem unlikely to offer much advantage. While, as noted in Chapter 2, there are some groups (e.g., minorities and government employees) in which unions have gained in either absolute membership or density, the overall challenge remains daunting, as the decline in union density is demographically, industrially, and occupationally wide.

Environmental and Organizational Contingencies

The various environmental and organizational contexts within which unions operate will affect the viability of any particular strategic or tactical approaches taken. Also, they will affect the viability of target growth areas. In this regard, the demographic and economic contexts which will affect the composition and structure of the workforce have been discussed in terms of where unions must target growth if density is to be noticeably enhanced.

In a broader sense, unions will continually face the economic realities of competitiveness, corporate restructuring, and globalization, which will greatly affect the approaches used to organize. As an illustration, the recently announced merger between Bell Atlantic and Nynex has provoked concerns that some of the 127,000 jobs in the combined $27 billion telecommunication giant will be lost. The CWA and IBEW have both pledged to resist the merger in order to preserve their members' jobs (McElroy and Morrison 1996: A10). Encouraged by the recently enacted deregulation of telecommunications, the announced merger must still receive approval from various state and federal regulators, before whom the unions intend to press their opposition. In any event, this situation demonstrates the potential import of the legal–political environment. The economic deregulation of such industries as trucking, the airlines, and telecommunications arguably intensifies competitive pressures, which affect jobs and the unions which represent displaced workers. The CWA has lost thousands of members in the telecommunications industry since the divestiture of AT&T in 1984, which was brought about by an antitrust suit initiated by the U.S. Department of Justice in 1974. In response, the CWA has aggressively organized, adding 85,000 new members in the "information" industry through organizing campaigns and mergers (Keefe and Boroff 1994: 341). In this regard, the CWA's efforts to organize "wall-to-wall" within this ever-broadening industry have resulted in its merger with the International Typographical Union (adding 40,000 members) in 1987, the addition of 9,100 new members from organizing under "neutrality" agreements, and 3,300 new members in the face of stiff corporate opposition (Keefe and Boroff 1994: 342).

Also, the prevailing ideology within the political climate will greatly affect not only labor's capacity to influence elections but also the likelihood of public-policy changes that will reduce the costs of unionizing, thus increasing the demand for and supply of union-organizing initiatives. To the extent that the national mood makes it unlikely that Congress, regardless of which party is in control, will revamp labor law to facilitate organizing, unions will have to consider political alternatives (e.g., concentrate on state and local lawmakers, where they might have greater influence) or leverage bargaining and organizing strategies to greater advantage.

Obviously, the technological context will affect unions through short and long term impacts on the structure of employment. While union jobs may be lost through restructuring, opportunities for organizing may materialize. Technological change, given its rapidity, generates enormous pressure on employees and employers to train and upgrade skill levels. Unions, as Rogers (1995) indicates, might significantly benefit from participating in this process.

A central theme here is that the human, financial, and political capital of unions will affect, at any given time, the capacity of unions to shape certain outcomes. The availability of these forms of capital will also directly impact the strategic and tactical options available to unions. Deficits in one area (e.g., a union is cash poor) may need to be compensated for in another (deployment of human capital, including the current membership and activists in allied groups).[10] Also, unions may have to expand the pie by broadening their base of grassroot alliances, taxing their members more for additional revenue, and educating rank and file as to the need to give more to their PACs, particularly where PAC contributions can have maximum impact (which may often be at the state and local level more so than in national politics).

Strategic and Tactical Options

Within each of the primary strategic areas unions may exercise power to grow, at least five conceptually distinguishable tactical options exist: community-based activism; economic retaliation; interest-group alliances; union consolidation; and alternative representation forms. These options, as suggested earlier, may be pursued exclusively or in conjunction with each other. Again, their objective, in an intermediate sense, is to reduce the costs of organizing and increase the commitment of resources to achieve the ultimate purpose of substantially higher levels of density.

Bargaining Strategy. This strategy leverages labor's extant relationships with employers to facilitate unionization. While in practice it revolves principally around units where unions have achieved formal recognition based on majority status, it need not be so restricted in concept. Alternative forms of worker representation might be established from which unions could extract additional advantage. The focus here, however, is leveraging current bargaining relationships in a formal sense to achieve agreements that promote union growth, perhaps through non-traditional union-management relations shy of majority recognition.

More specifically, a bargaining strategy would emphasize utilizing various tactics to achieve three types of agreements (or negotiating objectives): (1) to preserve and expand union jobs; (2) to expedite recognizing new units; and (3) to recognize new forms of worker representation in nonunion settings where a minority union presence exists. The first set of agreements would reduce or bar those employment-related practices that jeopardize union jobs in recognized units; namely, outsourcing, hiring temporary and part-time employees, and exploiting overtime. It would also involve investments in existing unionized facilities to upgrade technology, limit the relocation of unionized facilities to nonunion locales, and establish joint labor–management training programs to improve the skills (and hence job security and mobility) of unionized workers who face displacement. Such training programs might also create a pool of qualified workers from which employers might recruit for their various sites.

A second bargaining objective aims to expedite the organizing process. Three forms of facilitating provisions might be negotiated into bargaining agreements: accretion, neutrality, and card-checking. The objective is to circumvent the cumbersome certification process and minimize employer opposition, which is widely regarded as substantial hinderance to union success in achieving formal majority status and, hence, exclusive representation rights.

The third type of agreement is more novel or nontraditional. Recognizing that firms may open nonunion facilities in the process of expanding and that it may be extremely difficult to achieve majority status in many of these facilities, unions might nonetheless seek to secure worker rights in these settings that create incentives for employees to join a labor organization or association. For instance, unions might secure an agreement to establish formal grievance procedures in nonunion settings as a way of giving employees a voice and mitigating employment-related (e.g., equal employment opportunity [EEO]) litigation. Unions might offer associate membership status to employees in such sites, providing grievance representation should the need arise among associate members. Unions thus demonstrate their commitment to worker rights and provide an individual-specific, work-related reason for someone to join the ranks (e.g., pay partial or full dues). These benefits might encourage workers to vote for union certification at some point down the road, thus representing a more popular inducement than the consumer benefits (e.g., insurance, credit cards) typically conferred by associate membership. Along this line, research among local government employees suggests that *associations* of current employees which concentrate on work-related services may be linked to eventual bargaining representation. As Ichniowski and Zax (1990: 205–206) note:

> Associations encourage the formation of bargaining units in several ways. They reduce the costs of organizing; they offer an opportunity to introduce ideas of collective action without conforming to the legal regulations of recognition drives; and they offer an opportunity to demonstrate the importance of collective action to employers.... The ability of associations to promote collective bargaining in the private sector, however, could be limited because private sector associate membership programs... currently lack certain characteristics of public sector associations. Perhaps most important, associations in the local public sector are workplace-specific with current employees as members. In contrast, most private sector associations are not workplace-specific, and many members of private sector associations are retirees and workers on layoff. Associations that have no workplace-specific identity, and that may not even include working members, are unlikely to be called upon to be bargaining agents.

Relatedly, associations of employees or associate membership programs that concentrate on the work-related representation of current employees may enhance the overall image of unions. Such image-building, in turn, could bolster unions' chances of achieving majority status recognition. Jarley and Fiorito (1990: 223) found a correlation between "general attitudes toward unions" and support for both associate membership status and union representation in a more formal sense, concluding that "to the extent that unions can improve their general image, membership levels via both traditional and nontraditional avenues are likely to rise."

It is recognized that this is a form of backdoor union involvement. Promoting the use of minority forms of nonexclusive union representation and employee involvement programs that cover a wide array of areas (e.g., quality, productivity, safety, and health) may run afoul of existing labor law (i.e., section 8(a)(2)) which unions vigorously protect. Unions might, however, consider sponsoring such alternative forms of representation, while protecting exclusive bargaining rights in formally recognized units. The NLRA could be amended to explicitly allow such representation, requiring employee participation in the selection of employee representatives and protecting union rights to help service such alternative involvement forums (for broader discussions of NLRA amendment along these lines, see Weiler 1993; Delaney 1996; Coxson 1996; and Gould 1993).

To pursue these specific objectives, unions might use a combination of the five tactics enumerated earlier. In particular, they could launch a multi-union, grassroots coordinated bargaining campaign in a community or even wider geographical region to pressure employers across industries to support these goals. In the process, union members and their families would become activists, "lobbying" owners, managers, and community leaders to support their job-preserving, workplace-justice priorities. A second tactic would be to threaten or actually retaliate against recalcitrant employers. Such a tactic might include job actions (strikes or slowdowns), boycotts, public protests, or economic disinvestment initiatives (e.g., mobilizing shareholders or potential investors to withdraw support).

Third, unions might form various interest-group alliances to support their goals. They might ally themselves with consumer-protection, minority, religious, and civic action groups on an ad hoc basis to pressure employers. Closely related to a community action campaign, this tactic leverages whatever influence these groups might have over recalcitrant employers, whether it is the capacity to sway public opinion, persuade important business suppliers and customers, or enhance capacity to finance an expensive battle of litigation against an employer.

Fourth, unions could agree to merge or combine ranks within an industry or particular region to maximize their bargaining clout. Finally, they might seek representation on various corporate and other business-related boards of directors to gain a broader economic voice that might be directed to serve these specific bargaining (organizing!) interests.

Political Strategy. In the realm of politics (or the legal-enactment process), unions could seek three public-policy goals that would directly or indirectly encourage unionism. Two have already been noted: (1) securing policies, such as an increase in the minimum wage, that raise the cost of labor of nonunion employees; and (2) reducing the costs of organizing by reforming labor relations law. Reforms could include granting automatic recognition upon a majority-status petition, increasing the sanctions against employers who violate employees' right to organize, prohibiting certain employer practices (e.g., captive audience speeches) that may hinder union success, mandating arbitration of first-contract impasses (thus strengthening unions' ability to convince workers that unit representation will result, quickly rather than slowly, in contractual protection), and prohibiting the replacement of economic strikers.

A third policy objective, as previously suggested, might be to promote minority-status forms of worker representation. Public policy might encourage alternative dispute resolution procedures which facilitate union membership. It might also experiment with a worker-council type of arrangement that would explicitly permit or even encourage minority union representation. While these policy options certainly run counter to conventional union views, they may nonetheless serve the ultimate goal of increasing union membership.

Toward these ends, unions could again adopt the same array of tactics. Various interest groups might be allied and encouraged to mobilize on a community-wide basis to influence lawmakers. (Ironically, alternative dispute resolution and union-supported employee involvement policies might garner the support of conservative groups.) These efforts might focus on encouraging lawmakers to retaliate against anti-union, anti-employee participation employers. Such retaliation could come in the form of denying government contracts or licenses. In this regard, special attention might be given to influencing city councils and state legislatures with these powers, as well as presenting cases to regulatory bodies with jurisdiction over employers. Finally, unions might combine resources to influence elections and policy-making. In this vein, they might seek to promote labor-groomed candidates (as the UMWA has done in West Virginia (see *Wall Street Journal*, June 18, 1996: A1) and secure the appointment of labor supporters to various important regulatory agencies. This would give them a more direct form of representation than is often the case today. Obviously, special attention would have to be given to states, counties, and localities where unions are in a position to form the strongest grassroots, interest-group alliances.

Organizing Strategy. In this regard, the strategic objective is new membership per se, or, simply put, growth in numbers. Growth will eventually translate into economic and political power, including greater levels of workplace representation. While labor cannot and should not be expected to abandon formal forms of bargaining representation, it must weigh the costs of such attainment against those alternatives which might also secure additional members.

In tactical terms, unions should consider forming multigroup, interunion efforts to organize across industries and occupations on a scale broader than has heretofore been done (McDonald 1987; 1992). In consolidating these efforts, they might experiment creatively with incentives for employers to hire union-trained workers. As noted, labor–management sponsored training programs might be used to recruit, train, and select employees for firms in a regional area. Special services might be offered to unionized firms or firms that pledge neutrality in union-organizing initiatives. Such a mechanism would operate not as a closed shop but rather as a vehicle for creating a positive labor relations climate in which unions might flourish because of the competitive edge they have helped firms secure in the human resources area.

In the process of providing such talent, unions would benefit from alliances with groups in communities that have an interest in promoting employment among their members. Economic retaliation could come in the form of reduced recruiting opportunities among skilled employees for firms in the impacted regions. Further, trainees could become associate members and receive union services upon employment regardless of whether the firm in which they obtained a job has a formally recognized bargaining unit. More generally, unions might promote alternative forms of representation (worker training, occupational safety and health, and grievance counseling) in nonunion settings by offering their considerable expertise in these areas. They could help set up such mechanisms and persuade workers to join as full or associate members. As suggested, this activity could well serve the image-building that would promote union growth even further.

CONCLUSIONS

The ubiquitous decline in the labor movement suggests that unions have little choice but to think expansively about how to promote growth. The framework presented here builds on the notion that unions must concentrate on growth per se lest they will lose the future. Toward this end, they must creatively deploy their strategic resources.

Moreover, these resources must be used in a broad-based societal effort that recognizes that new forms of worker representation may be necessary and the only way to grow. Unions can ill afford an organizing strategy that focuses on minorities rather than whites, or women rather than men. Similarly, they cannot afford a strategy that fails to include minorities and women. Unions must balance their organizing pitch to serve the common needs of workers of various ages and races and both genders across industrial and occupational groups.

In pursuit of new recruits, bargaining, political action, and organizing, strategies and tactics should be well orchestrated and integrated to provide maximum leverage. Flexibility, adaptability, and responsiveness may well be the key to success. Bold, new approaches that give labor the chance to attract workers without visceral encounters with employers deserve attention, given the scope of the union decline and the breadth of renewal required. At the same time, unions may need to play hardball, using their powers at the bargaining table, in political arenas, and in organizing to raise the costs of employer resistance, misconduct, and indifference. In the final analysis, it is hard to imagine how unions can come out of their shrinkage if they continue the practices of the past and fail to devote the time, resources, and energy to renew their status.

NOTES

1. Newt Gingrich (Republican-Georgia) is the Speaker of the U.S. House of Representatives of the 104th Congress. Dick Armey (Republican-Texas) is the Majority Leader of that body.

2. McDonald (1992: 27) makes this point vividly, arguing for a fundamental shift in union-organizing philosophy: "Union organizing in the United States is a high-stakes game. Given current employer conduct, employees risk a lot of time, money, and emotional energy. Their jobs are on the line throughout the process and victory is not so much a money proposition as significant leverage for bargaining for major improvements." Accordingly, he (1992: 29) advocates increased reliance on nonmajority representation: "The labor movement is in a better position to retain and build membership in either an employee representation committee or minority union setting. The new AFL-CIO membership benefit program—credit cards, legal services, life insurance, associate membership—offers organizational tools that are especially suited to attracting independent unions or associate members in an open shop or employee committee situation."

3. Section 8(a)(2) of the NLRA forbids company-dominated unions, making it an unfair labor practice for an employer to "dominate or interfere with the formation or administration of any labor organization or to contribute financial or other support to it." This provision has been used to nullify certain employee-involvement programs in nonunion settings. In its 1992 *Electromation* decision, the NLRB invalidated Electromation's employee committees, which were created by management to address such issues as pay, pay progression, attendance, and communications (U.S. Commission on the Future of Worker–Management Relations 1994a: 54). McDonald (1992: 27) has recommended a legislative sanctioning of nonmajority union representation status (perhaps via employee committees) that would serve the purpose of facilitating organizing: "A second prescription is to lower the stakes of the organizing game legislatively by creating a minority representation system to supplement the current model. Under such a system, employee representation would be achieved with less than majority support and without a serious contest, but also without requiring the employer to negotiate a comprehensive bargaining agreement." McDonald (1992: 28) went on to comment that minority-status union representation "may also become a more facile group for developing employee involvement programs (EIPs) and for improving the employer's competitive position."

4. In 1994, for instance, union density was 29 percent in New York, 23 percent in New Jersey, 19.6 percent in Pennsylvania, and 18 percent in California. In contrast, union density was 8.2 percent in Florida, 8 percent in Georgia, 5.2

percent in South Carolina, and 7 percent in Texas. These data are from the Bureau of National Affairs (1995).

5. The U.S. DOL, BLS (1993b) projected labor-force and employment growth levels for the 1992–2005 period. Its projections include low, moderate, and high alternatives. Data on gender, age, and race refer to expected labor-force levels. Data on occupation and industry refer to expected employment.

6. U.S. DOL, BLS (various years) data indicate that "persons of Hispanic origin may be of any race" (white or nonwhite).

7. It is assumed that white non-Hispanics will constitute 73 percent of the 136,285,000 wage and salary workforce (including those in the agricultural sector).

8. In 1995, the U.S. DOL, BLS (1996a) reported 2,519,000 African-American union members and 1,357,000 Hispanic union members.

9. Current labor law excludes supervisors and managers from protections afforded to "employees." As managerial and supervisory duties are devolved in companies that promote teams and employee involvement, this distinction may become less justifiable. As the U.S. Commission on the Future of Worker-Management Relations (1994a: 55) noted: "If a more cooperative conception of the employer-employee relationship is embodied in labor law so that representation does not necessarily imply the existence of an adversarial relationship, it may be necessary to consider whether supervisors or middle managers should be denied the right to union representation or collective bargaining" under the NLRA.

10. McDonald (1987: 279) recognized the potential for using human capital, noting that the "use of union members as volunteer organizers has become a key ingredient for several major unions, including the UFCW, Carpenters, CWA, Sheet Metal, and ACTWU . . . . Expansion of this concept to other unions is an essential organizing goal."

Chapter 13

The Future of U.S. Unions

Unions have faced difficult circumstances in the past fifteen years. While the decline in union membership during this period is neither unique to this country nor of unparalleled scale by historical standards, it has followed several decades of continual shrinkage in workforce density. Today, only one in ten private sector workers belongs to a union, the lowest percentage since the depths of the Great Depression more than sixty years ago.

Faced with such a diminishing presence, labor unions can be expected to fight back with almost the same instinctiveness and intensity as any living being would when confronted with a hostile natural environment. A forceful response appears to be underway, the success of which will depend upon many circumstances, not the least of which are the resources unions can marshal to compete for workers' loyalties. In this regard, unions must allocate their human, financial, and political capital in such a way as to pursue strategies and tactics with maximum impact. Regardless of whether they ultimately succeed, unions will grapple with questions on the availability and deployment of resources as they fight to overcome barriers to expansion. As dynamic complex organizations, their responses to serious challenges may be both intellectually rational and highly guttural, confrontational and cooperative, defiant and compliant. *At the Crossroads* is about the perimeters within which unions will make important choices—on strategy, tactics, and resource allocation.

Does it matter what choices unions make and whether they are wise ones?

Is society harmed by a weak or nil labor movement, or better off with a vibrant (and responsible) one? The presumption here is that the answer to both questions is a decided yes. The strategic, tactical, and allocation decisions unions make do matter, if not in ultimately reversing the gears in union decline then in the way labor will interact with thousands of employers and millions of employees in the years to come. And society is benefited if unions do succeed. Not that unions have a place for everyone everywhere. Rather, unions serve as important countervailing economic and political institutions to balance the interests of workers with myriad but also common, concerns against the impersonality and brutality of unconstrained market forces. They also provide a collective mechanism for solving disputes in a nonviolent way outside the adversarial and restrictive embellishments of legal proceedings.

THE CHALLENGE

Unions stare directly at a weighty challenge. The decline is evident on the bargaining, organizing, and political fronts. Environmental conditions, including global competition, corporate restructuring, and the changing nature of work and the workforce, apply seemingly relentless downward pressure on organized labor. The litany of defeat, setback, and deterioration is almost crushing:

- Union density dropped by 34 percent in the 1980s and has continued to fall in the 1990s, despite two consecutive years of absolute membership growth;
- Union membership fell 25 percent in the 1980s, and has actually declined in fourteen of the past sixteen years;
- The major twenty-eight U.S.-based unions lost 14 percent of their ranks between 1979 and 1993. The seventeen private sector unions lost 30 percent, with the UAW, USW, ACTWU, and ILGWU losing more than half;
- Public sector union membership growth is far too anemic, however impressive it might appear on the surface, to compensate for the private sector downfall;
- Just to maintain current membership levels, the major unions will have to attract millions of new recruits over the next few years. To increase their current workforce density from 12 to 18 percent by the year 2000, these twenty-eight unions will have to double their ranks.

Unsurprisingly, union bargaining strength waned. In the 1980s, labor conceded to employment cutbacks, productivity increases, wage freezes, and two-tier pay structures on an unprecedented scale (Rose and Chaison 1996). Organizing activity plummeted. Strikes became infrequent and increasingly ineffectual. Employers unabashedly took measures to avoid unions, resist organizing drives, and squash strikes. Public opinion turned conservative, opposing government per se and interventionist economic and regulatory policies. The free market mantra gained appeal, Republicans swept Congress, and labor's public-policy agenda got turned on its head. Altogether, labor unions would appear to be in a vicious catch-22. As their bargaining, organizing, and political clout has waned, their capacity to use bargaining, organizing, and political strategies to extricate themselves from the doldrums would appear problematic at best.

A COMEBACK?

Amid these conditions, labor exhibits clear signs of new life and a willingness to fight back. Unions are undergoing their own transformations, setting new priorities, reallocating resources accordingly, and otherwise positioning themselves to deal better with the juggernaut of decline. Recent developments were almost unthinkable a few years ago:

- The old guard at the AFL-CIO was ousted and replaced by aggressive new leadership, with John Sweeney, former head of the SEIU, at the helm;
- The AFL-CIO and numerous unions—LIU, IBT, SEIU, to name a few—have dramatically accelerated their organizing efforts. SEIU hopes to triple its new recruits. Federation leaders hope that unions will devote a third of their budgets to organizing, as the SEIU has done;
- The AFL-CIO has embarked upon a $35 million campaign to retake control of the Congress from the Republicans. Boldly, the federation is financing this campaign from the *treasuries* of its affiliated unions;
- Major union mergers have taken place, led by the planned Mega-Metals union to be comprised of the UAW, USW, and IAM. The ACTWU and ILGWU have merged, and the AFT and NEA are still talking, having pledged a mutual no-raid agreement;
- Grassroots union activism is on the rise. Efforts are underway to copy the "Justice for Janitors" campaign. The AFL-CIO's Union Summer work program for 1,500 college students is underway. Organizers, political activists, and volunteers are being recruited and trained at a much accelerated pace;
- Vigorous corporate campaigns, such as the UFCW's public embarrassment of Food Lion, are being pursued to tax or financially cripple those employers who aggressively maintain their union-free status; and
- The UAW has adopted a militant bargaining position in its negotiations with the Big Three automakers (GM, Ford, and Chrysler) to bar outsourcing and reduce layoffs, thus preserving union jobs.

To succeed, these and various other initiatives will require that labor commit precious human, financial, and political capital. A critical issue, therefore, is the availability and allocation of such resources to achieve strategic objectives.

TRENDS IN HUMAN, FINANCIAL, AND POLITICAL CAPITAL

As democratic, political–economic institutions, unions acquire and allocate human, financial, and political capital to serve their own institutional well-being and the interests of current and prospective members. Decisions about the mobilization and allocation of these resources inherently reflect organizational priorities. As Weil (1994: 154) observes:

> The state of a labor union's finances impact the strategic choices available to its leaders. In the most simplistic case, a small union with a declining membership will be severely constrained as to what policies and strategies it can pursue. At the other end of the spectrum, a union with substantial reserves has the opportunity to engage in new programs, but also might face pressure from its members to redistribute those reserves in the form of dues reductions or even rebates (rebates are not unknown even to the labor movement). A union's finances can also send important signals to the membership . . . . Finally, union finances send messages to management. The accumulation of money in a strike fund is a well-known device to indicate a union's preparation for tough negotiations.

In addition, the availability—or lack thereof—of resources may have implications for the possibility and likelihood of union mergers.

The data demonstrate several important trends in the status of union resources. First, while membership has declined significantly among the twenty-eight unions as a whole, substantial interunion variation exists. As is widely known, public-employee union membership has grown appreciably since 1979; nine of the eleven unions studied in that sector experienced growth. Within each sector, however, the differences are extreme. While SEIU, for instance, grew by 74 percent, comparing 1993 to 1979, NFFE lost half its members and AFGE lost more than a third. In the private sector, UFCW, CWA, IUOE, and PPI held their losses to a minimum, staying more or less even in terms of total membership. In stark contrast, several major manufacturing unions literally lost their shirts: ILGWU's membership dropped by nearly 60 percent in a mere fifteen-year period.

Second, despite this decline in membership, union wealth held steady, comparing 1993 to 1979. In fact, the twenty-eight unions ended the period with slightly more wealth than they recorded in 1993. On a per-member basis, their total assets and wealth actually increased by a significant amount. However, both assets and wealth are relatively concentrated among a handful of even these major unions. Five unions of the major twenty-eight (UAW, USW, IBT, ILGWU, and CWA) held almost two-thirds of the wealth over the 1979–1993 period. In the main, public sector unions at the national level do not hold wealth that is comparable to their private sector counterparts, but, again, within each sector, considerable variation exists.

Third, while the unions' aggregate assets and wealth held up relatively well, notwithstanding membership losses, their general-purpose income plummeted. Operating income, approximately three-fourths of which is from member-based sources, fell by almost 25 percent, forcing a major reduction in union expenditures. Several unions, in fact, had their income more than halved. The IBT, for instance, had 55 percent less operating income in 1993 than it did in 1979, or 35 percent less to spend on a per-member basis. Except for AFGE, however, public sector unions' income grew, reflecting underlying membership trends. SEIU's income more than doubled, as did the AFT's.

Fourth, despite the loss of income, the twenty-eight unions' overall capacity to withstand a strike—or at least finance a major job action—improved. Their aggregate reserve ratios reflected a liquid asset base sufficient to fund nearly 75 percent of a year's budget in the 1990s compared to roughly 50 percent fifteen years earlier. Given the concentration in these unions' assets, however, it is unsurprising that a few unions stand as outliers. With more than $1 billion in U.S. Treasury securities, the UAW holds the largest strike fund, the greatest reserve ratio, and the strongest capacity to fund a strike.

Fifth, the unions were also able to increase their PAC fundraising while membership fell. In both the private and public sector, PAC receipts increased significantly in absolute real dollars on a per-member basis and relative to operating union income. Eighteen of the major unions actually raised more PAC money in real terms in 1994 than in 1980. The IBT's growth was well-nigh miraculous, and its PAC coffers had a nineteenfold jump in this period. In the public sector, the postal unions also recorded sizable gains, but the federal service employee unions registered steep losses. At the same time, unions raised relatively little PAC money, particularly if the situation is viewed in terms of per-member donations. In the 1994 federal election cycle, only two unions (IAM and NALC) raised more than $5 per member in real PAC money; most raised less than $3 per member.

THE FUTURE

Despite membership losses, unions remain viable in situations. They have a sizable membership base: Total union membership in the United States exceeds sixteen million; the major twenty-eight unions have more than thirteen million members. By any reasonable standard, this is a source of human capital which, if properly mobilized, can have a significant impact on the workplace and broader economic and political affairs. In addition, unions have kept their financial house in order and expanded their political presence through increased PAC activity.

The strategic issue before labor unions is whether they are willing to break away from the status quo. Are they willing to depart from traditional practice, which has allegedly paid too little attention to organizing and put all the eggs in the exclusive representation basket, and make the commitment to a bold agenda of action? In short, are labor unions willing to leverage the bulk of their resources and mobilize untapped sources of strength? While the labor movement may not be able to arrest shrinkage that is driven by environmental conditions, the past ebb and flow in union membership suggests that revival is far from unthinkable. The future of organized labor in the United States will depend in substantial part on whether unions take the following kinds of steps:

- Establish an organizing and political action cadre of volunteers equivalent to one-tenth of their ranks. These volunteers, on average, should devote one day a month to relevant purposes, building a grassroots network in areas where unions have had trouble in the past;
- Allocate at least one-third of their operating budget to organizing activity, part of which would be devoted to recruiting and training volunteers;
- Leverage pension funds and other investment sources to induce corporations and policy makers to lessen their animosity toward unions;
- Set the goal of raising $10 per member in PAC money and target political activity toward a work-related policy agenda that will maximize rank-and-file support and benefit labor's public image;
- Focus on organizing—recruiting—rather than certification as exclusive bargaining agents;
- Promote employer involvement and alternative dispute resolution procedures in employment settings that can be leveraged to induce union membership;
- Adopt an inclusive organizing strategy that stresses the benefits to employers and employees in geographic regions, offering to provide services that are beneficial to both and that enhance competitiveness;
- Form superunions that would combine resources and focus on organizing broad classes of workers within these regions. The objective of mergers should be growth, with resources mobilized and allocated accordingly.

Even with taking these steps, unions face a daunting task; and their success requires that some events break in their favor. Without such concerted effort, however, unions are certain to glide continually downward.

Bibliography

Aaron, Benjamin. 1984. Future trends in industrial relations law. *Industrial Relations* 23: 52–57.

Aaron, Benjamin, Joseph R. Grodin, and James L. Stern, eds. 1979. *Public sector bargaining*. Washington, D.C.: The Bureau of National Affairs.

Aaron, Benjamin, Joyce M. Najita, and James L. Stern, eds. 1988. *Public sector bargaining*. Washington, D.C.: The Bureau of National Affairs.

AFL-CIO. 1992. *North American Free Trade Negotiations: The jobs debate: Fiction and reality*. Washington, D.C.: AFL-CIO.

———. 1994a. *A labor perspective on the new American workplace—A call for partnership*. Washington, D.C.: AFL-CIO.

———. 1994b. *AFL-CIO Housing Investment Trust*. June 30. Washington, D.C.: AFL-CIO.

———. 1995a. Repeal of service contract attacks low-wage workers. *AFL-CIO legislative fact sheet*. November 28. Washington, D.C.: AFL-CIO.

———. 1995b. Say good-bye to the 40-hour week and overtime. *AFL-CIO legislative fact sheet*. November 28. Washington, D.C.: AFL-CIO.

———. 1995c. The Davis-Bacon Act protects workers and wages. *AFL-CIO legislative fact sheet*. November 28. Washington, D.C.: AFL-CIO.

———. 1995d. The minimum wage is not a living wage. *AFL-CIO legislative fact sheet*. November 28. Washington, D.C.: AFL-CIO.

———. 1995e. Workers' safety at risk with OSHA reform. *AFL-CIO legislative fact sheet*. November 28. Washington, D.C.: AFL-CIO.

———. 1996. *Talking points on the Team Act*. July 24. Washington, D.C.: AFL-CIO.

AFL-CIO Committee on the Evolution of Work. 1985. *The changing situation of workers and their unions*. Washington, D.C.: AFL-CIO.

Allen, Steven G. 1994. Developments in collective bargaining in construction in the 1980s and 1990s. In *Contemporary collective bargaining in the private sector*, edited by Paula B. Voos, 411–446. Madison, Wisc.: Industrial Relations Research Association.

Allison, Elisabeth K. 1975. Financial analysis of the local union. *Industrial Relations* 14: 145–155.

Andrews, Martyn, and Robin Naylor. 1994. Declining union density in the 1980s: What do panel data tell us? *British Journal of Industrial Relations* 32: 413–426.

Arrowsmith, J. David. 1992. *Canada's trade unions: An information manual.* Kingston, Ontario: Industrial Relations Centre, Queen's University.

Arthur, Jeffrey B., and Suzanne K. Smith. 1994. The transformation of industrial relations in the American steel industry. In *Contemporary collective bargaining in the private sector*, edited by Paula B. Voos, 135–180. Madison Wisc.: Industrial Relations Research Association.

Atkin, Robert S., and Marick F. Masters. 1995. Union democracy and the Labor-Management Reporting and Disclosure Act: An alternative reform proposal. *Employee Responsibilities and Rights Journal* 8: 193–208.

Axelrod, Robert. 1982. Communication. *American Political Science Review* 76: 393–396.

Banks, Andy. 1991–1992. The power and promise of community unionism. *Labor Research Review* 18: 17–31.

Barbash, Jack. 1956. *The practice of unionism.* New York: Harper and Row.

———. 1965. The structure of union political action—a trial analytic framework. *Labor Law Journal* 16: 491–496.

———. 1984. Trade unionism from Roosevelt to Reagan. *Annals of the American Academy* 473: 11–22.

Barth, James R., and Joseph J. Cordes. 1981. Nontraditional criteria for investing pension assets: An economic appraisal. *Journal of Labor Research* 2: 219–247.

Belzer, Michael H. 1994. The motor carrier industry: Truckers and teamsters under siege. In *Contemporary collective bargaining in the private sector*, edited by Paula B. Voos, 259–302. Madison, Wisc.: Industrial Relations Research Association.

Bennett, James T. 1991. Private sector unions: The myth of decline. *Journal of Labor Research* 12: 1–12.

———. 1996. Comprehensive corporate campaigns. *Journal of Labor Research* 17: 327–328.

Bennett, James T., and John T. Delaney. 1993. Research on unions: Some subjects in need of scholars. *Journal of Labor Research* 14: 95–110.

Bennett, James T., and Manuel H. Johnson. 1981. Union use of employee pension funds: Introduction and overview. *Journal of Labor Research* 2: 181-90.

Bernstein, Aaron. 1994. Why America needs unions but not the kind it has now. *Business Week*, May 23, 70–82.

———. 1995a. Can a new leader bring labor back to life. *Business Week*, July 3, 87.

———. 1995b. Now departing for China: Boeing jobs. *Business Week*, November 27, 46.

———. 1996. Andy Stern's mission impossible: The new service workers' union head aims to triple its recruits. *Business Week*, June 10, 73.

Bernstein, Aaron, Zachary Schiller, and Edith Hill Updike. 1995. Rubber workers with nerves of steel. *Business Week*, December 18, 44.

Berry, Jeffrey M. 1989. *The interest group society*. Glenview, Ill.: Scott, Foresman and Company.

Bierman, Leonard, and Marick F. Masters. 1985. The need for Hatch Act clarification. *Labor Law Journal* 36: 313–318.

Blair, Jeffrey. 1994. USW leader leaves legacy of job losses, board gains. *Pittsburgh Post-Gazette*, February 27, B9.

Block, Richard N. 1980. Union organizing and the allocation of union resources. *Industrial and Labor Relations Review* 34: 101–113.

———. 1995. Labor law, economics, and industrial democracy: A reconciliation. *Industrial Relations* 34: 402–416.

Blume, Norman. 1970. The impact of a local union on its membership in a local election. *Western Political Quarterly* 23: 138–150.

Blumenstein, Rebecca. 1996. Final whistle: A GM plant closes, scattering workers around the country. *Wall Street Journal*, June 26, A1, A6.

Blumenstein, Rebecca, Nichole M. Christian, and Gabriella Stern. 1996. GM to break with peers in UAW talks. Auto maker ready to risk another strike on cost issue. *Wall Street Journal*, April 26, A2, A4.

Bok, Derek C., and John T. Dunlop. 1970. *Labor and the American community*. New York: Simon and Schuster.

Bradsher, Keith. 1996a. UAW is setting bargaining strategy. *New York Times*, January 23, C6.

———. 1996b. UAW sets hard stance in bargaining. Talks in summer may be toughest in years. *New York Times*, April 4, C1.

Brimelow, Peter, and Leslie Spencer. 1995. Comeuppance. *Forbes*, February 13, 121–127.

Budd, John W., and Paul K. Heinz. 1996. Union representation elections and labor law reform: Lessons from the Minneapolis Hilton. *Labor Studies Journal* 20: 3–20.

Bureau of Labour Information, Canada. 1992. *Directory of labour organizations in Canada*. Ottawa, Canada: Canadian Government Publishing Center.

Bureau of National Affairs (BNA). 1991. *BNA's quarterly report on job absence and turnover, 4th quarter, 1990*. Washington, D.C.: The Bureau.

———. 1995. *Union membership and earnings data book*. Washington, D.C.: The Bureau.

Burkins, Glenn. 1996a. Labor's bid to aid Democrats faces one hurdle: Many of its members often vote for Republicans. *Wall Street Journal*, April 9, A20.

———. 1996b. Teamsters leaders head for showdown. *Wall Street Journal*, July 12, A2, A6.

———. 1996c. Teamsters chief Carey loses straw poll of delegates to rival candidate Hoffa. *Wall Street Journal*, July 19, A14.

Burton, John F., Jr., and Terry Thomas. 1988. The extent of collective bargaining in the public sector. In *Public Sector Bargaining*, edited by Benjamin Aaron, Joyce M. Najita, and James L. Stern, 1–51.

Carlisle, Anthony T. 1996a. Paying the dues. *Pittsburgh Business Times*, January 29, 11.

———. 1996b. With the new century's approach, unions face a challenge to reinvent. *Pittsburgh Business Times*, April 1, 10.

———. 1996c. Merger of metals: The steel workers union comes home next month for a convention vote that will determine its future. *Pittsburgh Business Times*, July 15–21: 1, 30.

Chaison, Gary N. 1982. Union mergers and the integration of union governing structures. *Journal of Labor Research* 3: 139–52.

———. 1986. *When unions merge*. Lexington, Mass.: Lexington Books.

Chaison, Gary N., and Dileep G. Dhavale. 1990. The changing scope of union organizing. *Journal of Labor Research* 11: 307–322.

Chaison, Gary N., and Joseph B. Rose. 1991. The macrodeterminants of union growth and decline. In *The state of the unions*, edited by George Strauss, Daniel G. Gallagher, and Jack Fiorito, 3–46. Madison, Wisc.: Industrial Relations Research Association.

Chaykowski, Richard P., Terry Thomason, and Harris L. Zwerling. 1994. Labor relations in American textiles. In *Contemporary collective bargaining in the private sector*, edited by Paula B. Voos, 373–410. Madison, Wisc.: Industrial Relations Research Association.

Christian, Nichole M. 1996. UAW targets outsourcing and layoffs. *Wall Street Journal*, June 20, A2, A4.

Clark, Paul F. 1989. Organizing the organizers: Professional staff unionism in the American labor movement. *Industrial and Labor Relations Review* 42: 584–599.

———. 1992. Professional staff in American unions: Changes, trends, implications. *Journal of Labor Research* 13: 381–392.

Clark, Paul F. and Lois G. Gray. 1991. Union administration. In *The State of the unions*, edited by George Strauss, Daniel G. Gallagher, and Jack Fiorito, 175–200. Madison, Wisc.: Industrial Relations Research Association.

———. 1992. The management of human resources in national unions. In *Proceedings of the forty-fourth annual meeting of the Industrial Relations Research Association*, edited by John F. Burton, Jr., 414–423. Madison, Wisc.: Industrial Relations Research Association.

Clark, Paul, and Marick F. Masters. 1996. *Pennsylvania COPE union member survey: A final report*. Unpublished monograph.

Cloke, Kenneth. 1981. Mandatory political contributions and union democracy. *Industrial Relations Law Journal* 4: 527–586.

Cobble, Dorothy S., and Michael Merrill. 1994. Collective bargaining in the hospitality industry in the 1980s. In *Contemporary collective bargaining in the private sector*, edited by Paula B. Voos, 447–490. Madison, Wisc.: Industrial Relations Research Association.

Conant, John L., and David L. Kaserman. 1989. Union merger incentives and pecuniary externalities. *Journal of Labor Research* 10: 243–254.

Cook, Alice H. 1991. Women and minorities. In *The state of the unions*, edited by George Strauss, Daniel G. Gallagher, and Jack Fiorito, 237–258. Madison, Wisc.: Industrial Relations Research Association.

Cooke, William N., and Frederick H. Gautschi. 1982. Political bias in NLRB unfair labor practice decisions. *Industrial and Labor Relations Review* 35: 539–549.

Coxson, Harold P. 1996. Workplace cooperation: Current problems, new approaches—comment on Delaney. *Journal of Labor Research* 17: 63–68.

Craft, James A., and Marian M. Extejt. 1983. New strategies in union organizing. *Journal of Labor Research* 4: 19–32.

Craypo, Charles. 1994. Meatpacking: Industry restructuring and union decline. In *Contemporary collective bargaining in the private sector*, edited by Paula B. Voos, 63–96. Madison, Wisc.: Industrial Relations Research Association.

Cutcher-Gershenfeld, Joel, and Patrick P. McHugh. 1994. Collective bargaining in the North American auto supply industry. In *Contemporary collective bargaining in the private sector*, edited by Paula B. Voos, 225–258. Madison, Wisc.: Industrial Relations Research Association.

CWA. 1993. *Mobilizing for the '90's*. Washington, D.C.: CWA.

———. 1996. *The CWA triangle*. Washington, D.C.: CWA.

———. undated. *Changing information services: Strategies for workers and consumers*. Washington, D.C.: CWA.

DaParma, Ron. 1994. Cost-saving measures boost USW. *Pittsburgh Tribune-Review*, December 4, H1, H6.

Delaney, John T. 1991. The future of union's as political organizations. *Journal of Labor Research* 12: 373–387.

Delaney, John T. 1996. Workplace cooperation: Current problems, new approaches. *Journal of Labor Research* 17: 45–62.

Delaney, John T., Jack Fiorito, and Marick F. Masters. 1988. The effects of union organizational and environmental characteristics on union political action. *American Journal of Political Science* 32: 616–642.

Delaney, John T. and Marick F. Masters. 1991a. Union characteristics and union political action. *Labor Law Journal* 42: 467–472.

———. 1991b. Union and political action. In *The State of the Unions*, edited by George Strauss, Daniel G. Gallagher, and Jack Fiorito, 277–312. Madison, Wisc: Industrial Relations Research Association.

Delaney, John T., Marick F. Masters, and Susan Schwochau. 1988. Unionism and voter turnout. *Journal of Labor Research* 9: 221–236.

———. 1990. Union membership and voting for COPE-endorsed candidates. *Industrial and Labor Relations Review* 43: 621–635.

Delaney, John T., Paul Jarley, and Jack Fiorito. 1996. Planning for change: Determinants of innovation in U.S. national unions. *Industrial and Labor Relations Review* 49: 597–614.

Delaney, John, and Susan Schwochau. 1993. Employee representation through the political process. In *Employee representation: Alternatives and future directions*, edited by Bruce Kaufman and Morris Kleiner, 265–304. Madison, Wisc.: Industrial Relations Research Association.

Derber, Milton. 1970. *The American idea of industrial democracy: 1865–1965*. Urbana, Ill.: University of Illinois Press.

Dertouzos, Michael L., Richard K. Lester, and Robert M. Solow. 1989. *Made in America: Regaining the productive edge*. Cambridge, Mass.: MIT Press.

Dickens, William T., and Jonathan S. Leonard. 1985. Accounting for the decline in union membership, 1950-1980. *Industrial Labor Relations Review* 38: 323–334.

DiLorenzo, Thomas J. 1996. The corporate campaign against Food Lion: A study of media manipulation. *Journal of Labor Research* 17: 359–376.

Dunlop, John T. 1958. *Industrial relations systems.* New York: Holt.

Eaton, Adrienne, and Jill Kriesky. 1994. Collective bargaining in the paper industry: Developments since 1979. In *Contemporary collective bargaining in the private sector,* edited by Paula B. Voos, 25–62. Madison, Wisc.: Industrial Relations Research Association.

Epstein, Edwin M. 1976. Labor and federal elections: The new legal framework. *Industrial Relations* 15: 257–274.

———. 1980. Labor's eroding position in American electoral politics: The impact of the Federal Election Campaign Act of 1971. In *Employment and labor relations policy*, edited by Charles Bulmer and John J. Carmichael, Jr., 151–177. Lexington, Mass.: D.C. Heath.

Erickson, Christopher L. 1994. Collective bargaining in the aerospace industry in the 1980s. In *Contemporary collective bargaining in the private sector,* edited by Paula B. Voos, 97–134. Madison, Wisc.: Industrial Relations Research Association.

Estey, Martin S., Philip Taft, and Martin Wagner. 1964. *Regulating union government.* New York: Harper and Row.

Ewing, David W. 1989. *Justice on the job: Resolving grievances in the nonunion workplace.* Boston, Mass.: Harvard Business School Press.

Farber, Henry S. 1985. The extent of unionization in the United States. In *Challenges and choices facing American labor,* edited by Thomas A. Kochan, 15–44. Cambridge, Mass.: MIT Press.

Farber, Henry S., and Alan B. Krueger. 1993. Union membership in the United States: The decline continues. In *Employee representation: Alternatives and future directions*, edited by Bruce E. Kaufmann and Morris M. Kleiner, 105–134. Madison, Wisc.: Industrial Relations Research Association.

Feuille, Peter. 1991. Unionism in the public sector: The joy of protected markets. *Journal of Labor Research* 11: 357–367.

Fields, Mitchell W., Marick F. Masters, and James W. Thacker. 1987. Union commitment and membership support for political action: An exploratory analysis. *Journal of Labor Research* 8: 143–157.

Fiorito, Jack. 1987. Political instrumentality perceptions and desires for union representation. *Journal of Labor Research* 8: 271–290.

Fiorito, Jack, and Charles R. Greer. 1982. Determinants of U.S. unionism: Past research and future needs. *Industrial Relations* 21: 1–32.

Fiorito, Jack, Cynthia L. Gramm, and Wallace Hendricks. 1991. Union structural choices. In *The state of the unions*, edited by George Strauss, Daniel G. Gallagher, and Jack Fiorito, 103–138. Madison, Wisc.: Industrial Relations Research Association.

Fiorito, Jack, Lee P. Stepina, and Dennis P. Bozeman. 1996. Explaining the unionism gap: Public-private sector differences in preferences for unionization. *Journal of Labor Research* 17: 463–478.

Fiorito, Jack, Paul Jarley, and John T. Delaney. 1995. National union effectiveness in organizing: measures and influences. *Industrial Labor Relations Review* 48: 613–635.

Fitzpatrick, Tracy, and Weezy Waldstein. 1994. Challenges to strategic planning in international unions. In *Proceedings of the forty-sixth annual meeting of the*

Industrial Relations Research Association, edited by Paula B. Voos, 73–84. Madison, Wisc.: Industrial Relations Research Association.

Foner, Philip S. 1947. *From colonial times to the founding of the American Federation of Labor*. New York: International Publishers (1978 reprint).

Foulkes, Fred. 1979. *Personnel policies of large nonunion companies*. Englewood Cliffs, N.J.: Prentice-Hall.

Franklin, Stephen. 1995. Decatur labor wars are over, but peace is still a long way off. *Chicago Tribune*, December 27, section 3, p.1.

———. 1996. For Caterpillar workers, scars are deep. *Chicago Tribune*, February 11, section 5, pp. 1–2.

Fraser, Lynn M. 1988. *Understanding financial statements*. Englewood Cliffs, N.J.: Prentice-Hall.

Freeman, Richard B., and Morris M. Kleiner. 1990. Employer behavior in the face of union organizing drives. *Industrial and Labor Relations Review* 43: 351–365.

Freeman, Richard B., and James L. Medoff. 1984. *What do unions do?* New York: Basic Books.

Freeman, Richard B., and Joel Rogers. 1993. Who speaks for us? Employee representation in a nonunion labor market. In *Employee representation: Alternatives and future directions*. Edited by Bruce E. Kaufman and Morris M. Kleiner, 13–80. Madison, Wisc.: Industrial Relations Research Association.

Fullagar, Clive, and Julian Barling. 1987. Toward a model of union commitment. In *Advances in industrial and labor relations*, vol. 4, edited by David Lewin, David B. Lipsky, and Donna Sockell, 43–78. Greenwich, Conn.: JAI Press.

Galenson, Walter. 1960. *The CIO challenge to the AFL. A history of the American labor movement, 1935–1941*. Cambridge, Mass. Harvard University Press.

Gangemi, Columbus R., Jr., and Joseph J. Torres. 1996. The corporate campaign at Caterpillar. *Journal of Labor Research* 17: 377–394.

Garland, Susan B., Kevin Kelly, Dave Sedgwick, and Stephen Baker. 1995. Breath of fire or last gasp? *Business Week*, August 14, 42.

Garland, Susan B., and Mary Beth Regan. 1996. Workers unite . . . against the GOP. *Business Week*, June 24, 34–35.

Gely, Rafael, and Timothy D. Chandler. 1995. Protective service unions' political activities and departmental expenditures. *Journal of Labor Research* 16: 171–186.

Gerhart, Paul F. 1974. *Political activity by public employee organizations at the local level: Threat or promise*. Chicago: International Personnel Management Association.

Gifford, Courtney D. 1982. *Directory of U.S. labor organizations, 1982–1983 edition*. Washington, D.C.: The Bureau of National Affairs.

———. 1984. *Directory of U.S. labor organizations, 1984–1985 edition*. Washington, D.C.: The Bureau of National Affairs.

———. 1986. *Directory of U.S. labor organizations, 1986–1987 edition*. Washington, D.C.: The Bureau of National Affairs.

———. 1988. *Directory of U.S. labor organizations, 1988–1989 edition*. Washington, D.C.: The Bureau of National Affairs.

———. 1990. *Directory of U.S. labor organizations, 1990–1991 edition*. Washington, D.C.: The Bureau of National Affairs.

———. 1992. *Directory of U.S. labor organizations, 1992–1993 edition*. Washington, D.C.: The Bureau of National Affairs.

———. 1994. *Directory of U.S. labor organizations, 1994–1995 edition*. Washington, D.C.: The Bureau of National Affairs.

Goldfield, Michael. 1987. *The decline of organized labor in the United States*. Chicago: University of Chicago Press.

Gould, William B., IV. 1993. *Agenda for reform*. Cambridge, Mass.: MIT Press.

Grabelsky, Jeffrey, and Richard Hurd. 1994. Reinventing an organizing union: Strategies for change. In *Proceedings of the forty-sixth annual meeting of the Industrial Relations Research Association*, edited by Paula B. Voos, 95–104. Madison, Wisc.: Industrial Relations Research Association.

Gramm, Cynthia L. 1992. Labor's legislative initiatives to restrict permanently replacing strikers. In *Proceedings of the forty-fourth annual meeting of the Industrial Relations Research Association*, edited by John F. Burton, Jr. Madison, Wisc.: Industrial Relations Research Association, 95–104.

Greenhouse, Steven. 1995a. Unions propose penalties for companies that flee northeast. *New York Times*, November 26, A17.

———. 1995b. After merger, garment union's heart is still on Seventh Avenue. *New York Times*, December 4, A16.

———. 1996. Labor chief takes assertive stance. *New York Times*, June 2, A17.

Greenstone, J. David. 1977. *Labor in American politics*. Chicago: University of Chicago Press.

Griffith, Pat. 1994. AFL-CIO pension money may fuel city housing. *Pittsburgh Post-Gazette*, January 16, A6.

———. 1995. Three unions trying to forge a powerhouse. *Pittsburgh Post-Gazette*, July 28, A1, A6.

Gunset, George. 1995. Strike's bitter end: UAW gives in to Caterpillar. *Chicago Tribune*, December 10, section 7, p 1.

Gustafson, Fred. 1994. Pumping: George Becker aims to build up the Steelworkers. *Pittsburgh Newsweekly*, December 15–21, 12–14.

Harbridge, Raymond, and Anthony Honeybone. 1996. External legitimacy in unions: Trends in New Zealand. *Journal of Labor Research* 17: 425–444.

Hendricks, Wallace, Cynthia L. Gramm, and Jack Fiorito. 1993. Centralization of bargaining decisions in American unions. *Industrial Relations* 32: 367–390.

Hendricks, Wallace, and Lawrence M. Kahn. 1982. The determinants of bargaining structure in U.S. manufacturing industries. *Industrial and Labor Relations Review* 35: 181–195.

Heneman, Herbert G., III, and Marcus H. Sandver. 1983. Predicting the outcome of union certification elections: A review of the literature. *Industrial and Labor Relations Review* 36: 537–359.

———. 1989. Union characteristics and organizing success. *Journal of Labor Research* 10: 377–390.

Herndon, James F. 1982. Access, record, and competition as influences on interest group contributions to congressional campaigns. *Journal of Politics* 44: 996–1020.

Hershey, William. 1996. With male ranks thinning, unions looking elsewhere. *Pittsburgh Post-Gazette*, July 21, C-4.

Hoekstra, Pete. 1996. Corporate campaigns: A view from Capitol Hill. *Journal of Labor Research* 17: 411–416.

Holley, William H., and Kenneth M. Jennings. 1994. *The labor relations process*. Fort Worth, Tex.: Dryden Press.

Hudson, Ruth A., and Hjalmar Rosen. 1954. Union political action: The member speaks. *Industrial and Labor Relations Review* 7: 404–418.

Hunt, James W., and Patricia K. Strongin. 1994. *The law of the workplace: Rights of employers and employees.* 3rd ed. Washington, D.C.: The Bureau of National Affairs.

Hurd, Richard W. 1989. Learning from clerical unions: Two cases of organizing success. *Labor Studies Journal* 14: 30–51.

Hurd, Richard W., and Adrienne M. McElwain. 1988. Organizing clerical workers: Determinants of success. *Industrial and Labor Relations Review* 41: 360–373.

Ichniowski, Casey, and Jeffrey S. Zax. 1990. Today's associations, tomorrow's unions. *Industrial and Labor Relations Review* 43: 191–208.

Ivancevich, John M. 1992. *Human resource management foundations of personnel* Homewood, Ill.: Irwin.

Jacoby, Mary. 1996. Labor works around edges of election law. *Chicago Tribune,* June 27, 1.

Jarley, Paul, and Cheryl Maranto. 1990. Union corporate campaigns: An assessment. *Industrial and Labor Relations Review* 43: 505–524.

Jarley, Paul, and Jack Fiorito. 1990. Associate membership: Unionism or consumerism? *Industrial and Labor Relations Review* 43: 209–224.

Jarley, Paul, John Delaney and Jack Fiorito. 1992. Embracing the Committee on the Evaluation of Work report: What have unions done? In *Proceedings of forty-fourth annual meeting of the Industrial Relations Research Association,* edited by John F. Burton, Jr., 500–511. Madison, Wisc.: Industrial Relations Research Association.

Jennings, Ken, and Jeffrey W. Steagall. 1996. Unions and NAFTA's legislative passage: Confrontation and cover. *Labor Studies Journal* 21: 61–79.

Juravich, Tom, and Peter R. Shergold. 1988. The impact of unions on the voting behavior of their members. *Industrial and Labor Relations Review* 41: 374–385.

Katz, Harry, and John P. MacDuffie. 1994. Collective bargaining in the U.S. auto assembly sector. In *Contemporary collective bargaining in the private sector,* edited by Paula B. Voos, 181–224. Madison, Wisc.: Industrial Relations Research Association.

Katz, Harry C., and Thomas A. Kochan. 1992. *An introduction to collective bargaining and industrial relations.* New York: McGraw-Hill.

Kau, James P., and Paul H. Rubin. 1981. The impact of labor unions on the passage of economic legislation. *Journal of Labor Research* 2: 133–146.

Kaufman, Bruce, and Morris M. Kleiner, eds. 1993. *Employee representation: Alternatives and future directions.* Madison, Wisc.: Industrial Relations Research Association.

Keefe, Jeffrey, and Karen Boroff. 1994. Telecommunications labor–management relations after divestiture. In *Contemporary collective bargaining in the private sector,* edited by Paula B. Voos, 303–372. Madison, Wisc.: Industrial Relations Research Association.

Kelly, Kevin. 1995. Caught in Cat's claws: The UAW may have to accept terms it went on strike to avoid. *Business Week,* December 4, 38.

Kilborn, Peter. 1995. Union capitulation shows strike is now dull sword. *New York Times,* December 5, A18.

The Kiplinger Washington Letter. August 25, 1995.

———. May 24, 1996a.

———. June 14, 1996b.

———. June 28, 1996c.

Kochan, Thomas A., and Harry C. Katz. 1988. *Collective bargaining and industrial relations*. Homewood, Ill.: Irwin.

Kochan, Thomas A., Harry C. Katz, and Robert B. McKersie. 1986. *The transformation of American industrial relations*. New York: Basic Books.

Kochan, Thomas A., and Paul Osterman. 1994. *The mutual gains enterprise*. Boston: Harvard Business School Press.

Koziara, Karen Shallcross, Michael H. Moskow, and Lucretia Dewey Tanner, eds. 1987. *Working women: Past, present, future*. Washington, D.C.: The Bureau of National Affairs, Industrial Relations Research Association Series.

The largest industrial and service corporations. *Fortune*, April 29, 1996.

Lawler, John J. 1990. *Unionization and deunionization strategy, tactics, and outcomes*. Columbia, S.C.: University of South Carolina Press.

LeRoy, Michael H. 1990. The 1988 elections: Re-emergence of the labor bloc vote? *Labor Studies Journal* 15: 5–32.

———. 1995. The changing character of strikes involving permanent striker replacements, 1935–1990. *Journal of Labor Research* 16: 423–438.

Levitan, Sar A., and Joseph J. Loewenberg. 1964. The politics and provisions of the Landrum-Griffin Act. In *Regulating union government*, edited by Martin S. Estey, Phillip Taft, and Martin Wagner, 28–64.

Levitt, Martin J. (with Terry Conrow). 1993. *Confessions of a union buster*. New York: Crown Publisher.

Lewin, David, Peter Feuille, Thomas A. Kochan, and John T. Delaney. 1988. *Public sector labor relations: Analysis and readings*. Lexington, Mass.: Lexington Books.

Lewin, David, David B. Lipsky, and Donna Sockell, eds. 1987. *Advances in industrial and labor relations*. Vol 4. Greenwich, Conn.: JAI Press.

Lipset, Seymour M. 1995. Trade union exceptionalism: The United States and Canada. *Annals of the American Academy* 538: 115–130.

Lublin, Joann S. 1996. Unions brandish stock to force change. *Wall Street Journal*, May 3, B1, B2.

Maranto, Cheryl L. 1988. Corporate characteristics and union organizing. *Industrial Relations* 27: 352–370.

Marcus, Ruth, and Thomas B. Edsall. 1995. Labor targets 55 House Republicans. *Washington Post*, December 10, A12.

Masters, Marick F. 1983. Federal-sector labor relations and the political activities of three federal-employee unions. Ph.D. diss., Institute of Labor and Industrial Relations, University of Illinois at Urbana-Champaign.

———. 1984. Federal employee unions: Bargaining or political agents? *Journal of Collective Negotiations in the Public Sector* 13: 191–202.

———. 1985. Federal-employee unions and political action. *Industrial and Labor Relations Review* 38: 612–628.

Masters, Marick F., and Asghar Zardkoohi. 1987. Labor unions and the U.S. Congress: PAC allocations and legislative voting. In *Advances in industrial and labor relations*, vol. 4, edited by David Lewin, 79–117. Greenwich, Conn.: JAI Press.

———. 1988. Congressional support for unions' positions across diverse legislation. *Journal of Labor Research* 9: 149–166.

Masters, Marick F., and Gerald D. Keim. 1985. Determinants of PAC participation among large corporations. *The Journal of Politics* 47: 1158–1173.

Masters, Marick F., and John T. Delaney. 1984. Interunion variation in congressional campaign support. *Industrial Relations* 23: 410–416.

———. 1985. The causes of union political involvement: A longitudinal analysis. *Journal of Labor Research* 6: 341–362.

———. 1987a. Contemporary labor political investments and performance. *Labor Studies Journal* 11: 220–237.

———. 1987b. Union legislative records during President Reagan's first term. *Journal of Labor Research* 8: 1–18.

———. 1987c. Union political activities: A review of the empirical literature. *Industrial and Labor Relations Review* 40: 336–353.

Masters, Marick F., and Leonard Bierman. 1985. The Hatch Act and the political activities of federal employee unions: A need for policy reform. *Public Administration Review* 45: 518–526.

Masters, Marick F., and Robert S. Atkin. 1989. Bargaining representation and union membership in the federal sector: A free rider's paradise. *Public Personnel Management* 18: 311–324.

———. 1990. Public policy, bargaining structure, and free-riding in the federal sector. *Journal of Collective Negotiations in the Public Sector* 19: 97–112.

———. 1992. Labor's legislative agenda in the 1990s. In *Proceedings of the forty-fourth annual meeting of the Industrial Relations Research Association*, edited by John F. Burton, Jr., 309–313. Madison, Wisc.: Industrial Relations Research Association.

———. 1993a. A financial analysis of major unions: Implications for financial reporting reform under the Labor–Management Reporting and Disclosure Act. *Labor Law Journal* 44: 341–350.

———. 1993b. Financial and bargaining implications of free riding in the federal sector. *Journal of Collective Negotiations in the Public Sector* 22: 327–340.

———. 1993c. *The status of public sector unions.* Unpublished monograph. Pittsburgh, Pa.: University of Pittsburgh Graduate School of Business.

———. 1995. Bargaining, financial, and political bases of federal sector unions. *Review of the Personnel Administration* 15: 5–23.

———. 1996a. Financial and political resources of nine major public sector unions in the 1980s. *Journal of Labor Research* 17: 183–198.

———. 1996b. Local union officers' donations to a political action committee. *Relations Industrielles* 51: 40–61.

———. 1996c. The financial power of public-employee unions. In *Advances in industrial and labor relations*, vol. 7, edited by David Lewin, Bruce Kaufman, and David Sockell, 177–205. Greenwich, Conn.: JAI Press.

Masters, Marick F., Robert S. Atkin, and Gary W. Florkowski. 1989. An analysis of union reporting requirements under Title II of the Landrum-Griffin Act. *Labor Law Journal* 40: 713–722.

Masters, Marick F., Robert S. Atkin, and Gerald Schoenfeld. 1990. A survey of USWA local officers' commitment-support attitudes. *Labor Studies Journal* 15: 51–80.

Masters, Marick F., Robert S. Atkin, and John T. Delaney. 1990. Unions, political action, and public policies: A review of the past decade. *Policy Studies Journal* 18: 471–480.

Masters, Nicholas A. 1962. The organized bureaucracy as a base of support for the Democratic party. *Law and Contemporary Problems* 27: 252–265.

Mathis, Robert L., and John H. Jackson. 1991. *Personnel/human resource management.* St. Paul, Minn.: West Publishing Company.

McCallion, Gail. 1990. *The changing role of strike activity in labor–management disputes.* Washington, D.C.: Congressional Research Service.

McClendon, John A., Jill Kriesky, and Adrienne Eaton. 1995. Member support for union mergers: An analysis of an affiliation referendum. *Journal of Labor Research* 16: 9–24.

McDonald, Charles. 1992. U.S. union membership in future decades: A trade unionist's perspective. *Industrial Relations* 31: 13–30.

McDonald, Charles. 1987. The AFL-CIO blueprint for the future—A progress report. In *Proceedings of the thirty-ninth annual meeting of the Industrial Relations Research Association,* edited by Barbara D. Dennis, 276–282. Madison, Wisc.: Industrial Relations Research Association.

McElroy, Colleen, and Dan Morrison. 1996. Phone unions fight merger. *Pittsburgh Post-Gazette,* April 21, A8.

McGuiness, Jeffrey C. 1996. Legal and regulatory responses to corporate campaigns. *Journal of Labor Research* 27: 417–424.

McKay, Jim. 1995. Merger a bid to shift labor out of reverse. *Pittsburgh Post-Gazette,* July 28, A1, A6.

———. 1996. Teachers union truce. *Pittsburgh Post-Gazette,* July 7, C2.

McKay, Jim, and Steve Halvonik. 1996. CWA drives into bill's info-bahn. *Pittsburgh Post-Gazette,* January 23, D8, D12.

Miller, James P. 1996. Household to pay $575 million for head start on AFL-CIO card. *Wall Street Journal,* June 18, B4.

Moe, Terry M. 1981. Toward a broader view of interest groups. *Journal of Politics* 43: 531–543.

Moore, William J., Denise R. Chachere, Thomas D. Curtis, and David Gordon. 1995. The political influence of unions and corporations on COPE votes in the U.S. Senate, 1979–1988. *Journal of Labor Research* 16: 203–22.

Morand, David A. 1994. The changing situation of U.S. labor law: Alternative legislative initiatives for workers and workplaces. *Labor Studies Journal* 19: 40–58.

Murmann, Kent F., and Andrew A. Porter. 1983. Employer campaign tactics and NLRB election outcomes: Some preliminary evidence. In *Proceedings of the thirty-fifth annual meeting of the Industrial Relations Research Association,* edited by Barbara D. Dennis, 67–72. Madison, Wisc.: Industrial Relations Research Association.

Needleman, Ruth. 1993. Building an organizing culture of unionism. In *Proceedings of the forty-fifth annual meeting of the Industrial Relations Research Association,* edited by John F. Burton, 358–366. Madison, Wisc.: Industrial Relations Research Association.

Needleman, Ruth, and Lucretia Dewey Tanner. 1987. Women in unions. In *Working women: Past, present, future,* edited by Karen Shallcross Koziara, Michael H. Moskow, and Lucretia Dewey Tanner, 187–224. Washington, D.C.: The Bureau of National Affairs, Industrial Relations Research Association Series.

Newsday. 1996. Carey edges Hoffa in Teamsters funding battle. *Pittsburgh Tribune-Review*, July 20, A12.

Nomani, Asra Q., and Robert L. Rose. 1995. AFL-CIO presidential hopefuls focus on organizing, politicizing workers. *Wall Street Journal*, July 29, C13.

Northrup, Herbert R. 1984. The rise and demise of PATCO. *Industrial and Labor Relations Review* 37: 167–184.

———. 1996. Corporate campaigns: The perversion of the regulatory process. *Journal of Labor Research* 17: 345–358.

Northrup, Herbert R., and Arnie D. Thornton. 1988. *The federal government as employer: The Federal Labor Relations Authority and the PATCO challenge.* Philadelphia: Wharton School Industrial Research Unit.

Northrup, James P., and Herbert R. Northrup. 1981. Union divergent investing of pensions: A power, non-employee relations issue. *Journal of Labor Research* 2: 191–208.

Norton, Ernie. 1996a. From investment banker to union man. *Wall Street Journal*, January 23, B1, B8.

———. 1996b. New blood for the USW. *Pittsburgh Post-Gazette*, January 26, C6.

Novak, Robert. 1996. Labor activism now provoking GOP retaliation. *Pittsburgh Tribune-Review*. May 16, A6.

Olson, Mancur, Jr. 1965. *The logic of collective action: Public goods and a theory of groups*. Cambridge, Mass.: Harvard University Press.

Organisation for Economic Co-Operation and Development (OECD). 1994. *OECD Employment Outlook.* Paris: Organisation for Economic Co-Operation and Development.

Perlman, Selig. 1928. *A theory of the labor movement*. New York: MacMillan.

Perry, Charles R. 1996. Corporate campaigns in context. *Journal of Labor Research* 17: 329–344.

Perusek, Glenn. 1989. The U.S.–Canada split in the United Automobile Workers. In *Proceedings of the forty-first annual meeting of the Industrial Relations Research Association*, edited by Barbara D. Dennis, 272–278. Madison, Wisc.: Industrial Relations Research Association.

Peterson, Florence. 1963. *American labor unions: What they are and how they work.* New York: Harper and Row.

Peterson, Richard B., Thomas W. Lee, and Barbara Finnegan. 1992. Strategies and tactics in union organizing campaigns. *Industrial Relations* 31: 370–381.

Reed, Thomas F. 1990. Profiles of union organizers from manufacturing and service unions. *Journal of Labor Research* 11: 73–80.

———. 1992. Incidence and patterns of representation campaign tactics: A comparison of manufacturing and service unions. *Relations Industrielles* 47: 203–217.

Rehmus, Charles M., and Benjamin A. Kerner. 1980. The agency shop after Abood: No free ride, but what's the fare? *Industrial and Labor Relations Review* 34: 90–100.

Rogers, Joel. 1995. A strategy for labor. *Industrial Relations* 34: 367–381.

Rose, Joseph B., and Gary N. Chaison. 1985. The state of unions: United States and Canada. *Journal of Labor Research* 6: 97–112.

———. 1990. New measures of union organizing effectiveness. *Industrial Relations* 29: 457–468.

———. 1995. Canadian labor policy as a model for legislative reform in the United States. *Labor Law Journal* 46: 259–272.

———. 1996. Linking union density and union effectiveness: The North American experience. *Industrial Relations* 35: 78–105.

Rose, Robert L. 1995a. AFL-CIO's Donahue finds he's choice of many who want Kirkland to retire. *Wall Street Journal*, February 17, B4.

———. 1995b. The Enforcers: Federal labor board gets more aggressive to employers' dismay. *Wall Street Journal*, June 1, A1.

———. 1995c. Donahue succeeds Kirkland as head of the AFL-CIO. *Wall Street Journal*, August 2, A7.

———. 1995d. Caterpillar seen as big winner in UAW talks. *Wall Street Journal*, November 30, A4.

———. 1996. AFL-CIO President John Sweeney pushes on aggressive agenda. *Wall Street Journal*, February 20, A1.

Rose, Robert L., and Glenn Burrins. 1996. AFL-CIO reclaims aggressive union, signaling change. *Wall Street Journal*, February 21, C22.

Sabato, Larry J. 1985. *PAC power inside the world of political action committees*. New York: W.W. Norton.

Salisbury, Robert H. 1969. An exchange theory of interest groups. *Midwest Journal of Political Science* 13: 1–32.

Schneider, B. V. H. 1988. Public-sector labor legislation: An evolutionary analysis. In *Public Sector Bargaining*, edited by Benjamin Aaron, Joyce M. Najita, and James L. Stern, 189–228. Washington, D.C.: The Bureau of National Affairs.

Schnell, John F., and Cynthia L. Gramm. 1994. The empirical relations between employers' striker replacement strategies and strike duration. *Industrial and Labor Relations Review* 47: 189–206.

Schurman, Susan J., and Hal Stack. 1994. From strategic planning to organizational change in local unions. In *Proceedings of the forty-sixth annual meeting of the Industrial Relations Research Association*, edited by Paula B. Voos, 85–94. Madison, Wisc.: Industrial Relations Research Association.

Seeber, Ronald L. 1991. Trade union growth and decline: The movement and the individual. In *The state of the unions*, edited by George Strauss, Daniel G. Gallagher, and Jack Fiorito, 93–100. Madison, Wisc.: Industrial Relations Research Association.

Seib, Gerald F. 1996. Organized labor shows a pulse: GOP feels ill. *Wall Street Journal*, April 24, A16.

Seidman, Joel. 1964. Emergence of concern with union government and administration. In *Regulating union government*, edited by Martin S. Estey, Phillip Taft, and Martin Wagner, 1–27. Madison, Wisc.: Industrial Relations Research Association.

Sheflin, Neil, and Leo Troy. 1983. Finances of American unions in the 1970's. *Journal of Labor Research* 42: 149–158.

Sheppard, Harold L., and Nicholas A. Masters. 1959. The politics of union endorsement of candidates in the Detroit area. *American Political Science Review* 53: 437–447.

Soffer, Benson. 1964. Collective bargaining and federal regulation of union government. In *Regulating union government*, edited by Martin S. Estey, Phillip

Taft, and Martin Wagner, 91–129. Madison, Wisc.: Industrial Relations Research Association.

Steagall, Jeffrey, and Ken Jennings. 1996. Unions, PAC contributions, and the NAFTA vote. *Journal of Labor Research* 17: 515–521.

Stein, Emanuel. 1964. Union finance and LMRDA. In *Regulating union government*, edited by Martin S. Estey, Phillip Taft, and Martin Wagner, 150–173. Madison, Wisc.: Industrial Relations Research Association.

Stern, James L. 1979. Unionism in the public sector. In *Public sector bargaining*, edited by Benjamin Aaron, Joseph R. Grodin, and James L. Stern, 44–79. Washington, D.C.: The Bureau of National Affairs.

———. 1988. Unionism in the public sector. In *Public sector bargaining*, edited by Benjamin Aaron, Joyce M. Najita, and James L. Stern 52–89. Washington, D.C.: The Bureau of National Affairs.

Stratton, Kay, and Robert B. Brown. 1989. Strategic planning in U.S. labor unions. In *Proceedings of the forty-first annual meetings of the Industrial Relations Research Association*, edited by Barbara D. Dennis, 523–531. Madison, Wisc.: Industrial Relations Research Association.

Stratton-Devine, Kay. 1990. Interorganizational relationships among U.S. labor unions: Mergers and affiliations. In *Proceedings of the forty-second annual meeting of the Industrial Relations Research Association*, edited by John F. Burton, Jr., 155–162. Madison, Wisc.: Industrial Relations Research Association.

———. 1992. Union merger benefits: An empirical analysis. *Journal of Labor Research* 13: 133–143.

———. 1995. Surveying unions: Lessons from studies of union strategy and planning. In *Proceedings of the forty-seventh annual meeting of the Industrial Relations Research Association*, edited by Paula B. Voos, 163–168. Madison, Wisc.: Industrial Relations Research Association.

Strauss, George. 1991. Union democracy. In *The state of the unions*, edited by George Strauss, Daniel G. Gallagher, and Jack Fiorito, 201–236. Madison, Wisc.: Industrial Relations Research Association.

———. 1995. Is the New Deal system collapsing? With what might it be replaced? *Industrial Relations* 34: 329–349.

Strauss, George, Daniel G. Gallagher, and Jack Fiorito, eds. 1991. *The state of the unions*. Madison, Wisc.: Industrial Relations Research Association.

Suris, Oscar, and Robert L. Rose. 1996. UAW is boasting efforts to organize workers at major auto parts supplier. *Wall Street Journal*, June 28, A2, A4.

Swoboda, Frank. 1996. Teamsters not to be confused with choirboys. *Pittsburgh Post-Gazette*, July 21, C6.

Swoboda, Frank, and Martha M. Hamilton. 1996. Labor looks to grow from the grass roots: New AFL-CIO chief brings in cadre of younger activists in effort to restore movement's clout. *Washington Post*, February 18, H1, H6.

Tasini, Jonathan. 1995. Labor's last chance: What the union can do to help the American workers—and save themselves. *Washington Post*, February 12, C3.

Troy, Leo. 1975. American unions and their wealth. *Industrial Relations* 14: 134–144.

———. 1990. Is the U.S. unique in the decline of private sector unionism? *Journal of Labor Research* 11: 111–144.

———. 1995. Private-sector unionism weakens. *Wall Street Journal*, September 1, A6.

Troy, Leo, and Neil Sheflin. 1985. *U.S. union sourcebook: Membership, finances, structure directory*. West Orange, N.J.: Industrial Relations Data and Information Services.

United Steelworkers of America. 1986. *Then and now: The road between*. Pittsburgh: United Steelworkers of America.

U.S. Commission on the Future of Worker–Management Relations. 1994a. *Fact finding report*. Washington, D.C.: Government Printing Office.

———. 1994b. *Report and recommendations*. Washington, D.C.: Government Printing Office.

U.S. Department of Labor, Bureau of Labor Statistics (DOL, BLS). 1970. *Directory of national and international labor unions in the United States, 1969*. Washington, D.C.: Government Printing Office.

———. 1974. *Directory of national unions and employee associations, 1973*. Washington, D.C.: Government Printing Office.

———. 1977. *Directory of national unions and employee associations, 1975*. Washington, D.C.: Government Printing Office.

———. 1979. *Directory of national unions and employee associations, 1977*. Washington, D.C.: Government Printing Office.

———. 1980. *Directory of national unions and employee associations, 1979*. Washington, D.C.: Government Printing Office.

———. 1986. *Employment and earnings*. Washington, D.C.: Government Printing Office.

———. 1988. *Employment and earnings*. Washington, D.C.: Government Printing Office.

———. 1989. Union membership in 1988. *News Release USDL 89–45*, January 27.

———. 1990. *Employment and earnings*, Washington, D.C.: Government Printing Office.

———. 1992. *Employment and earnings*. Washington, D.C.: Government Printing Office.

———. 1993a. Union members in 1992. *News Release USDL 93–43*, February 8.

———. 1993b. BLS releases new 1992–2005 Employment Projections. *News Release 1992–2005 employment projections. News Release USDL 95–485*, November 24.

———. 1994. Union members in 1993. *News Release USDL 94–58*, February 9.

———. 1995. *Compensation and working conditions*. Washington, D.C.: Government Printing Office.

———. 1996a. Union members in 1995. *News Release USDL 96–41*, February 9.

———. 1996b. Major work stoppages, 1995. *News Release USDL 96-59*, February 21.

U.S. Department of Labor, Labor–Management Standards Enforcement. Undated. *LMRDA reports*. Washington, D.C.: Department of Labor.

U.S. Department of Labor, Office of Labor–Management Standards. 1994. Instructions for Form LM-2. Washington, D.C.: Department of Labor.

U.S. Federal Election Commission (FEC). 1982. *FEC reports on financial activity 1979–1980. Final report party and non-party political committees*. Washington, D.C.: Federal Election Commission.

———. 1983. *FEC reports on financial activity 1981–1982: Final report party and non-party political committees*. Washington, D.C.: Federal Election Commission.

———. 1985. *FEC reports on financial activity 1983–1984: Final report party and nonparty political committees.* Washington, D.C.: Federal Election Commission.
———. 1988. *FEC reports on financial activity 1985–1986: Final report party and nonparty political committees.* Washington, D.C.: Federal Election Commission.
———. 1989. *FEC reports on financial activity 1987–1988: Final report party and nonparty political committees.* Washington, D.C.: Federal Election Commission.
———. 1991. *FEC reports on financial activity 1989–1990: Final report party and nonparty political committees.* Washington, D.C.: Federal Election Commission.
———. 1992. *Campaign guide for corporations and labor organizations.* Washington, D.C.: Federal Election Commission.
———. 1993. PAC activity rebounds in 1991–1992 election cycle: Unusual nature of contests seen as reason. *FEC Press Release*, April 29.
———. 1995a. *FEC reports on financial activity 1993–1994: Final report party and nonparty political committees.* Washington, D.C.: Federal Election Commission.
———. 1995b. 1994 PAC activity shows little growth over 1992 level, final FEC report finds. *FEC Press Release*, November.
U.S. National Labor Relations Board. 1996. *NLRB annual report for 1995.* Washington, D.C.: Government Printing Office.
U.S. Office of Personnel Management (OPM). 1992. *Union recognition in the federal government.* Washington, D.C.: Government Printing Office.
Vigilante, Richard. 1996. The *Daily News* War of 1990–1991. *Journal of Labor Research* 17: 395–410.
Voos, Paula B. 1983. Union organizing: costs and benefits. *Industrial and Labor Research Review* 36: 576–591.
———. 1984a. Does it pay to organize? Estimating the cost to unions. *Monthly Labor Review* June, 43–44.
———. 1984b. Trends in union organizing expenditures, 1953–1977. *Industrial and Labor Relations Review* 38: 52–63.
———. 1987. Union organizing expenditures: Determinants and their implications for union growth. *Journal of Labor Research* 8: 19–30.
———. 1994a. An economic perspective on contemporary trends in collective bargaining. In *Contemporary collective bargaining in the private sector*, edited by Paula B. Voos, 1–24. Madison, Wisc.: Industrial Relations Research Association.
———. 1994b. *Contemporary collective bargaining in the private sector.* Madison, Wisc: Industrial Relations Research Association.
Wachter, Michael L. 1995. Labor law reform: One step forward and two steps back. *Industrial Relations* 34: 382–401.
Wall Street Journal. 1996. Union members are mining for local votes. June 18, A1.
Walton, Richard, Joel Cutcher-Gershenfeld, and Robert B. McKersie. 1994. *Strategic negotiations.* Boston: Harvard Business School Press.
Webb, Sidney, and Beatrice Webb. 1897. *Industrial democracy.* New York: Augustus M. Kelley (1965 reprint).
Weil, David. 1994. *Turning the tide: Strategic planning for labor unions.* New York: Lexington Books.
Weiler, Paul C. 1990. *Governing the workplace: The future of labor and employment law.* Cambridge, Mass.: Harvard University Press.

———. 1993. Governing the workplace: Employee representation in the eyes of the law. In *Employee representation: Alternative and future directions*, edited by Bruce Kaufman and Morris M. Kleiner, 81–104. Madison, Wisc.: Industrial Relations Research Association.

Wellington, Harry H., and Ralph K. Winter, Jr. 1971. *The unions and the cities*. Washington, D.C.: Brookings Institution.

Wheeler, Hoyt N., and John A. McClendon. 1991. The individual decision to unionize. In *The state of the unions*, edited by George Strauss, Daniel G. Gallagher, and Jack Fiorito, 47–84. Madison, Wisc.:; Industrial Relations Research Association.

Williamson, Lisa. 1995. Union mergers: 1985–1994 update. *Monthly Labor Review* February, 18–25.

Willman, Paul, and Alan Cave. 1994. The union of the future: Super-unions or joint ventures? *British Journal of Industrial Relations* 32: 395–412.

Willman, Paul, and Timothy Morris. 1995. Financial management and financial performance in British trade unions. *British Journal of Industrial Relations* 33: 289–298.

Willman, Paul, Timothy Morris, and Beverly Aston. 1993. *Union business: Trade union organisation, and financial reform in the Thatcher years*. Cambridge: Cambridge University Press.

Wolfe, Arthur C. 1969. Trends in labor union voting behavior, 1948–1968. *Industrial Relations* 9: 1–10.

Zachary, G. Pascal. 1995. Some unions step up organizing campaigns and get new members. *Wall Street Journal*, September 1, A1, A3.

———. 1996a. Unions talk tough but face big hurdles. *Wall Street Journal*, January 22, A1.

———. 1996b. Sweeney to give AFL-CIO leadership his blueprint for reform at meeting. *Wall Street Journal*, January 24, A5.

———. 1996c. Chief AFL-CIO organizer to try civil rights tactics. *Wall Street Journal*, February 8, B1, B10.

Index

Airline Pilots Association (ALPA), 63, 71
Amalgamated Clothing and Textile Workers Union(ACTWU), 12, 26, 60, 64, 67, 72, 78, 80, 82, 84, 87, 98, 99, 103, 107, 111, 114, 115, 136, 137, 138, 140, 142, 146, 154, 169, 180, 202, 204, 205
American Federation of Government Employees (AFGE), 8, 67, 68, 70, 79, 82, 98, 111, 126, 129, 135, 138, 148, 155, 169, 206, 207
American Federation of Labor (AFL), 35, 43, 60, 61, 163
American Federation of Labor–Congress of Industrial Organizations (AFL-CIO), 4, 6, 8, 9, 10, 12, 13, 14, 16, 18, 25, 28, 29, 31, 32, 35, 41, 54, 119, 123, 124, 131, 142, 158, 177, 179, 185, 201, 205
American Federation of State, County, and Municipal Employees (AFSCME), 67, 70, 71, 82, 84, 90, 101, 111, 126, 134, 146, 149, 166, 179
American Federation of Teachers (AFT), 12, 67, 70, 72, 82, 84, 87, 90, 98, 103, 114, 152, 166, 180, 205, 207
American Postal Workers Union (APWU), 8, 64, 70, 72, 80, 82, 84, 87, 98, 103, 111, 114, 126, 138, 148, 149, 152, 180
American Telephone & Telegraph (AT&T), 132, 159, 195
Ameritech, 132
Armey, Dick, 186, 201
Association of Trial Lawyers, 132

Becker, George, 143
Bell Atlantic, 194
Bensinger, Richard, 6, 158
Bush, George, 18, 59

Carey, Ronald, 142, 156
Carpenters and Joiners of America (CJA), 27, 62, 67, 79, 80, 82, 84, 98, 99, 101, 111, 114, 146, 149, 152, 155, 180, 202
Caterpillar, 1, 30, 41, 150

Christian Coalition, 123
Clinton, Bill, 18, 25, 58, 185
Committee on Political Education (COPE), 8, 119
Communications Workers of America (CWA), 19, 26, 62, 66, 67, 79, 84, 87, 99, 101, 118, 146, 149, 152, 155, 159, 166, 180, 194, 195, 202, 206
Congress of Industrial Organizations (CIO), 35, 43, 60, 163

Daily News strike (Detroit newspapers strike), 41, 150, 156
Davis–Bacon Act, 2, 29, 41
Donahue, Thomas, 9, 29
Dunlop, John, 3

Eastern Airline strike, 7
Economically Targeted Investments, 27
Electromation, 201

Fair Labor Standards Act, 2, 29, 41
Federal Aviation Authority (FAA), 25
Federal Election Campaign Act (FECA), 37, 40, 120
Federal Election Commission, 131
Federal Labor Relations Authority, 41
Federal Service Labor–Management Relations Statute (FSLMRS), 25, 41, 42, 67
Food Lion, 27, 35, 41, 205
Ford Motor Company, 143

General Motors, 7, 143, 171
Gerard, Leo, 143
Gingrich, Newt, 186, 201
Gould, William, IV, 35, 56
Greyhound strike, 7

Hatch Act, 2, 8
Hoffa, James, Jr., 156
Hormel strike, 160
Hotel Employees and Restaurant Employees (HERE), 25, 62, 67, 79, 80, 82, 84, 99, 101, 114, 154, 169

International Association of Fire Fighters (IAFF), 84, 87, 98, 101, 135, 146, 149
International Association of Machinists (IAM), 5, 9, 12, 35, 60, 62, 64, 72, 79, 80, 82, 84, 98, 99, 111, 114, 126, 139, 146, 149, 152, 155, 166, 178, 180, 205, 207
International Brotherhood of Electrical Workers (IBEW), 62, 66, 67, 79, 80, 82, 84, 87, 98, 99, 106, 111, 114, 131, 137, 152, 155, 166, 169, 180, 194
International Brotherhood of Teamsters (IBT), 16, 27, 62, 67, 71, 80, 82, 84, 87, 90, 98, 99, 101, 103, 106, 111, 114, 115, 123, 134, 136, 137, 138, 139, 142, 146, 149, 152, 154, 155, 156, 158, 166, 178, 180, 205, 206, 207
International Ladies Garment Workers Union (ILGWU), 5, 12, 60, 67, 72, 79, 80, 82, 84, 98, 99, 100, 101, 111, 114, 126, 134, 136, 139, 140, 146, 148, 149, 152, 155, 156, 180, 204
International Union of Electrical Workers (IUE), 62, 67, 79, 80, 84, 98, 99, 114, 146, 169, 180
International Union of Operating Engineers (IUOE), 62, 66, 67, 79, 84, 87, 99, 114, 138, 152, 169, 180, 206

J. P. Stevens, 26, 27
Justice for Janitors, 27, 148, 165, 178, 205

Kirkland, Lane, 9, 54
Knights of Labor, 43, 60

Labor–Management Reporting and Disclosure Act (LMRDA), 12, 14, 37, 42, 103, 106
Laborers International Union (LIU), 62, 64, 66, 72, 79, 82, 84, 87, 99, 111, 114, 142, 149, 166, 180, 205
Lewis, John L., 60

Marine Engineers Beneficial Association (MEBA), 63, 71
McDonald, David, 103

Mega-Merger (Auto Workers, Machinists, Steelworkers), 9, 12, 64, 158, 178, 180, 205
Merit Systems Protection Board, 18
Minimum Wage, 25
Mondale, Walter, 18
Murray, Philip, 33

National Association of Government Employees (NAGE), 70
National Association of Letter Carriers (NALC), 8, 63, 70, 71, 79, 80, 82, 84, 87, 98, 101, 103, 111, 114, 126, 138, 148, 149, 152, 180, 207
National Cash Register (NCR), 159
National Education Association (NEA), 12, 14, 16, 64, 66, 67, 70, 72, 78, 80, 82, 84, 86, 98, 111, 126, 134, 139, 146, 149, 163, 166, 169, 180, 205
National Federation of Federal Employees (NFFE), 14, 16, 64, 66, 67, 68, 70, 72, 78, 80, 84, 98, 99, 111, 114, 126, 129, 134, 135, 138, 139, 140, 148, 155, 169, 180, 206
National Labor Relations Act (NLRA), 2, 25, 41, 189, 198, 201, 202
National Labor Relations Board (NLRB), 5, 8, 35, 55, 159, 173, 201
National Rifle Association (NRA), 123, 124, 132
National Rural Letter Carriers Association (NRLCA), 2, 14, 16, 64, 66, 67, 70, 80, 82, 84, 87, 98, 99, 101, 103, 111, 126, 134, 135, 137, 138, 139, 146, 149, 152, 166, 169, 180
National Treasury Employees Union (NTEU), 14, 16, 64, 66, 67, 70, 72, 80, 82, 84, 99, 101, 103, 111, 126, 129, 134, 135, 138, 146, 148, 152, 155, 166, 169, 180
North American Free Trade Agreement (NAFTA), 1, 2, 9, 18, 28, 41, 58
Nynex, 194

Occupational Safety and Health Act, 41

Patterson, William, 27
Phelps–Dodge strike, 7, 160
Pittston Coal Company strike, 151
Plumbing and Pipefitting Industry (PPI), 66, 67, 79, 80, 82, 84, 98, 99, 111, 146, 149, 152, 180, 206
Political action committees (PACs), 11, 15, 16, 17, 18, 28, 33, 34, 35, 36, 37, 38, 39, 40, 42, 63, 71, 90, 119, 120, 121, 122, 123, 124, 126, 129, 131, 132, 133, 138, 139, 140, 143, 149, 155, 160, 166, 168, 169, 171, 178, 180, 182, 195, 207, 208
Postal Reorganization Act of 1970, 42
Professional Air Traffic Controllers Organization (PATCO), 7, 25, 41, 56, 68, 132, 160

Racketeer Influenced and Corrupt Organizations Act (RICO), 27
Reagan, Ronald, 8, 10, 45, 56, 59, 132
Retail, Wholesale Department Store Union (RWDSU), 67, 72, 79, 84, 87, 98, 99, 101, 106, 111, 114, 134, 138, 146, 152, 169, 180
Right-to-work laws (RTWs), 42

Service Employees International Union (SEIU), 4, 19, 27, 33, 35, 62, 64, 71, 72, 82, 84, 90, 98, 99, 101, 103, 111, 114, 134, 146, 148, 154, 155, 163, 165, 166, 169, 178, 179, 205, 206, 207
Stern, Andy, 155, 165, 178
Sweeney, John, 4, 9, 29, 32, 35, 41, 119, 155, 158, 185, 205

Taft–Hartley Act, 42, 56
TEAM Act, 2, 18

Union of Needletrades Industrial and Textile Employees (UNITE), 12, 180
United Auto Workers (UAW), 1, 5, 7, 9, 12, 18, 29, 30, 37, 41, 60, 62, 64, 67, 72, 78, 79, 80, 82, 83, 84, 87, 98, 99, 101, 103, 107, 111, 114, 115, 126, 136, 137, 139, 143, 146, 149, 150, 152, 155, 156, 163, 166, 178, 180, 204, 205, 206, 207
United Food and Commercial Workers Union (UFCW), 12, 27, 35, 41, 62, 64, 66, 67, 72, 80, 82, 84,

United Food and Commercial Workers Union *(continued)* 98, 99, 111, 114, 134, 136, 140, 152, 154, 166, 169, 179, 180, 202, 205, 206
United Mine Workers of America (UMWA), 60, 151, 152, 199
United Paper Workers Internaional Union (UPIU), 62, 64, 72, 79, 84, 98, 99, 111, 114, 138, 152, 169, 180
U.S. Postal Service, 135
United Rubber Workers (URW), 12, 60, 71, 155
United Steelworkers of America (USW), 5, 9, 12, 19, 29, 33, 60, 62, 64, 67, 71, 72, 79, 80, 82, 84, 90, 98, 99, 103, 111, 114, 132, 136, 139, 143, 146, 152, 155, 158, 166, 169, 178, 180, 204, 205, 206

ABOUT THE AUTHOR

MARICK F. MASTERS is Professor of Business Administration at the Joseph M. Katz Graduate School of Business, University of Pittsburgh. Dr. Masters has written widely on labor issues in several journals.

ISBN 1-56720-129-6
90000>
EAN
9 781567 201291
HARDCOVER BAR CODE